TRANSFORMATION OF ARCHIVES AND HERITAGE EDUCATION

in Post-apartheid South Africa

Geraldine Frieslaar & Olusegun Morakinyo

Transformation of Archives and Heritage Education in Post-apartheid South Africa

Published by African Sun Media under the SUN PReSS imprint
Place of publication: Stellenbosch, South Africa

All rights reserved

Copyright © 2023 African Sun Media and the authors

This publication was subjected to an independent double-blind peer evaluation by the publisher.

The authors and the publisher have made every effort to obtain permission for and acknowledge the use of copyrighted material. Refer all enquiries to the publisher.

No part of this book may be reproduced or transmitted in any form or by any electronic, photographic or mechanical means, including photocopying and recording on record, tape or laser disk, on microfilm, via the Internet, by e-mail, or by any other information storage and retrieval system, without prior written permission by the publisher.

Views reflected in this publication are not necessarily those of the publisher.

First edition 2023

ISBN 978-1-991260-40-6
ISBN 978-1-991260-41-3 (e-book)
https://doi.org/10.52779/9781991260413

Set in Assistant Regular 10/14

Cover design, typesetting and production by African Sun Media

SUN PReSS is an imprint of African Sun Media. Scholarly, professional and reference works are published under this imprint in print and electronic formats.

This publication can be ordered from:
orders@africansunmedia.co.za
Takealot: bit.ly/2monsfl
Google Books: bit.ly/2k1Uilm
africansunmedia.store.it.si *(e-books)*
Amazon Kindle: amzn.to/2ktL.pkL
JSTOR: https://bit.ly/3udc057

Visit africansunmedia.co.za for more information.

Contents

Acknowledgements ii
Abbreviations iv
Introduction 1

1. The Aura of Archives: Innocuous Charms, Fevers and Afflictions 19
2. Transforming the Archive: Archivist as Historian/Historian as Archivist ... 45
3. The Configuration of Archives in Post-apartheid South Africa 61
4. A History of Museum and Heritage Studies in Africa 99
5. The Transformation of Museum and Heritage Studies in South Africa 123
6. Public History and Heritage Studies in South Africa 149

Conclusion 181
References 187
Index 201

Acknowledgements

This book is the outcome of a collective and collaborative effort for which we have accumulated a debt of gratitude over the past few years. Within this vein, we would like to especially acknowledge, with deep gratitude, the financial support of the National Institute for Humanities and the Social Sciences (NIHSS) when it awarded a grant to our book project under the Working Groups Programme for 2021-2022, and thus enabled focused research, capacity building of two postgraduate students during the preparation of the manuscript, and the subsequent completion of our manuscript. The genesis of this book spans more than a decade and we acknowledge that it would not have been possible without the guidance and insights of Prof Ciraj Rassool and Prof Leslie Witz at the Department of History, University of the Western Cape, who were the co-convenors of the African Programme in Museum and Heritage Studies (APMHS).

We are grateful to many individuals and organisations that have enriched our thinking and praxis and framed our approach to this book through their shared experiences, expertise, and insights. In this regard, we would like to acknowledge the following institutions that have informed our praxis through either employment or collaborative engagement and dialogue: Cape Town Holocaust and Genocide Centre, District Six Museum, Robben Island Museum, UWC Robben Island Museum Mayibuye Archives, South African History Archive, National Heritage and Cultural Studies Centre at the University of Fort Hare, Historical Research Papers Archive and History Workshop at the University of the Witwatersrand, Department of History and Centre for Humanities Research at the University of the Western Cape, Constitution Hill and Mzala Nxumalo Centre for the Study of South African Society, Iziko Museums, and Ditsong Museums of South Africa. We would also like to acknowledge Horst Kleinschmidt for his mentorship, friendship and support during the last decade. We owe an enormous debt of thanks to our colleagues far and wide for their engagement, collegial support, and guidance during the research and synthesis of our findings. We would like to especially thank Prof Luvuyo Dondolo, Prof Neo Lekgotla Laga Ramoupi, Dr Sipokazi Madida, Dr Mary Mbewe, Sinazo Mtshemla, Dr Sibongiseni Mkhize, Catherine Snel, Dr Noel Solani and other colleagues in the archival and heritage field that have contributed towards the writing of this book. We are grateful for the professional and dedicated assistance that we received at the various archives, in particular the UNISA archives that we visited during the duration of our research.

Acknowledgements

We owe a special vote of thanks to Stellenbosch University for the invaluable support during the writing of this book. Specifically, we acknowledge the quiet, behind-the-scenes support of the Stellenbosch University Museum that administered the financial side of the project, our two postgraduate research assistants, Robynne Boonzaaier and Curtley Solomons, and lastly for the supportive environment that our colleagues provided during the preparation and writing of this book.

We would like to thank African Sun Media for their professionalism and patience during the long writing process of this book and for facilitating the blind review process that enabled us to chisel and improve the manuscript. We acknowledge with sincere appreciation the unwavering support and love from our families and friends without whose encouragement and understanding none of this would have been possible.

Finally, we acknowledge and dedicate this book to our daughter, Feyijimi Morakinyo, who designed the cover of this publication and has spent many days alongside us touring archives and museums, and has been part of several iterations of this book. We thank her for her love, intuitiveness, and natural inclination towards a thirst for knowledge.

Abbreviations

ACTAG	Arts and Culture Task Group
AHD	Authorised Heritage Discourse
AFRICOM	International Council of African Museums
AMHS	African Museum and Heritage Studies
ANC	African National Congress
APMHS	African Programme in Museum and Heritage Studies
AWHF	African World Heritage Fund
AZAPO	Azanian People's Organisation
BCM	Black Consciousness Movement
BMA	British Museums Association
CCNY	Carnegie Corporation New York
CCS	Centre for Cultural Studies
CER	Centre for Research in Ethnic Relations
CHDA	Centre for Heritage Development in Africa
CHR	Centre for Humanities Research
CMMH	Commission for Museums, Monuments and Heraldry
CMS	Centre for Museum Studies
CPSA	Communist Party of South Africa
DACST	Department of Arts, Culture, Science and Technology
EPA	l'Ecole du Patrimoine Africain
GALA	Gay and Lesbian Archives
IAAM	International Anti-Apartheid Movement
ICCROM	International Centre for the Study of the Preservation and Restoration of Cultural Property
ICOM	International Council of Museums
ICS	Institute of Commonwealth Studies
ICTOP	International Committee for the Training of Personnel
IHR	Institute for Historical Research
IDAF	International Defence and Aid Fund

Abbreviations

IMF	International Monetary Fund
MCHC	Mayibuye Centre for History and Culture
NAHECS	National Heritage and Cultural Studies Centre
NHC	National Heritage Council
NGO	Non-Governmental Organisation
NUB	National University of Benin
PAC	Pan Africanist Congress
PAIA	Promotion of Access to Information Act
PDMA	Programme for Museum Development in Africa
PIA	Protection of Information Act
PREMA	Prevention Conservation in Museums in Africa
RIM	Robben Island Museum
RITP	Robben Island Training Programme
SAHA	South African History Archive
SAHO	South Africa History Online
SAMA	South African Museums Association
SAMP	Swedish-African Museum Programme
SANROC	South African Non-Racial Olympic Committee
SAP	Structural Adjustment Programme
SAS	State Archives Service
SIDA	Swedish International Development Cooperation Agency
SOMAFCO	Solomon Mahlangu Freedom College
SU	Stellenbosch University
TRC	Truth and Reconciliation Commission
UCT	University of Cape Town
UFH	University of Fort Hare
UM	Unity Movement
UNESCO	United Nations Educational, Scientific and Cultural Organisation
UP	University of Pretoria
UWC	University of the Western Cape
UWC RIM	University of the Western Cape Robben Island Museum
WESTAG	Western Province Task Group
WHL	World Heritage List

Introduction

> Today, museum directors throughout the continent and, indeed, most of the staff themselves, are indigenous Africans. However, the basic set-up of the museums remains the same: endless glass cases with (often) dusty natural history or ethnographic specimens. Does this type of exhibit truly satisfy the needs of today's African museum visitor, whether a member of the local community or a tourist? The answer, increasingly, is 'no'.[1]

Lorna Abungu, former executive director of the now defunct International Council of African Museums (AFRICOM), succinctly described the challenge of transformation and decolonisation of the museum and, more broadly, the heritage sector in Africa and specifically South Africa, which is the focus of this study. Although there have been significant strides to change the demographics of museum personnel and develop new museums and heritage institutions in post-apartheid South Africa, the Eurocentric model of the museum and heritage sector has largely remained intact and the same. Despite the euphoria around the transformation of heritage in the beginnings of post-apartheid South Africa, it can be argued that the transformation of heritage institutions has been superficial and cosmetic with the ideological foundation of the colonial archive and museum, as well as Eurocentric modalities of heritage education remaining solid, largely unmoved, and under continuing challenge.

There is therefore a need to reflect on the extent of the success of transformation through a study that revisits the history of the underlying reasons for archival transformation and the kind of education and training required to accomplish transformation. More importantly, we argue for a study that meticulously identifies what exactly was to be transformed, the criteria for its evaluation, and the extent to which cultural institutions are transformed. Framed within the epistemological uncertainty of the post-apartheid South African heritage complex, there is a need to reflect on questions around the challenges and possibilities of the transformation of archives, both through its processes and the education and training of heritage professionals. The book provides an alternative discursive perspective on post-apartheid heritage transformation through an emphasis on the changing meaning of the archivist through a different heritage education orientation by critically interrogating existing histories, policies, and epistemologies of the transformation of the heritage complex in post-apartheid South Africa. The question we address in this book is to what extent has the heritage complex been transformed or is it a case of the more things change the more they remain the same? We look at the state of transformation of the archive and heritage education sector through selected institutions to answer these questions.

At the heart of a society in transition, particularly one that was built on institutionalised racism, inequality, human rights violations, and state-imposed amnesia characteristic of the apartheid era, are its cultural, heritage, and memory institutions. However, these institutions are never quite central in public debates and collective memory except when they are used by the state as vehicles to foster nation-building, political unity, and inclusivity. The newly adopted International Council of Museum's (ICOM) definition of the museum defines the museum as:

> a not-for-profit, permanent institution in the service of society that researches, collects, conserves, interprets and exhibits tangible and intangible heritage. Open to the public, accessible and inclusive, museums foster diversity and sustainability. They operate and communicate ethically, professionally and with the participation of communities, offering varied experiences for education, enjoyment, reflection and knowledge sharing.[2]

While the current definition was finally approved in August 2022 (which is incidentally not very different from the former definition of 2007 with the exception of inclusivity and community participation), there seems to have been a missed opportunity with the non-incorporation of the proposed definition that was tabled at ICOM's General Conference in Kyoto, Japan in 2019. This definition emphasised the role of the museum as "democratising, inclusive and polyphonic spaces for critical dialogue about the pasts and the futures … with a goal of contributing to human dignity and social justice, global equality and planetary wellbeing."[3] However, while the approved definition suggests that museums are "neutral containers, custodian[s] of a universal heritage, displaying a common global cultural patrimony … ",[4] we argue that from an Afrocentric decolonial perspective the museum as product of the colonial era is rather a weapon for subjugation of Africans and the exploitation of Africa observed from the history of its modes of collection and exhibition making. This is because in contrast to Western museums that were established to encourage scholarship and provide education in the making of its citizenry, African museums were created as storehouses for curios and 'tribal' artefacts that were often collected through the use of violence, conquest, looting, and pillage but also through the seemingly less violent influence of religion which gradually led to indigenous communities discarding objects associated with belief systems and cultures.[5]

Similar to museums in Europe which were adjuncts of the colonial enterprise in the destruction and distortion of African epistemic systems, the museum and its collections in South Africa not only houses the physical evidence of the conquest of Africa, but also serves as a device for the enduring projection of racist white supremacy as we argue in this book, following Dan Hicks' theory of the museum as weapon.[6] According to Hicks, the museum is "a project put to work in the name of brutal colonial and racial violence",[7] a "monument to the violent propaganda of western superiority above African civilisation erected in the name of 'race science'"[8] with intimate links to the "enduring processes of militarist-corporate colonialism in 21st-century global capitalism."[9]

It is significant that the South African Museum in Cape Town, established in 1825, was the first museum in Africa, even predating the Egyptian Museum in Cairo in 1858 despite the historical root of the museum reputed to be in the devastating loss of the Alexandria library complex in Egypt in 48 BCE. The history of museums in South Africa reveals the intrinsic interconnectedness of empire, colonialism, and the invention of Africa. It also shows how the museum developed as a weapon for the subjugation of Africa and in the construction of the colonial archive of Africa. Paradoxically, while the philosophy of the Egyptian museum was premised on suppressing the Africanity and Africanness of ancient Egyptian civilisations, the philosophy of the colonial museum is aimed at exploring Africa in all its details to construct instrumental knowledge for its exploitation for the benefits of the empire. It was through the activities of the museum as an institution in South Africa that the colonial archive of knowledge of Africa was constructed, and it was the knowledge gathered and collected through the expeditions and field studies of the museum which provided the information that enabled and assisted the colonial conquest of Africa. It is important at this stage to note that the establishment of the South African Museum also predates the Great Trek of 1835, the 6th Frontier War 1834-1835, the looting of Benin in 1897, and the Anglo-Zulu wars of 1879. This reveals how the museum was employed as a device of knowledge gathering and surveillance, which in turn enabled the conquest and colonisation of Africa.

The histories of the development of museums in South Africa indicate its centrality to the colonial project as an epistemic device to construct the colonial knowledge archive of Africa through the collection, systematisation, and categorisation of knowledge about Africa, primarily its conquest and exploitation. Following Hicks' theory of how the museum was employed as a weapon; it is not far-fetched to follow this argument when casting a cursory glance at the biographies of the earliest directors of the South African Museum. Although there were claims that Willem Adriaan van der Stel, Governor of the Cape Colony from 1699 to 1707, was reputed to have a museum that displayed zoological and other curiosities from his collections until 1806, the first museum in South Africa was established in Cape Town in 1825. This was followed by the Albany Museum in Grahamstown in 1855, which formally inaugurated the museum in South Africa as we know it at present. These museums were followed by the Port Elizabeth Museum in 1856, and the Free State Republic Museum in Bloemfontein in 1877, the King William's Town Museum in 1884, the Durban Museum in 1887, the Pretoria Museum in 1893, and the Pietermaritzburg Museum in 1903.

This timeline of the establishment of museums in South Africa shows their importance in South Africa as a source of knowledge and information which was required for the colonial project to conquer Africa. Thus, in contrast to Europe where the museum started from private collections of the 'cabinet of curiosities' in the 15th and 16th centuries, almost all of the museums in Africa were established by the colonial empire at the height of the European conquest of Africa as an epistemological device for the construction of alterity knowledge of Africa and weapon for the subjugation of Africans. Most of the museums were established by the colonial administration as an epistemic platform to know and define Africa as a prelude to its conquest, subjugation, and eventual colonisation. The beginning of museums in South Africa was strictly for scientific specialist research in natural history, geographical mapping, archaeology, and racist ethnographic study of Africans as a species to be tamed, categorised, and exploited.

The work of Andrew Smith (1797-1872), appointed as the first Superintendent of the South African Museum of Natural History in Cape Town by Lord Charles Somerset in 1825, reveals this foundational museum ethos of the era, which determined the type of training that was required and undertaken for working in the museum. Andrew Smith is widely recognised as the father of South African zoology and stands out as an "impressive figure in the history of African zoology."[10] His reputation as a serious naturalist is definitely based on his multi-volume *Illustrations of the Zoology of South Africa*, which stands out as one of the very early authoritative work of descriptions of African reptiles, amphibians, fishes, and some of the rarer mammals and birds.[11] Apart from being a natural scientist, ethnologist, and anthropologist, he was trained as a soldier and a medical doctor, and most crucially an intelligence expert, which intimates the way the museum was employed as an epistemic device and the type of studies and training that was required to be eligible to work in the museum during that era. As indicative of the ethos of the museum as an epistemic device for the acquisition of knowledge of Africa through surveillance and covert intelligence gathering, Smith travelled to Namaland immediately after his appointment as Superintendent of the South African Museum in 1825 and to the Zulu kingdom in 1832-1833 on 'intelligence missions' on behalf of the Government of the Cape Colony under the cover of scientific natural history collection expeditions.

The wars of dispossession that followed his expeditions are well documented. As observed by R.F.H. Summers, it was routine museum work during this period to use scientific excuses as cover for gathering intelligence on people and areas of interest to the colonial government. Thus, central to the ethos inculcated to train museum workers of the era was using the scientific mission of collection for the museum as a cover to covertly gather intelligence of the people, environment, and languages for the colonial project. This further confirms the museum as a platform of knowledge generation for the purpose of conquest and subjugation during this era.[12] Smith was the leader of the Expedition for Exploring Central Africa in 1834-1836. This was the era of expeditions as part of the construction of the colonial archive of knowledge of Africa and reconnaissance as a precursor to subsequent military invasion where not only African objects, flora, and fauna, but live Africans were collected as part of nature, based on racist science.[13] In line with the prevailing ethos of the museum to further the colonial project through knowledge construction of Africa, objects collected on the expeditions were generally sent to Europe, apparently for further study and research.[14] The main objective and guiding ethos of the museum during this era was the search for and construction of knowledge of Africa through scientific expedition and ethnographic studies of African culture.[15]

Smith left the service of the Museum in 1837 and eventually sold his 'South African Museum' at an auction in London mainly to the British Museum, giving a new meaning to museum as an assemblage of collections: "any public exhibition of scientific or historical interest, especially if it were spectacular and contained mounted animals"[16] that can be packed and sold. Smith was replaced by Leopold Layard and the museum was eventually reorganised in 1855, marking the beginning of the South African Museum in Cape Town, now part of the Iziko Museums as renamed in the post-apartheid.

The ethos of the museum as an institution for colonial episteme was further solidified through the archive it constructed to acquire knowledge of Africa. Although traces of archives were around before the arrival of European colonialism in the mid-17th century when colonial recordkeeping supplanted these forms of archiving, the latter has been habitually ignored. According to Verne Harris, pre-eminent scholar on archiving and archivist to Nelson Mandela in South Africa:

> There has been 'archive' in South Africa for as long as humans have inhabited this part of the world. Collective stories, passed from generation to generation; rock paintings; signs patterned into dwellings, clothing, shields and so on; markings, temporary and permanent, on human bodies; these and many other forms of archive carried the narratives, messages and beliefs of people for millennia. Their traces can still be found in South Africa today.[17]

The arrival of European colonialism signalled the beginning of formal repositories to manage the resources and administrative challenges of the respective Dutch and British projects of empire-building. The most important reason for developing formal repositories during colonial times was the centrality of the archive in the formation and creation of the nation. Colonial archives were as much products of state machinery as technologies that bolstered the production of those states themselves, as argued by Ann Laura Stoler in her insightful study on 19th century Dutch colonial archives.[18] Taking her argument further, Stoler contended that "[c]olonial archives were both sites of the imaginary and institutions that fashioned histories as they concealed, revealed, and reproduced the power of the state."[19] Akin to museums in South Africa, archives were designed to "celebrate official white narratives of progressive control and understanding, with racist tropes like 'bringing civilisation to Africa,' and 'the White man's burden' ever-present."[20] Following the modest pre-national, administrative colonial beginnings, the archival holdings underwent a major development in 1910 with the establishment of the Union of South Africa. The national archives service, under the auspices of the Department of the Interior, legislatively came into being in 1922 and was later configured as part of the project of building an Afrikaner nation. The custodial mandate of the newly established State Archives Service (SAS) included the archival records of national and provincial government offices, which was further expanded in 1962 to encompass the archival records of local government offices, as well as the records of the former self-governing homelands. Further to its mandate, SAS was also empowered to augment its public archival record holdings with private records.

With the institutionalisation of apartheid in 1948, and especially after the implementation of the Archives Act in 1962, the SAS was transformed into a formidable bureaucratic system with wide-ranging regulatory powers and "an extraordinary capacity to secure the support of most white South Africans, as well as the acquiescence or collaboration of significant sections of the black population."[21] In a similar vein to colonialism, the apartheid state also sought to control social memory and the production of knowledge, as well as who had access to knowledge. Focused on legitimising apartheid rule and building support for their ideology, the apartheid state gave attention to constructing state-funded memory institutions such as archives, museums, libraries, and monuments through which they collected and constructed official narratives focused on entrenching a dominant ideology of white minority rule. The rigidity of the apartheid bureaucratic structures moulded the state archives into an apparatus in the service of the apartheid system as access to the state archives and employment opportunities within the state archives mirrored the enforced apartheid-era legislation. The adoption of an apartheid bureaucratic culture contributed to a skewed representation of historical memory in South Africa as the approach of the state archives to archival practices was informed by an ideology that sought to racially exclude, omit, and elide the struggles and experiences of colonialism, segregating apartheid's marginalised and oppressed.[22] It is also significant that in examples where documentation of black experiences or other marginalised voices took place, scant as it may be, this was subject to the subjectivities of white archival professionals.

This situation of apartheid fashioned gaps within historical memory and state imposed public amnesia through censure and restricted access prevailed until the end of apartheid which, formally at least, culminated in 1994 with the first democratic elections and the adoption of an Interim Constitution. Reflecting on this period of transition, Harris noted that the transformation discourse in archives was constructed "around a commitment to redressing inherited imbalances and rectifying the exclusions of the past."[23] According to Harris, the impetus of the construction of a transformation discourse around archives was to take the archives to the people.[24] Although there was a fervent desire to redefine archives during the 1990s, this reimagining had to occur within the constraints posed by an inherited bureaucratic system built upon the injustices and inequality of apartheid, as well as the confines of a reconciliation narrative as set out by the agenda of a new democracy in the making.

It is against this background that the *National Archives of South Africa Act* came into being in 1996, which usurped the SAS and established the National Archives in response to the shifting political changes and the need for transformation within the national archival system. As newly established and reconstituted archival and memory projects were positioning themselves to assume possession of the counter archives, the National Archives had to work harder to establish their credibility in respect of representation, access, and active documenters. Central to transforming the national archival system were issues of representation within the public service that had been at the forefront since 1994, and which have seen changes brought about through the application of affirmative action policies in the recruitment of racially diverse candidates in the National Archives.

Parallel to the transformation of the national archival system was the question of transparency and accountability and the degree to which public records should be made accessible to the public while also considering the interests of the state in safeguarding sensitive national issues. In balancing the interest of the state with the responsibility of providing access of public records to the public, the Promotion of Access to Information Act (2000), also known as PAIA, was passed which gives effect to the constitutional right of access to information held by public and private bodies as outlined in the South African Constitution.[25]

However, as Veronique Rioufol and others have argued, the new democratic dispensation of 1994 brought its own conditions to reshape representations of South Africa as a country "promoting democratisation, fostering reconciliation and national unity,"[26] through which South Africa was represented within the lens of a reconciled and unified rainbow nation. Drawing on Rioufol's argument of the positive and universalist terms in which South Africa was recast "to fit the new political situation and to foster cohesion,"[27] it can be argued that in the project of transformation and recasting South Africa as a unified nation, it necessarily involved the silencing, forgetting, or marginalising of certain voices and narratives. In his reflections on the relationship between the archive and the making of the nation state, Kwame Anthony Appiah made a similar argument where he noted that, "[n]ational history is a question of what we choose to remember, not just in the sense of which facts we use for our public purposes, but equally in the sense that we choose which facts actually count as ours."[28] Furthermore, the widespread destruction of records and the entrenchment of an apartheid culture built on secrecy within the national archival system, which was further shaped by the compromises reached as a result of the negotiated settlement between the apartheid regime and the liberation movements, impacted heavily on the work of transitional justice and truth recovery in the post-apartheid era.

As the history of the South African Museum Association's (SAMA) origin indicates, this orientation of museums in South Africa as a weapon and device for the promotion of white supremacy ideology and subjugation of Africans was enhanced and expanded to support and promote the apartheid ideology through the museums and heritage institutions from the 1930s up until 1994. Thus, while Dan Hicks' theory of museums as a weapon is hyped-up here as the Martin Bernal[29] of African Museum and Heritage Studies, it is worth revisiting then president Nelson Mandela's 1997 speech at the formal opening of the Robben Island Museum (RIM) as the first national cultural institution of democratic South Africa, and the foremost intervention of the Legacy Project Programme where the violence of the museum in South Africa was confronted. In the speech, Mandela in a critique of current museums and exhibitions, laid out the work to be done in overturning the legacy of "colonial and apartheid times, when our museums and monuments reflected the experiences and political ideals of a minority to the exclusion of others."[30] In his blistering speech, Mandela stated:

> During colonial and apartheid times, our museums and monuments reflected the experiences and political ideals of a minority to the exclusion of others, which glorified mainly white and colonial history … The demeaning portrayal of black people in particular – that is African, Indian and Coloured people – is painful to recall, … the small glimpse of black history in the others was largely fixed in the grip of racist and other stereotypes. … can we afford exhibitions in our museums depicting any of our people as lesser human beings, sometimes in natural history museums usually reserved for the depiction of animals? Can we continue to tolerate our ancestors being shown as people locked in time? … Such degrading forms of representation inhibit our children's appreciation of the value and strength of our democracy, of tolerance and of human rights. They demean the victims and warp the minds of the perpetrators.[31]

Mandela lamented that "the demeaning portrayal of black people in particular – that is African, Indian and Coloured people – is painful to recall", noting how all South African museums in 1994 glorified mainly white and colonial history except only three percent, which itself "was largely fixed in the grip of racist and other stereotypes."[32] Through these statements, Mandela provided the ideological, cultural, political, and historical background of the rationale for the work of transforming or restructuring the then existing orientation of the cultural institutions in South Africa from its white supremacist agenda to a more inclusive, democratic orientation geared towards the realisation of nation-building, reconciliation, and inclusivity. Mandela thus strongly and forcefully challenged the Eurocentric notion of the museum that exoticised indigenous people, presenting them alongside fauna and flora as frozen in time as this outmoded and racist museological practices of collecting and representation is not representative of the human rights enshrined in the South African Constitution nor in the Bill of Rights as befitting of a newly formed democracy.

Giving scholarly erudition to Mandela's statement quoted above on the colonial legacy of the museum and heritage sector in pre-1994 South Africa, Amareswar Galla listed several problems within the inherited apartheid museum and heritage structures.[33] The democratic aversion to the racist and undemocratic orientation of the colonial-apartheid heritage policies and practices were bolstered by the determination and commitment to change it through equitable redress by democratic activists. This is the historical-ideological genesis of the establishment of the Arts and Culture Task Group (ACTAG) as a policy framework for the implementation of democratisation, representation, and accountability in the cultural and heritage sector. As Galla argued and as we advance in our argument throughout the book, it was through the process of museum and heritage transformation in South Africa that "the legitimacy of the hegemonic Western discourse and its apartheid manifestations began to be challenged and issues of politics of heritage discourse, the blatant discrimination under apartheid and the myth of professional detachment was deconstructed and their limitations exposed."[34] According to Galla, the work that thus needs to be done through transformation beyond the deconstruction of the racist apartheid legacy is the reconstructive process of creating an integrated, holistic, and interactive mechanism for transforming heritage management on the democratic pillars of inclusive multicultural community and nation-building.[35] The scope of the ACTAG report was broad, covering exhaustively virtually all the arts, culture, and heritage spheres, which has received equally massive scholarly and public engagements. However, we focus here on its policies on archives and museum and heritage studies.

One of the reasons for our focus specifically on archives and Museum and Heritage Studies is based on the inter-connectedness of our professional experiences as a former archivist at the University of the Western Cape Robben Island Museum (UWC RIM) Mayibuye Archives and the former academic coordinator of the African Programme in Museum and Heritage Studies (APMHS), a postgraduate diploma in Museum and Heritage Studies co-convened by UWC and RIM, and our respective doctoral studies, which focused on the transformation of the archive through the evolution of liberation archives and an historical and philosophical study of heritage education in post-apartheid South Africa. The impetus for the book specifically developed from a joint seminar and conference paper: 'The UWC Robben Island Museum Mayibuye Archives and the African Programme in Museum and Heritage Studies (APMHS) in the nexus of public historical scholarship' delivered at the Centre for Humanities Research (CHR), South African Contemporary History and Humanities Seminar at the University of the Western Cape (UWC), and at the National Heritage Council's (NHC) 'Archives for Deepening Democracy' Conference in East London in 2012. A further imperative for the study is to emphasise the importance of heritage education and training as one of the ways to effect transformation and the subsequent decolonising of heritage institutions. Furthermore, we believe that the heritage sector requires more focused engagement because despite the acknowledgement of the importance of critical Museum Studies in the transformation of the sector, as well as issues around the appropriate education and training needed to operationalise and sustain this transformation project, it has received little critical attention in the study of the transformation of the archive and Museum and Heritage Studies in South Africa.

We argue that within the framework of the more expansive restructuring processes of a transformation discourse, Mandela's 1997 speech on Heritage Day set in motion a formalised process in which the inherently racist meaning of the museum was challenged and the transformation of the museum and heritage sector in South Africa started on its course, which in turn had global reverberations within the heritage field.[36] Crucial in Mandela's admonishment of the museum as device for the projection of white supremacy and racism was his recognition of the violence of the display and representation of Africans, which Hicks also echoed, when he argued that for as long as museums continue to display African looted objects through the prism of museums, they will remain monuments to white supremacist ideology of racial science.[37]

Against the backdrop of a transformation discourse that offered a way for existing heritage institutions to be reimagined in alignment with the democratic ideals of a new South Africa, and to reflect the cultural sensibilities of the changing political conditions within the country, the early 1990s saw a flowering of new heritage institutions, national museums, community museums, memorial projects, monuments, archival institutions, and a host of intellectual and academic programmes. Alongside these new developments were also the refashioning or reinvention of existing institutions through renaming, reclaiming, and redress primarily through the addition of previously racially marginalised persons to the staff bases of research and heritage projects. These various initiatives of redress as we argue, did not really disrupt the deeply entrenched racist modalities which forms the foundation of these institutions. Informed by the newly adopted ethos of the democratic government, these institutions focused on forging a shared and collective sense of history and heritage aligned to the new democratic government's commitment to reconciliation, social cohesion, redress, and nation-building.

The political developments and intense transformation processes saw the emergence of various post-apartheid heritage institutions and training programmes such as the Mayibuye Centre for History and Culture which was later absorbed into the Robben Island Museum (RIM), the Robben Island Training Programme (RITP) – African Programme in Museum and Heritage Studies (APMHS) jointly convened by UWC, University of Cape Town (UCT) and RIM, the District Six Museum, the Lwandle Migrant Labour Museum, the South African History Archive (SAHA), the Gay and Lesbian Archives (GALA), and the National Heritage and Cultural Studies Centre (NAHECS) at the University of Fort Hare (UFH) among a host of institutions formed during the 1990s. Most of these institutions played a key role in the transformation discourse by leading discussions in heritage transformation on the national stage, however transformation has been painfully slow and where it has happened, there have been varying degrees of success especially when framed by political and socio-economic considerations.

Although this study is broadly concerned with the transformation of the museum and heritage sector, it focuses primarily on the evolution of the intricate connection between post-apartheid archives and Museum and Heritage Studies in post-apartheid South Africa, specifically from 1994 to 2014. Through an exposition and critical analysis of the history of the Mayibuye Centre for History and Culture as an activist space of public historical knowledge production and scholarship, we trace how the project of Public History developed through the activist activities of the Mayibuye Centre and opened discussions around frictions, contestations, and contradictions in and around archives, museums, heritage professionals, and academics, which was not only radical for its time but also had a global impact in respect of the increased call for the restitution of looted objects, arguably similar to the #RhodesMustFall movement and subsequent fallist movements that emanated from South Africa. In responding to Mandela's challenge to transform the museum and heritage sector in alignment with the ideals of democracy, human rights, and the Constitution, which was a culmination of the activities of the Mayibuye Centre, various policy initiatives were set in motion to redress this racist anomaly of the legacy of museums and the heritage landscape in South Africa. These initiatives were codified in the report of the ACTAG White Paper of 1996 as previously discussed above, which in turn gave rise to other pieces of heritage policies and legislation.

We further our contribution to this field by going back to the fundamental questions of: What is being transformed in archives and Museum and Heritage Studies in South Africa? How has the archives and Museum and Heritage Studies sectors specifically been transformed? Why is it being transformed? Who benefits from this transformation? From a hypothesis that transformation is not necessarily a metaphor or conveniently translates into decolonisation and that it is possible to transform institutions without decolonisation, we agree with Galla's position which could be applied broadly that the "[t]ransformation of museums is not about chameleon-like adaptation to a democratic and multicultural South Africa but an active engagement in shared cultural spaces informed by contested and empowering discourse for all South Africans."[38] We further this understanding of transformation through a critical conceptual analysis of the relationship between transformation and decolonisation. The question we ask is in the context of the history of colonialism and apartheid: Is it possible to transform without decolonising and does decolonisation unavoidably entail transformation? Is transformation a euphemism for decolonisation or to avoid decolonisation?

Our hypothesis is that since transformation is a specialised work of decolonisation as a process of deconstruction and re-construction, it will need people not only to be trained in specialised technical skills for the purpose, but also an ideological orientation and re-orientation. This training will ideally be situated in a decolonial ethos of Museum and Heritage Studies and training. The question we thus ask is: What and where are the archives of these decolonised ethos for training of the specialised skills needed to overturn the existing colonial apartheid legacy of Museum and Heritage Studies in South Africa? While the history of the origin and development of South African museums is well documented and gives ample glimpses into what ethos of the museum are inculcated at different stages in the archival configuration and Museum and Heritage Studies in South Africa from 1825 to 1994, the work of the Mayibuye Centre documents the underbelly of this period, especially its role as a space of public historical knowledge production that provides a credible counter archive for museum and heritage training and study in South Africa.

The Mayibuye Centre launched in 1991 at UWC can be described as the incubator and engine of transformation of archives and Museum and Heritage Studies in South Africa. As narrated by André Odendaal, the evolution of UWC as the 'intellectual home of the democratic left', because of the activities of its faculty members and students in challenging and questioning the system of knowledge production in South Africa, which has hitherto served to defend and shore-up the apartheid system under the guise of apolitical academic scholarship, was the background to the establishment of the Mayibuye Centre.[39] As against the apolitical illusion of other universities, UWC declared that the university cannot be politically neutral by breaking "with a colonially rooted university system that had traditionally privileged either Afrikaner nationalism or liberal capitalism" by redefining its mission to a commitment to "serve the Third world communities of South Africa through an open and critical alignment with the political movements and organisations committed to the struggle for liberation of South Africa."[40]

One of the initiatives of realising this mission was the People's History Project, initiated by UWC's Department of History, this initiative as Odendaal explained "was perhaps the first in the country to identify formally with and attempt to institutionalise at university level the demands of the mass-based democratic movement for people's education."[41] It is this connection and interaction between academic history and the society-in-the-making beyond the confines of the campus as an exclusive academic space that gave rise to the Mayibuye Centre as a critical space of public historical knowledge production and development of the archive of the liberation struggle in South Africa and "provided a conceptual base" for the transformation of archives and Museum and Heritage Studies in South Africa, as we discuss in this book. As further noted by Odendaal apart from his own efforts at relocating the records of the International Defence and Aid Fund (IDAF) from London to Cape Town, which constituted a counter archive of South African history from the perspectives of international solidarity, resistance, and the liberation struggle, the construction of the post-apartheid archive through "the intense community and struggle-based enterprise of material collection and activities"[42] of ordinary people who donated hidden material is an aspect that has been ignored in the study of the construction of the post-apartheid archive. What further distinguishes the Mayibuye Centre as a platform of archive and Museum and Heritage Studies through public historical knowledge production was its activities which "cut across traditional boundaries between 'town and gown' or in other words challenged the traditional monastic notion of a university separated from the world around it."[43] As discussed in this book, these "activities and the Public History experience of the 1980s and early 1990s gave rise to an awareness in the centre of the exciting opportunities to work in diverse, multi-media, cross-disciplinary ways, and brought across to its leadership the massive impact that technological revolution accompanying economic globalisation would have on traditional academic practices."[44] This is what Ciraj Rassool described as the transactional exchange of knowledge between the academy and the public which is definitive of the transformation of archives and Museum and Heritage Studies in South Africa we argue in this book.[45]

The book is structured into six chapters. Chapter One introduces a number of key historical, theoretical, and critical debates regarding the archive/archives. The departure point of this chapter is to firstly engage with the selected works of scholars such as Foucault and Derrida's articulations of the archive as it may be productive in exploring the positionality of archives within the transformation discourse. In addition to Foucault and Derrida's theories on the archive, there has been a steady proliferation of literature around the nature of archives, its functions, and its work. This has formed part of a wider interdisciplinary debate among scholars and now also increasingly among archival professionals. With the recent sustained interest in archives from especially outside the archive from various disciplines, this chapter reflects on the intellectual history of archival thought over the last century by engaging with the classical texts on archival theory by thinkers such Hilary Jenkinson and T.R. Schellenberg who shaped much of contemporary archival thinking. Drawing on this body of work that has been produced on the archive, this chapter suggests a reimagining of the archive by arguing for a deeper philosophical understanding of the archive and an appreciation of the epistemological meanings the archive holds. The chapter concludes by underlining the importance of an interdisciplinary conversation between archivists and scholars regarding the philosophical and practical underpinnings of the archive.

Chapter Two argues that one of the ways the archive can be transformed is through a fundamental paradigm shift in the way archivists approach their work in archives. As a way of negotiating the somewhat tenuous relationship between the archivist and historian, one of the aims of the chapter is to argue that archivists and scholars should become more self-aware of the mediation that takes place within archives as this will create a better understanding of the archival processes that records are subject to. More importantly, this chapter calls on archivists to abandon their antiquarian approach to the archive and instead become researchers actively involved in knowledge production and activists of social justice.

Chapter Three provides an analysis of the configuration of archives in South Africa, specifically NAHECS in relation to the UWC Robben Island Museum Mayibuye Archives. The chapter uncovers and addresses critical questions of the role of post-apartheid archives in the transition to democracy and reflects on the making of a new nation and in sustaining its narrative of reconciliation and triumph. By focusing on how post-apartheid archives have been deployed and for which purposes, this chapter examine the challenges and limitations that frame archives and their implication for the aspiration of nation-building and reconciliation.

Chapter Four provides an overview of the history of Museum and Heritage Studies in Africa by assessing the various training programmes on offer throughout the continent to situate the African Programme in Museum and Heritage Studies (APMHS). The APMHS which was part of the outcome of the UWC Robben Island Mayibuye Archives' incorporation into the Robben Island Museum (RIM) evolved from the Robben Island Training Programme (RITP), jointly convened by the UWC, UCT and RIM in 1998. This was the pilot initiative to transform South African Museum and Heritage Studies and training from its colonial and apartheid legacy into an inclusive democratic orientation through fast-track training in museum and heritage skills geared towards social justice. One of the distinctions it made between itself and other programmes of Museum and Heritage Studies in Africa was its rejection of concentrating on the acquisition of technical museum skills as the focus of Museum and Heritage Studies.

Chapter Five explores the extent to which the Robben Island Training Programme – African Programme in Museum and Heritage Studies' orientation to Museum and Heritage Studies was innovative, radical, and progressive compared to other pre-existing programmes in South Africa and the rest of the continent as discussed in the previous chapter. This exploration is necessary as it identify how it is different from other programmes of Museum and Heritage Studies in both South Africa and the continent and show the limits and the possibilities that it opens for a critical Afrocentric turn in African Museum and Heritage Studies (AMHS). Discussing the history of Museum Studies and training in South Africa also allows us to explore the kind of training and studies required and appropriate for dismantling the colonial museum as a means to transform and decolonise Museum and Heritage Studies from its racist exclusionary ethos to a decolonised African centred orientation that responds to the need for epistemic and social justice. Although more needs to be done in decolonising and transforming Museum and Heritage Studies, it is undeniable that there has been immense tangible transformation in the heritage sector in South Africa. However, the extent to which heritage is decolonised depends on how far it is on the Afrocentric turn of dismantling the colonial museum.

Lastly, Chapter Six explores the question of the interconnectedness of Public History to a programme in Museum and Heritage Studies, given the centrality of the Public History research project at UWC's Department of History, to the establishment and development of the RITP Diploma in Museum and Heritage studies. To answer this question, this chapter focus on the meaning and features of the distinct brand of Public History developed by the 'Troika' at UWC's History department and why it is definitive of the RITP-APMHS and of transformation of Museum and Heritage Studies in Africa, specifically in South Africa.

We conclude our book by reiterating that despite the transformative gains made in South Africa since 1994, heritage institutions and heritage training opportunities continue to be haunted by the legacies of their own colonial and apartheid history as they remain locked in their Eurocentric custodial cloisters reflected through their collections, exhibitions, and training opportunities. While there are significant issues of training, funding, poor leadership, and aging equipment and infrastructure which hinders transformation, it is our contention that there also seems to be a lack of political and public interest in heritage institutions and heritage training as they are competing with a host of other socio-economic and political challenges that the South African society has to grapple with. These are some of the failures of post-apartheid transformation, some systemic and some as unintentional consequences of limited funding, political interference, and limited professional training. However, as we argued, for transformation to be fully realised, there needs to be a rupture from the colonial vestiges that informs the approach to heritage on the African continent and in South Africa in particular. In moving towards transformation, one that is informed by an African-based decolonised approach to heritage, we should be able to have honest, in-depth, and critical self-reflections of policies, practices, roles, missions, visions, and continuing relevance. Rather than remaining spectators and passive custodians of history, collections should be cultivated and activated through research initiatives, pedagogy, and public programming to assist in knowledge production. Equally important to this is to enrich the lives of those around it and in this way ensure its sustainability and relevance in an evolving post-apartheid society.

Endnotes

1. L. Abungu. 2005. 'Museum and Communities in Africa: Facing New Challenges'. *Public Archaeology*, 4(2-3):151-154. https://doi.org/10.1179/pua.2005.4.2-3.151
2. *Newly approved ICOM definition of museum.* http://bit.ly/3lLrQE8 [Accessed 7 November 2022].
3. *One of the proposed ICOM definitions of museum.* http://bit.ly/3ZklVm9 [Accessed 28 April 2022].
4. D. Hicks. 2020. *The Brutish Museums: The Benin Bronzes, Colonial Violence and Cultural Restitution.* London: Pluto Press, 3.
5. E.N. Arinze. 1998. 'African Museums: The Challenge of Change'. *Museum International*, 50(1):31. https://doi.org/10.1111/1468-0033.00133
6. Hicks. *The Brutish Museums: The Benin Bronzes.*
7. Ibid., 16-17.
8. Ibid., 3.
9. Ibid., 16.
10. A. Smith, (1797-1872). 1849. *Illustrations of the Zoology of South Africa Collected During an Expedition to the Interior of South Africa 1834, 1835, and 1836.* London: Smith, Elder & Co. https://doi.org/10.5962/bhl.title.10416
11. K. Rookmaaker. 2017. 'The Zoological Contributions of Andrew Smith (1797-1872) with an Annotated Bibliography and a Numerical Analysis of Newly Described Animal Species'. *Transactions of the Royal Society of South Africa*, 72(2):152. https://doi.org/10.1080/0035919X.2016.1230078
12. See R.F.H. Summers. 1975. *A History of the South African Museum, 1825-1975.* Cape Town: Published for the Trustees of the South African Museum by A.A. Balkema, 10-12.
13. See R.H. Davis. 1977. 'Review of Andrew Smith's Journal of His Expedition into the Interior of South Africa, 1834-1836: An Authentic Narrative of Travels and Discoveries, the Manners and Customs of the Native Tribes, and the Physical Nature of the Country', by W.F. Lye. *The International Journal of African Historical Studies*, 10(2):320-322. https://doi.org/10.2307/217364;

    C. Rassool. 2015. 'Human Remains, the Discipline of the Dead, and the South African Memorial Complex'. In: D.R. Peterson, K. Gavua & C. Rassool (eds.), *The Politics of Heritage in Africa Economies, Histories, and Infrastructures.* London: Cambridge University Press, 133-156. https://doi.org/10.1017/CBO9781316151181.008
14. As revealed in Andrew Smith's diary edited by Percival R. Kirby and published by the Van Riebeeck Society in 1939-1940 under the title, *The Diary of Dr Andrew Smith, Director of the 'Expedition for Exploring Central Africa, 1834-1836.*
15. Summers. *A History of the South African Museum*, 11-12.
16. Ibid., 17.
17. V. Harris. 2000. *Exploring Archives: An Introduction to Archival Ideas and Practice in South Africa.* Pretoria: National Archives of South Africa, 6.
18. A.L. Stoler. 2002. 'Colonial Archives and the Arts of Governance'. *Archival Science*, 2, 98. https://doi.org/10.1007/BF02435632

19 Ibid., 97;
    Also read R.H. Brown & B. Davis-Brown. 1998. 'The Making of Memory: The Politics of Archives, Libraries and Museums in the Construction of National Consciousness'. *History of the Human Sciences*, 11(4):20. https://doi.org/10.1177/095269519801100402
20 S.H. Griffin & S. Timcke. 2021. 'Re-framing Archival thought in Jamaica and South Africa: Challenging Racist Structures, Generating New Narratives'. *Archives and Records*, 43(1):9. https://doi.org/10.1080/23257962.2021.2002137
21 Harris. *Exploring Archives*, 7.
22 V. Harris. 2002. 'The Archival Sliver: Power, Memory and Archives in South Africa'. *Archival Science* 2:73. https://doi.org/10.1007/BF02435631
23 V. Harris. 2001. 'Seeing (in) Blindness: South Africa, Archives and Passion for Justice'. *Archifacts*, 5. https://phambo.wiser.org.za/files/seminars/Harris2002.pdf
24 Harris. *Exploring Archives*, 5.
25 Section 32(1) of the Constitution of the Republic of South Africa, Act 108 of 1996 states that everyone has the right of access to records or/and information held by the state and any information held by another person and that is required for the exercise or protection of any rights.
26 V. Riouful. 2000. 'Behind Telling: Post-apartheid Representations of Robben Island's Past'. *Kronos*, 26:22.
27 Ibid., 26.
28 K.A. Appiah. 2011. 'Identity, Politics and the Archive'. In: X. Mangcu (ed.), *Becoming Worthy Ancestors: Archive, Public Deliberation and Identity in South Africa*. Johannesburg: Wits University Press, 106.
29 See M. Bernal. 1991. *Black Athena: The Afroasiatic Roots of Classical Civilization*. New Brunswick, NJ: Rutgers University Press.
    Bernal through his *Black Athena* theory dismantled the dominant paradigm which denied that ancient Egyptian civilisation was African.
30 Nelson Mandela Speech at the formal opening of Robben Island Museum, Heritage Day, 24th September 1997. http://bit.ly/42NIQLY [Accessed 21 April 2022].
31 Ibid.
32 Ibid.
33 A. Galla. 1999. 'Transformation in South Africa: A Legacy Challenged'. *Museum International*, 51(2):38-43. https://doi.org/10.1111/1468-0033.00203
    Galla was also the recipient of SAMA's inaugural presidential award for outstanding service for transformation planning and training in 1997.
34 Ibid., 38-43.
35 Ibid., 39.
36 See ongoing discourse of decolonising the museum and the restitution of African objects globally.
37 Hicks. *The Brutish Museums: The Benin Bronzes*, 3.
38 Galla. 'Transformation in South Africa', 42-43.
39 N. Lekgotla laga Ramoupi, N. Solani, A. Odendaal & K. ka Mpumlwana (eds.). 2021. *Robben Island Rainbow Dreams: The Making of Democratic South Africa's First National Heritage Institution*. Cape Town: HRSC Press, 19.

40 Ibid., 19.
41 Ibid., 20.
42 Ibid., 23.
43 Ibid., 23.
44 Ibid., 24.
45 C. Rassool. 2010. 'Power, Knowledge and the Politics of Public Pasts'. *African Studies*, 69(1):87. https://doi.org/10.1080/00020181003647215

The Aura of Archives – Innocuous Charms, Fevers, and Afflictions   1

> The archive is an excess of meaning, where the reader experiences beauty, amazement, and a certain affective tremor. The location will be secret, different for each person, but, in every itinerary, there will be encounters that will facilitate access to this secret place, and most of all to its expression.[1]

Archives are sites of contestation and political presence, yet like other forms of history, memory, and trace, archives are never quite central in public debates and collective memory. Archives in post-apartheid South Africa are "far from standing as enduring monuments to the past, instead they appear somewhat fragile, eternally subject to the judgement of the society in which they exist." They are "neither atemporal nor absolute, the meaning they convey may be manipulated, misinterpreted, or suppressed … [T]he archives of the past are also the mutable creations of the present."[2] Serving as a pedagogic tool and aide-mémoire of the past, archives as collective remembrance draws on elements from the past to speak to the present and an imagined future. However, the post-apartheid commemorative culture which has gripped South Africa since the mid-1990s has also accentuated the tensions, contestation, and compromise between remembering and forgetting, all intertwined with multiple stories of loss, triumph, sacrifice, heroism, victimhood, trauma, and violence. These are all located within the politics, socio-economics, and culture of a negotiated transition and settlement towards the building of democracy.

Despite South Africa's euphoric democratic dawn in 1994, it remains a country undergoing intense socio-economic, political, and cultural transition, particularly as it continues to grapple with the legacies of complex, contested, and fragmented colonial and apartheid pasts which the present must contend with. In trying to attend to the difficult legacies of a country built on institutionalised racism and discrimination, secrecy, inequality, gross human rights violations, and state-imposed amnesia, and in the recasting of a new nation, various mnemonic devices such as archives, museums, memorials, monuments, public holidays, public art and performances, historiographies, autobiographical writing, and recreational tourism among others, have been deployed in the service of the production of collective memory, social cohesion, reconciliation, and transformation in post-apartheid South Africa. More than two decades after the new democratic dispensation was ushered in, reality has set in with the sobering cognisance that there are limits to the South African 'miracle' and its liberation. Burdened with the legacies brought about by the oppressive, discriminatory, and violent acts of colonialism, apartheid, and resistance, the transformation discourse in some respects has become a dream deferred as the effects of these legacies continue to reverberate in post-apartheid South Africa. This is exacerbated by the deepening of race and class division, inequality, an incongruent ruling party, and the resultant, often violent, forms of protest actions with the focus primarily on basic rights such as land, housing, employment, healthcare, and education. Further contributing to these challenges facing the transformation of post-apartheid heritage is chronic budgetary constraints, lack of funding, and inadequate human resource capacity.

In recognising the impact left behind by colonial and apartheid systems of power, one can begin to understand the limitations and challenges that face the transformation of the archival system within post-apartheid South Africa. In deconstructing the challenges and successes of the transformation of archives in post-apartheid South Africa, this chapter engages with key historical, theoretical, and critical debates regarding the archive. There has been a steady proliferation of literature around the nature of archives, their functions, and their work. In post-apartheid South Africa, the debate on the archive was made explicit with the publishing of *Refiguring the Archive* (2002),[3] which was one of the outcomes of a project that focused on a series of thirteen seminars, workshops, and an exhibition hosted in 1998 by the University of the Witwatersrand's Graduate School for the Humanities and Social Sciences in partnership with Wits Historical Papers, the South African History Archive (SAHA), the Gay and Lesbian Archives (GALA), and the National Archives. The publication remains a definitive and compelling body of work in which a cross-disciplinary discussion unfolded about the nature of archives through debates around memory, power, visuality, truth and reconciliation, and other contestations, all of which pervade the archive. It has formed part of a wider interdisciplinary debate among scholars and now also increasingly among archival professionals who have written on the reconfiguration of the archive over the last two decades.

As a way of making a foray into this conversation, and to better understand the archive in respect of its positionality within the transformation discourse, one of the central tenets of this chapter is to interrogate the complex meanings of the archive both in the physical world and as an expression of the internal psyche. If archives are to remain relevant in an age of significant socio-economic, political, and technological changes, scholars and archivists need to dig deeper "to see the elastic, inexact character of truth, and symbolic interpretation rather than literalism that allows us to err, to change, [and] to adapt."[4] For this shift to occur, this chapter will argue for a deeper philosophical understanding of the archive and the epistemological meanings the archive holds. Much has been imagined, thought of, and written about the archive. Still, there remains much more to be imagined and written about it. The idea of the archive has become quite a contested concept both outside and within the archive as can be seen from ongoing debates percolating within academic discourses and among archivists about the archive as an institution, as a mode of thinking, and as a way of knowing. Problematically, the term 'archive', 'archives' and/ or 'collection' is often employed too easily without much cognisance of the complexities inherent in the notion of 'archive' or the conceptual differences between 'archives' as an ordered repository of preserved historical source material and 'archive' as a mode of thinking about and knowing the world. There has been a discernible awareness around 'archive' and 'archives', particularly from scholars with diverse theoretical formulations of the archive emerging across various disciplines in which the archive is either read in deconstructive terms or as a Foucauldian epistemology. Nonetheless, the 'archive' has remained contested territory.

Though few have attempted definitions of the archive, much critique is levelled against the archive, often with little recognition of the philosophy, theory, conventions, and practices that govern it. Often, much to the dismay of those in the archival profession, "the idea of the archive which the professional archivist is familiar with has become overlaid and blended, even diluted or adulterated, with concepts drawn from the newly engaged disciplines: the text, the ouvre, the corpus, the canon and the repertoire."[5] Nothing is less clear today, according to Jacques Derrida, than the word archive,[6] and it is in this sense that the archive has become contested territory which, in turn, has made archivists feel uneasy about the academic disciplines' advance into the field of archives.

The physical manifestation of archives as places of storage and preservation, where physical, documentary, visual, oral, virtual, or material fragments of the past are kept, has also become an intense source of contestation and debate as archives are shaped through acts of remembering and forgetting which, in turn, depends on changing public and political discourses.[7] Thus, in trying to think through the questions of the archive, and through the exploration of diverse theoretical and practical formulations of the archive by scholars and archivists, this chapter will build an argument that archives should be recognised as "an intellectual discipline based on the philosophical study of ideas, not [just as] an empirical discipline based on the scientific study of fact."[8] More than this, as a way of foregrounding a dialogue between scholars and archivists, perhaps it is pertinent to distinguish that this chapter will discuss two distinct genres of writing about the archive. Here, we are referring to the theoretical formulations of the archive juxtaposed with archival principles and practices of record-keeping, or what became known as archival science, which at times may have suggestive points of intersection and, at other times, seem to be wholly disjointed. Though theory and practice will be discussed as oppositional at some points in the chapter, there are also several points of intersection.

Writing about the perceived dichotomy between theory and practice, Terry Cook and Joan Schwartz argued that "these twins – theory and practice – should not be viewed as archival polarities."[9] They further argued that "theory, then, is the complement to practice, not its opposite. Theory and practice should cross-fertilize each other in the theatre of archives, rather than one being derivative of, or dependent on, the other."[10] Following Cook and Schwartz's argument, we argue that theory and practice should become integrated aspects of the work of the archivist as a means to understand the deeper contextual meanings of the archive and effect transformation within and of archives. We further argue that in imagining a different future for the archive, it is necessary that theory and practice should not be regarded as opposites but as complementary to each other.

Archives are troubled, and the trouble of archives, as perceived by Derrida, lies "at the unstable limit between public and private, between the family, the society, and the State, between the family and an intimacy even more private than the family, between oneself and oneself."[11] But perhaps it is not so much that this trouble is unsettling. Instead, this trouble should be deployed to unsettle and problematise the metaphorical, intellectual, and physical spaces that archives seem to inhabit so trouble-free. Archives are sites of mediation, complexity, power, and contestation as they are precariously suspended between the private, the public, the personal, and the political. Despite these tensions, archives remain paradoxically alluring. It has enticed some scholars and a growing number of archivists to think critically about its philosophy, history, politics, and poetics. This has sparked an interdisciplinary conversation, especially among scholars.

The lure of the archive

In her reflections as a researcher in the archive, Harriet Bradley emotively pointed to the philosophical nature of the archive when she noted:

> Even in an age of postmodern scepticism the archive continues to hold its alluring seductions and intoxications. There is the promise (or illusion?) that all time lost can become time regained. In the archive, there lingers an assurance of concreteness, objectivity, recovery, and wholeness. Caught up in the heady and powerful atmosphere of scholarship and professionalism we enter the rose garden, hearing the 'hidden laughter of children' in the leaves of the apple-tree. But as Eliot knew, we may only find that which we bring with us. In the end, what we hear is not, perhaps, the lost alterity; above all, what we find in the archive is ourselves.[12]

In stirring terms, through her reference to T.S. Eliot's *Burnt Norton*[13] in which he affectingly spoke about the elusiveness of time, Bradley alluded to the elusive and mysterious nature of the archive as it enthrals, seduces, and intoxicates those who enter its cloistered sanctum. Reference to the archive evokes images of a dusty, dark, forbidden, and mysterious place filled with insurmountable mountains of material stacked from floor to ceiling with a forlorn archivist diligently sieving through faded, disintegrating, yellow-stained records. Despite this romantic imagery, the archive has increasingly become central both to scholarly research and the existence of a democratic society. Political theorist, Irving Velody, reiterated this by arguing that "a[s] the backdrop to all scholarly research, stands the archive, [because it] appeals to ultimate truth [and] adequacy, and plausibility in the work of the humanities and social sciences rest on archival presuppositions."[14]

Echoing this sentiment, Thomas Osborne argued that there is a family of disciplines that surround the archive rather than just history or the historiographical disciplines.[15] Drawing on Michel Foucault's argument that clinical medicine is a discipline that is central to the epistemological structure of all the so-called human sciences, Osborne argued that the archive is central to the humanities. Ever since the innovations made by August Compte, Jules Michelet, and Leopold von Ranke, which focused on transforming the archive into a site of historical knowledge production, archival research has in effect provided the foundation for research in the humanities.[16] Though their approach to archival research was rooted in 19th-century positivism and empiricism to mirror the prevailing methodology of the natural sciences, they did much to advance the idea of exploring the archive as a site in which to pursue historical research, albeit based on the positivist modes of enquiry emphasising truth, evidence, and authenticity. It was only at the turn of the 20th century that this positivist and empiricist approach to historical research was challenged by the Frankfurt School in particular. Despite this challenge, the recalcitrant imagining of the archive as evidentiary, objective, and authentic has remained.

For example, in her meditative reflections on doing research in the police archives held at the Library of the Arsenal in Paris, Arlette Farge offered a way to understand the allure of archives. Farge beautifully articulated that "the taste for the archive is rooted in these encounters with the silhouettes of the past, be they faltering or sublime." According to her, "there is an obscure beauty in so many existences barely illuminated by words, in confrontation with each other, imprisoned by their own devices as much as they were undone by their era."[17] She also alerted us to the nuance that despite the deceptive beauty of the archives in the way they can ensnare and grip hold of the lone researcher, archival research becomes an obsession that captivates the historian with promises of untold discoveries, fragmented as they are. Farge explained that doing research in archives sometimes "gives rise to the naïve but profound feeling of tearing away a veil, of crossing through the opaqueness of knowledge and, as if after a long and uncertain voyage, finally gaining access to the essence of beings and things."[18] Further in her exploration of the police archives, Farge described the materiality of the archive to the reader through an account of her sensorial experiences of touching, seeing, smelling, and feeling the records placed in front of her. This is the allure of the archives that may entice historians to forget about the snares of archival research. Farge further suggested that the materiality of archives might be tied to the reason for the lingering image of the archives as truthful and impartial.[19] However, Farge emphasised that the aim of archival research is not "to unearth some buried treasure, but for the historian to use the archives as a vantage point from which she can bring to light new forms of knowledge."[20]

Harriet Bradley also recognised that part of the thrill of doing archival research for the historian is that it is considered a rite of initiation into the profession.[21] Apart from being filled with potential exhilarating discoveries and intimate pleasures where archives quite literally entrance and bewitch those who wander there through its haunting temporality, Bradley suggested that archives may even hold the promise (even if imaginary) of finding oneself. Bradley argued that "through the archive we strive to recover what we have lost, and to relive the lost past by retelling its stories."[22] But perhaps it is in this sometimes-frenetic pursuit of the archive to find this lost object, or in essence to find ourselves, that we are overcome by what Derrida termed the "archive fever" by falling under the spell of the archive. For Derrida, this is "the archive fever or disorder we are experiencing today, concerning its lightest symptoms or the great holocaustic tragedies of our modern history and historiography: concerning all the detestable revisionisms, as well as the most legitimate, necessary and courageous rewritings of history."[23]

Derrida further noted that an awareness of historical indeterminacy lies at the heart of this archive fever as an epistemic source, which compels us to persistently return to the archive as a source of knowledge. Put simply, "we are *en mal d'archive*: in need of archives."[24] More than this, according to Derrida we also burn for them. In trying to understand this need or desire to archive and for the archive, as it both tantalises and torments, it is worth remembering Derrida's words: "nothing is less reliable, nothing is less clear today than the word archive."[25] Yet, we continue to be obsessed by the seductive pleasures and fetishised qualities of the archive in our nostalgic yearnings to return to the past. Derrida poignantly described this desire by noting that "It is to burn with a passion. It is never to rest, interminably, from searching for the archive right where it slips away. It is to run after the archive. […] It is to have a compulsive, repetitive, and nostalgic desire for the archive, an irrepressible desire to return to the origin, a homesickness, a nostalgia for the return to the most archaic place of absolute commencement."[26]

Ironically, these fragments or remnants of the past only ever provide a "temporary satiation of the quest for full identity and narcissistic unity."[27] Within a similar vein as Derrida, Helen Freshwater argued that the allure of the archive can be tied to the seeming "promise [of] the recovery of lost time, the possibility of being reunited with the lost past, and the fulfilment of our deepest desires for wholeness and completion."[28] Derrida, Freshwater, and Bradley have compellingly argued that the fascination of archives lies at the heart of the nostalgic yet impossible search for the lost object, as the recovery of lost time will never be realised, and the lost object will never be found.[29] Drawing on Jean Laplanche, Freshwater argued that "what we are searching for in the archive, as in psychoanalysis, is, in fact, a lost object."[30] Freshwater further argued that "the narrative of the past event or evidence will have been transformed by our research in much the same way as the processes of displacement and repression alter the lost object."[31] Thus in the search for the lost object, what we potentially find in the archive is not just ourselves, but a substitute for the lost object which inevitably has been altered by our archival research. Also reflecting on her physical encounters with the archive, Carolyn Steedman perceptively remarked:

> In the project of finding an identity through the processes of historical identification, the past is searched for something [...] that confirms the searcher in his or her sense of self, confirms them as they want to be, and feel in some measure that they already are [...] [but] the object has been altered by the very search for it [...] what has actually been lost can never be found. This not to say that *nothing* is found, but that thing is always something else.[32]

More than just searching for something in the past, Steedman argued that part of the allure of archives can be found in the physical phenomenology of archives as spaces.[33] Explaining her argument, Steedman deployed Gaston Bachelard's psychological study in which he explored the intimate spaces of people's lives with a specific focus on the house. In *The Poetics of Space*, Bachelard argued that:

> In the theatre of the past that is constituted by memory [...] we think we know ourselves in time, when all we know is a sequence of fixations in the spaces of the being's stability – a being who does not want to melt away, and who, even in the past, wants time to 'suspend' its flight. In its countless alveoli space contains compressed time. That is what space is for.[34]

According to Steedman, "[t]he Archive belongs to the kind of oneiric spaces that Bachelard described: alone in the Archive, in the counting house of dreams"[35] where the historian goes to be at home, as well as to be alone.[36] For Steedman, this desire or fever for the archive is as much about wanting to know and have the past as it is about articulating a certain way of being in the world.

There has been a discernible awareness around archives in the form of very creative and diverse theoretical formulations of the archive that have emerged from various disciplines in the humanities and social sciences.[37] This interdisciplinary debate outside the archive has, in some ways, contributed much to the knowledge around archives but has also revealed several limitations in the exploration of the archival discourse across the disciplines. In a rethinking of the archive and as a way of addressing these limitations, it is of critical importance that a nuanced understanding of the practices, history, and theory is cultivated not only by scholars across the various disciplines, but also by those in the archival profession, especially regarding the (dis)juncture between archival theory and practice. In his essay on the archive and the human sciences, Velody asserted that "[a] science of the archive must then include a theory of its institutionalisation."[38] We would argue that an intellectual history of archives would thus not only improve the praxis of archivists but may be very productive in nurturing a more nuanced approach to the ethical, practical, and political intricacies that shape the record as it is framed within the power/knowledge paradigm of the metaphorical archive or the material archive. In wrestling with the meaning of the archive, historians, literary critics, philosophers, political scientists, and archivists have to find a way of engaging in a shared yet self-reflexive dialogue to "understand better the very ideas and assumptions about archives that have shaped their ethos, their concepts, their institutions, their collections, and their practices,"[39] and also their training, especially as it relates to Museum and Heritage Studies, as we show later in the book.

Transforming the archive

Apart from the archive's centrality to scholarly research, it is associated with power and control. This is because archival records may also be used as instruments of power in state formation through the silencing and suppression of records. Paradoxically, the same records can also be empowering and liberating as recordkeeping and documentation may ensure state accountability. Concerning the decisive role the archive plays in the formation and subsequent safeguarding of the nation and state, Derrida argued that "[t]here is no political power without control of the archive, if not memory. Effective democratisation can always be measured by this essential criterion: the participation in and access to the archive, its constitution, and its interpretation."[40] Drawing on Benedict Anderson's concept of the nation as an 'imagined community', Richard Harvey Brown and Beth Davis-Brown made a similar argument regarding the centrality of the archive in the formation and creation of the nation.[41]

However, in transforming the archive, the concept of the archive has to take on new and diverse readings, meanings, and forms as it stretches out over a vast terrain "tendering promises of the preservation of primordiality and primariness, origin and source, authority and identity, intention and meaning, durability and permanence."[42] In a paper presented at the 56th Annual Meeting of the Society of American Archivists in 1992, Canadian archivist, Brien Brothman, argued that the term 'archive' can refer both to an action or an object which can be translated into "the archive as edifice; the archive as text; the archive as record; the archive as institution; the archive as university; the archive as scene of dissimulation or manipulation; the archive as discourse; the archive as professional paradigm (knowledge)."[43]

Whereas Brothman touched more broadly on the diverse and often ambiguous meanings of the archive, another archivist, Eric Ketelaar, considerably narrowed his understanding of what the archive is and what it does. Ketelaar argued that archives often resemble temples and prisons, on both an architectural and procedural level. He argued that "archives resemble temples as institutions of surveillance and power architecturally, but they also function as such, because the panoptical archive disciplines and controls through knowledge-power."[44] Within a similar vein as Ketelaar, Velody noted that the archive is perceived as a "well defined data-holding facility, somewhat like a penitentiary."[45] While Brothman and Ketelaar, among others, viewed the archive as a place, space, institution, information, knowledge, or within the limits of Foucauldian discursivity,[46] there are others who viewed the archive within a more metaphorical and philosophical sense. Verne Harris, a leading archival professional and theoretician in South Africa, argued that "'the archive' is to be found whenever and wherever information is marked, or recorded, on a substrate through human agency […] It is to be found in a plethora of markings on the human body, from circumcision to facial scarification, from tattoos to amputations. 'The archive', in short, is all around us; it is on us and inside us."[47]

While these reflections on the archive enable a preliminary understanding of it, we argue that it would also be productive to engage with the many historical, philosophical, and corporeal complexities of the archive. Though the ideas of Michel Foucault and Jacques Derrida have informed and stimulated much of the debate and fervour around archives, Walter Benjamin preceded them. In his seminal essay, 'The Work of Art in the Age of Mechanical Reproduction', Benjamin proposed a way of thinking about the fascination that the archive holds for the historian as the aura of the object. Benjamin discussed the effects of modernity on the work of art by arguing that the mechanical reproducibility of photographs contributed to the loss of their aura as they now lacked the characteristics of art because they subsequently shifted in their use from ritual to political.[48] The aura for Benjamin represented the uniqueness, authenticity, and permanence to explain what is perceived as art. According to Benjamin, the aura can also be explained by drawing a correlation between art and the occurrence of beauty in nature. He illustrated this by asking the reader to imagine the experience of looking at a distant mountain or a branch, and in that sense, the aura of the mountain will be experienced.[49] Benjamin argued that a traditional work of art constitutes a similar experience because, ideally, it possesses the qualities of an aura because of its uniqueness – it cannot be reproduced with complete accuracy to its original form.

From this discussion, one can then argue that the idea of the aura can be applied to other forms of representation and be used to explain the allure of the archive. Unlike the value of an art object, which is largely derived from its exclusivity, the value conferred on the document is tied to its informational content which in turn bestows the document with an aura. Freshwater reiterated Benjamin's point by arguing that despite being "in an age of simulacra, which is rapidly completing its transfer of the production and dissemination of information on to the computer screen, we still privilege the paper document of documentation."[50] However, technological advances or the digitisation of archives at once threaten to destroy the aura of the document but also provide a post-custodial situation where one could imagine an archive without walls.[51]

But as much as Benjamin's aura may explain the fascination with the archive, he also regarded it with great suspicion because "[t]here is no document of civilisation which is not at the same time a document of barbarism."[52] Benjamin further argued that "just as such a document is not free of barbarism, barbarism taints also the manner in which it was transmitted from one owner to another […] He regards it as his task to brush history against the grain."[53] Here, Benjamin conveyed his concern about how the archive should be approached as he cautioned that the archive should be read against the grain. In this cautionary note, Benjamin also alluded to the relationship between power and knowledge in the archive, where knowledge can either be deployed as a means of suppression or liberation. Foucault similarly proposed an understanding of the archive which is based on the relationship between knowledge and power. Imbricated closely in this epistemic relationship is "knowledge and the shaping of archives" and "archives and the shaping of knowledge."[54]

In his very complex, challenging, yet interesting work, *The Archaeology of Knowledge*, Foucault was primarily concerned with systems of thought and knowledge which are governed by rules. Foucault argued that the contemporary study of the history of ideas rests on discontinuities in discourse. He further argued that discourses emerge and transform as the result of a complex set of discursive and institutional relationships which are defined as much by breaks and ruptures and as unified themes.[55] Through this methodological argument, Foucault proposed an understanding of the archive through the 'archaeological method' in which he aimed to describe discourse on its own terms and through its own terms. He reiterated this point by arguing that:

> Archaeology does not seek to rediscover the continuous, insensible transition that relates discourses, on a gentle slope, to what precedes them, surrounds them, or follows them […] its problem is to define discourses in their specificity; to show in what way the set of rules that they put into operation is irreducible to any other […] it is not a 'doxology'; but a differential analysis of the modalities of discourse.[56]

He continued his argument by stating that:

> Archaeology tries to define not the thoughts, representations, images, themes, preoccupations that are concealed or revealed in discourses; but those discourses themselves […] It does not treat discourse as *document* […] it is concerned with discourse in its own volume, as a *monument* […] It refuses to be 'allegorical'.[57]

In abandoning the traditional form of historical analysis, and in an attempt to practice a different history from what is said and known through archaeology, Foucault argued that discursive practices allow statements to emerge as events or things, through which the archive governs this system of statements or what he calls "the system of discursivity".[58] For Foucault:

> … the archive is first the law of what can be said, the system that governs the appearance of statements as unique events. But the archive is also that which determines that all these things said do not accumulate endlessly in an amorphous mass.[59]

Foucault thus read the archive as an epistemological experiment of critical inquiry in which the document is questioned rather than viewed as an excavation site of evidentiary knowledge retrieval. In arguing for a different approach to historical analysis, Foucault proposed that the statement rather than the document should be described, because the archive can no longer be regarded merely as a collection of documents. Instead, the archive is defined as "the general system of the formation and transformation of statements", where statements and discourses are subject to the conditions and relations that govern the archive.[60] Foucault's formulation of the archive called for the detailed description of historical discourses through the individual statement which also performs an enunciative function. Though some critics of Foucault may complain that the Foucauldian archive is too abstract, we would argue that Foucault's archaeological method for historical research may be productive in thinking about the underlying structures that have underpinned the thought systems, theory, practices, and values in the making of different archives and how these have impacted on issues of knowledge production and access for present and future use.

In *Archive Fever: A Freudian Impression,* a lecture originally delivered by Derrida at the Freud Museum in London at an international colloquium on the history of psychiatry in 1994, Derrida proposed a psychoanalytic reading of the concept of the archive through the works of Sigmund Freud. In his initial reflections on the archive, Derrida started off with an etymological explanation of the word 'archive'. Derrida traced its meaning from the Greek *arkhē* which at once names the commencement and the commandment.[61] Derrida summarised this double meaning by noting that "in a way, the term indeed refers […] to the *arkhē* in the physical, historical, or ontological sense, which is to say the original, the first, the principal, the primitive, in short to the commencement. But even more, and even earlier, 'archive' refers to the *arkhē* in the nomological sense, to the *arkhē* of the commandment."[62] This was because "the meaning of 'archive', its only meaning, comes to it from the Greek *arkheion*: initially a house, a domicile, an address, the address, the residence of the superior magistrates, the *archons*, those who commanded."[63] Derrida explained that the archons are the documents' guardians who not only have the power to interpret the archives but have been tasked with the responsibility of ensuring the physical security of the archives.[64]

Thus for Derrida, the archives "needed at once a guardian and a localization" where the "archives could do neither without substrate nor without residence."[65] And it is in this "*domiciliation*, in this house arrest, that archives take place."[66] Through this exploration of the archive from the Greek superior magistrates' responsibility as archons to protect and interpret the archive and the *domiciliation* of the archive as a physical location, Derrida underlined the power and authority vested in archives. He added that it is in this place of consignation that the institutional passage from the private to the public occurs.[67] Building on Derrida's etymology of the concept of the archive, Michael Lynch argued that archival data is never raw as it passes from private to public.[68] Lynch noted that:

> An institutional passage from the private to the public precedes the formation of an archive, and this passage can be a site of struggle, occasionally resulting in breach, abortion, or miscarriage of the nascent archive. Consequently, we can appreciate that archives are as much products of historical struggle as they are primary sources for writing histories.[69]

Although Derrida's theoretical formulation of the archive certainly invited its own share of critique, it is important to note that Derrida also offered a more complex view of archives beyond his initial literal description of the archive as a physical space framed within the architectural dimensions of a physical site. In his reading of the archive, Derrida argued that the archive is not only about the preservation of the past, but also in anticipation of the future.[70] He noted that "the archive has always been a pledge, and like every pledge, a token of the future."[71] Derrida elucidated this point by saying that each time the archive is interpreted, it expands the archive. In this sense, the meaning of the archive is never fixed as the boundaries keep shifting. This is the reason that "the archive is never closed" as "it opens out of the future."[72] Put another way, archives are almost always constituted out of a present concern about the future and the psychological, almost compulsive, desire to acquire, collect, and preserve remnants or traces of a past. One could even go as far as saying that archives, similar to other heritage projects, are not as much about the past as it is about the future.

In his Freudian psychoanalytic formulation of the archive, Derrida offered a way for us to understand the desire to assemble, organise, and preserve the record. According to Derrida, Freudian psychoanalysis offers a theory of the archive that rests on the two conflicting forces of the archive: the death drive and the archive drive. Derrida argued that this death drive (sometimes also called a drive towards aggression and destruction) "destroys to advance its own archive."[73] He further explained that the death drive "not only incites forgetfulness, amnesia, the annihilation of memory but also commands the radical effacement, in truth the eradication [of] the archive, consignation, the documentary or monumental apparatus"[74] they represent.

Derrida continued his lamentation by noting that the death drive's "silent vocation is to burn the archive and to incite amnesia, thus refuting the economic principle of the archive, aiming to ruin the archive as accumulation and capitalisation of memory on some substrate and in an exterior place."[75] Following Derrida's argument, there is contention between the death drive and the archive drive as the death drive attempts to destroy not only its own archive but also any desire to archive or conserve, while simultaneously the archive drive is subject to the limitations of finitude. Derrida remarked on this tension between the death drive and the archive drive when he argued that:

> The archive always works, and *a priori*, against it itself [...] There would indeed be no archive desire without the radical finitude, without the possibility of a forgetfulness which does not limit itself to repression. Above all, and this is the most serious, beyond or within this simple limit called finiteness or finitude, there is no archive fever without the threat of this death drive, this aggression and destruction drive.[76]

More than just being a space for the storage and conservation of traces of the past, through its technical and archival processes that Derrida called 'archivisation', both Derrida and Foucault saw the archive as "produc[ing] as much as it records the event."[77] Far from being inert, the archive, when read through a Foucauldian and Derridean lens, becomes an intentional apparatus in which power and knowledge can shape the way historical research is conducted and therefore affect our political reality.[78] Critics of Derrida would remark that while Foucault's articulation of the archive is predicated upon mnemonic reliability, Derrida's archive is mnemonically unreliable because of its feverish, hallucinatory, and fragmentary nature.[79]

Scholars such as Carolyn Steedman and Thomas Richards have provided a different but no less interesting understanding of the archive. In her contemplation of the archive, Steedman focused on the historian's romance with the archive through a somewhat nostalgic account of the historian's engagement with the archives by recounting Jules Michelet's visits to the Archives Nationales in France. Steedman revealed that it was by reading Michelet that she first understood history-writing in generic terms as a form of magical realism in which one gives life to the dead.[80] Thoroughly frustrated with Derrida's notion of the archive, Steedman argued that archives are nothing like Derrida described them to be. In fact, according to Steedman, Derrida's meditation on the archive is not about archives but rather a contemplation of the history of Freudian psychoanalysis through the work of Yosef Hayim Yerushalmi's *Freud's Moses: Judaism Terminable and Interminable*.[81] Offering a more prosaic view on the archive, Steedman argued that Derrida failed to understand the corporeal and experiential nuances involved in doing archival research.

In her critique of *Archive Fever*, Steedman argued that the archive fever that Derrida wrote about is quite different from the one experienced by the researcher in the archive in relation to the materiality and the intimacy of the archive. Deconstructing the title of Derrida's *Mal d' archive* to the English translation of *Archive Fever*, and finding the English translation particularly unfortunate, Steedman argued that archive fever is better described as an occupational hazard or an industrial disease rather than Derrida's search for origins in what he describes as archive fever.[82] Tracing the development of the occupational disease field in early 19th-century England, through an investigation of the side-effects which came from the processing and production of the leather and paper industries, Steedman described the potential threats and dangers that the researcher faced in contracting an occupational or industrial illness in the archive whilst working with such material.[83] To demonstrate her point, she used Jules Michelet's description of his own experience in the Archives Nationales in Paris. Quoting Michelet, she wrote:

> … softly my dear friends, let us proceed in order if you please […] as I breathed in their dust, I saw them rise up. They rose from a sepulchre […] as in the Last Judgment of Michelangelo or in the Dance of Death. This frenzied dance […] I have tried to reproduce in my work.[84]

For Steedman, the archive can be thought of as a physiological process in which research is undertaken, framed by the potential dangers of industrial maladies which are contrasted by the intimacies and pleasures that the material nature of the archive can offer. Steedman's sensorial engagement with the archive invites a particularly evocative way of thinking about the archive. Though Steedman offered quite a severe critique of Derrida, especially his failure to address the effects of archival research, we would differ with Steedman by arguing that Derrida's deconstruction of the archive may be productive in thinking through the limits and possibilities of the transformation of archives in post-apartheid South Africa.

Writing about the colonial archive of 19th-century Britain in *The Imperial Archive*, Thomas Richards argued that the vast expanse of the British Empire presented an immense administrative challenge. Richards argued that the British Empire could really be seen as the first information society as this administrative challenge was met by producing maps, surveys, and censuses. Drawing upon the work of Foucault and Edward Said, Richards argued that the "administrative core of the Empire was built around knowledge-producing institutions like the British Museum, the Royal Geographic Society, the India Survey, and the universities" in which "the imperial archive was a fantasy of knowledge collected and united in the service of State and Empire."[85] In this way, the administrators of the Empire helped shape an enduring relationship between knowledge and power, where the state was united through information rather than through coercive force. Richards thus saw the archive as "a utopian space of comprehensive knowledge" and argued that "the archive was not a building, nor even a collection of texts, but the collectively imagined junction of all that was known and knowable, a fantastic representation of an epistemological master pattern."[86] Through his arguments in *The Imperial Archive*, Richards sought to demonstrate how the knowledge and power axis developed in the British Empire through the accumulation and dissemination of information that was enlisted in the service of the state and the Empire. While Richards' focus was on the colonial archive, his ideas may be very suggestive when thinking about the axis between knowledge and power operating within and around the archive, in other words, who controls the archive and for what purpose is it being controlled in post-apartheid South Africa?

As briefly discussed earlier in the chapter, the debate on the archives in post-apartheid South Africa culminated with the publishing of *Refiguring the Archive*. This was the outcome of a project that focused on a series of seminars constituted around the visit by Derrida to South Africa and was conceived as an idea to address and interrogate urgent questions around archives that followed in the wake of the work of the Truth and Reconciliation Commission (TRC) and the transformation of institutions in South Africa after 1994. In their interrogation of the archive, the contributors to the publication proposed a (re)figuring of the archive by investigating the ethnographies and histories of archives, how institutions such as archives are implicated in creating a particular vision of society, and, very significantly, the conditions and processes of the record.[87] Most of the essays drew upon the work of Derrida, except for Ann Laura Stoler in her Foucauldian approach to the colonial archives in India. The volume provided productive insights into the workings of the archive.

Much has been written since *Refiguring the Archive* was published in 2002, yet exceptionally, this volume also placed the archivist into a critically engaged position alongside thinkers of other disciplines.[88] More than that, it actively called for a new way of thinking about archives, for a transformation of archives and the way we engage with archives. In a critique of this ambitious project, we would argue that *Refiguring the Archive* provided a beacon through the murkiness of the archive's unchartered, tempestuous waters but failed to actualise its goals of refiguring the archive. A refiguring of the archive in post-apartheid South Africa would have required us "to reimagine the boundaries of what we have come to believe are disciplines and to have the courage to rethink them."[89] As argued earlier, a reimagining or transformation of the archive would require a philosophical and investigative engagement with the archive that may take us into unfamiliar, unpredictable, and ever-shifting territory that may produce more questions than answers. Quoting Proust, Joan Schwartz implored archivists to realise that "the real voyage of discovery consists not in seeking new landscapes but in having new eyes."[90] Pushing this argument further, we argue that in acquiring a new sense of vision to seek out or to probe the intellectual, physical, practical, and metaphorical space of the archive will require an enquiry into the philosophy of the archive, not only by scholars but also crucially by archivists.

New archival thinking in South Africa

In a new way of thinking, seeing, and knowing the archive, both scholars and archivists need to deploy a methodology of ethical self-awareness and reflexivity and enter the archive cognitive of the social, cultural, and technological settings in which the archive exists.[91] Therefore, in imagining another way of thinking about the archive and in trying to answer some of the questions that this chapter is grappling with, it will be both interesting and potentially instructive to draw on the perspectives offered by those in the archival profession as another means of interrogating the transformation process in post-apartheid South Africa. With the growing interest in archives, especially from outside the archive, with what can be termed as the 'archival turn' or an 'archival impulse'[92] within various disciplines and from other spheres, it is crucial to reflect on the history of archival thought over the last century within the archival domain. As mentioned earlier, in addition to scholars such as Benjamin, Foucault, Derrida, and Steedman critically thinking about the contested and ambiguous nature of the archive, there has also been a steady proliferation of literature around the nature of archives, its functions, and its work which have emanated from archivists.

In the historical literature on the archive as a professional practice space, with special reference to the classic texts on archival theory by thinkers and practicing archivists such Hilary Jenkinson and T.R. Schellenberg, who shaped much of the thinking in terms of how archives are viewed within society today, it would be helpful to trace the intellectual history of archival thought over the last century. This is important because archival theory emerged from within the archival profession itself before the profession was stunted in its development. Though informed by their times, much of the supposed classic articulations of archival theory and practices have made a deep impact on the archive of which the reverberations are still palpable today as it continues to shape access, knowledge production, and modes of working in and around archives.

At this point, it might be fruitful to distinguish that there are different genres or types of writing on the archive. Within the professional practicing space of the archive, writing on archival theory has for the most part been divided into two strains. One strain is archival but not theoretical because of the focus on the practicalities – technical aspects of archival work. The second strain is theoretical but not archival and calls for archivists to be historians or theoreticians.[93] The crucial questions that comes to the fore is whether being an archivist is merely a practical endeavour (technical undertaking) or is the archival profession a mere practical application of different methodological processes? And why is it imperative for both archivists and researchers to study archival theory at all?

To answer these questions, we argue that it would be instructive to explore the relationship between theory and practice and to investigate archival analysis by practicing archivists and not just theorists. In analysing the relationship between archival theory and practice, Heather MacNeil explained that archival theory based on the continuum model "is the analysis of ideas about the nature of archives, *methodology* the analysis of the ideas about how to treat them, and *practice* the outcome of the application of methodology in particular instances."[94] The difficulty arises when theory and method cannot be aligned and actualised into practice which, in turn, results in a crisis of the existing archival theoretical discourse.

Put another way, if ever there was a time to relate practice and theory or to find a way of reconciling the two seemingly opposing forces, it would be now if those in the archival profession are to rethink their discipline and practice to meet the challenges of a postmodern world.[95] In moving closer towards an alignment between theory and practice, Cook and MacNeil, along with others, have argued that a paradigm shift is needed to think through the predicament of the archive, which has been "provoked by a number of societal, technological, and professional developments that have thrown into question, if not crisis, some of the basic tenets concerning the nature and value of archives."[96] Cook furthers this position when he argued that:

> At the heart of the new paradigm is a shift away from viewing records as static physical objects, and towards understanding them as dynamic virtual concepts; a shift away from looking at records as the passive products of […] administrative activity and towards considering records as active agents themselves in the formation of human and organisational memory; a shift equally away from seeing the context of records creation resting within stable hierarchical organisations to situating records within fluid horizontal networks of work-flow functionality.[97]

In this precarious time of deeply unsettling visions of the future for archives and archivists, it has become of absolute importance that the archival profession realises the significance of theoretically studying the archive, firstly as a way to develop and nurture archival theory and secondly to address their "lack of theoretical investigation" which seriously impedes their professional standards.[98] In rethinking and transforming the archive, part of the argument of this chapter is that to better understand the archive, the archive itself, as an object, needs to be anchored in its own intellectual history of theory, conventions, concepts, practices, and debates.[99] Arguing this point, Barbara L. Craig stated that "just as personal identity is anchored in a strong historical sense, so is our professional identity – both come from the ability to experience continuity. Surely, if you have nothing to look backward to, and with pride, you have nothing to look forward to with hope."[100]

In his analysis of the history of archival thought since 1898, Cook argued this point convincingly when he noted that "without understanding our predecessors' intellectual struggles, we lose the benefit of their experiences and are condemned to repeat their errors."[101] Along with Cook, archivists such as Frank G. Burke and F. Gerald Ham have also argued for archivists to become scholars concerned with historiography and developing "a new philosophy of archives."[102] According to Burke and Ham, in particular, the historiographical method would allow the archivist to focus on the content and context of the record, which will assist in making informed decisions about the appraisal and description of collections.

Clearly at odds with Burke and Ham, John Roberts and Lester Cappon provided a pragmatic view on the nature of archives. While Cappon thoroughly critiqued the approach of especially Burke to the archive, by saying that Burke is confused between archival theory and the theory of history, Cappon still conceded that the archivist is, at heart, an historian.[103] Roberts, on the other hand, rejected the view that history should be tied to archival practices at all, as he disparagingly only regarded it as a "fairly straightforward, down to earth service occupation."[104] Demonstrating his narrow view of archives and the work of archivists, Roberts argued that it is "extreme intellectual silliness to boggle oneself with such preposterous phantoms as archival paradigms […] and other prostheses that some archivists would thrust forward as credentials to sit at the grown-ups' table."[105]

Though some of Roberts and Cappon's criticisms are valid, such as the viability of a historiographical focus given the practical limitations and frameworks that beset archives and archivists, we argue that Burke and Ham have resuscitated a call to rethink the archive. However, within a similar vein as Cook and others, we too would argue that to come to terms with the ever-changing, evolving nature of the archive, its past needs to be thoroughly explored not only because "what is past is prologue"[106] but also to transform the epistemological foundations of the archive. In explaining this, one of the seminal works that archivists are required to engage with is the *Manual for the Arrangement and Description of Archives*, published more than a century ago in 1898 by a group of three practicing Dutch archivists: Samuel Muller, Johan Feith, and Robert Fruin. While the *Manual* was a consolidated and standardised response to issues faced by archivists in the Netherlands during the 19th century, it widely became an important treatise on archival theory and is still regarded as such.[107] Laying a solid foundation for later books by Hilary Jenkinson (1922, 1966) and Theodore R. Schellenberg (1956, 1965), the Dutch *Manual*, as in the words of Schellenberg, became "a Bible for modern archivists."[108]

Primarily focusing on the practices and methodology of archival work by especially outlining the archival concepts of arrangement and description, the *Manual* solidified the use of the concept of *respects des fonds* in archival practice and created a new concept of provenance, which provided a framework for how records would be arranged and described in concordance with how it was arranged by the records' creator.[109] This being said, the *Manual* allowed the archivist to make subjective decisions regarding the arrangement of records that considered issues such as preservation, storage, and usage. Though the authors of the *Manual* may have been visionary, Muller, Feith and Fruin were mainly preoccupied with the arrangement and description of the archive in terms of provenance and original order at the expense of the other archival functions of appraisal and selection. John Ridener argued that "[t]he epistemological boundaries of the *Manual* are, for the most part, focused on creating practical unity, prescription of methods, and delineation of specific instructions to archivists."[110] Ridener further argued that this allowed the authors to circumvent more philosophical and theoretical questions of the archive, which is crucial to understand the nature of the archive, especially given the challenges brought about by changing contexts of politics, technologies, and historiographies. He concluded, however, along with Cook, that the *Manual* is important because it codified European archival theory and enunciated a methodology for treating archives which has shaped much of the archival profession's collective theory and practice.[111]

More than two decades later, the Dutch *Manual* set the stage for Hilary Jenkinson's positivist ideology on archives in his book, *A Manual of Archive Administration* (1922), in which he argued for the administrative importance of archives. Here, the archive is presented as impartial, authentic, evidential, and trustworthy, and the archivist was regarded as the passive, objective, and invisible servant and guardian of the archive.[112] Whereas the Dutch archivists only subtly engaged in some theorising in their *Manual*, Jenkinson's *Manual* focused on constructing a theory of archives which was based on the moral and theoretical reasons for keeping archives.[113] Building on some of the core concepts of the Dutch *Manual* such as original order and provenance, Jenkinson expanded on the practical guidelines offered by the Dutch archivists but found the *Manual's* almost exclusive focus on practice acutely lacking in its theoretical orientation regarding the new challenges brought about by technological innovation.

Primarily informed by Darwinian evolutionary theory and positivist historiography,[114] Jenkinson postulated the four qualities of the archive: impartiality; authenticity; naturalness; and interrelationship. Considered to be one of the classic thinkers on archival theory during the early 20th century (however contested his theory might be), Jenkinson proposed a methodology which saw archives as "simply written memorials authenticated by the fact of their official preservation" in which "the Archivist's career is one of service", devoted to being a voiceless and invisible servant and custodian.[115] Jenkinson posited a theory that sought to avoid the question of appraisal as he perceived the role of the archivist as one of keeping, but not selecting archives. According to Jenkinson, the task of selecting or appraising records should be left to the judgment of the records' creator as any appraisal done by the archivist would taint the innocence of records in their archival setting. While Jenkinson posited a theoretical approach to archives, his treatise unequivocally separated theory from practice.[116] Jenkinson's theoretical guide irrevocably changed the landscape of archives as he continues to cast a long shadow over the field of archival education and practice as most of the standards he set for the profession remains significant, even if no longer relevant, given the ongoing evolution of archival theory. Perhaps Jenkinson's most crucial contribution to the field of archival theory was that his *Manual* delineated the distinct boundaries between "the role of the archivist and its professional status as a discipline distinct from the study and writing of history."[117]

Following closely behind Jenkinson were the two works of American archival theorist T.R. Schellenberg, *Modern Archives: Principles and Techniques* (1956) and *The Management of Archives* (1965). In contrast to the Dutch archivists and Jenkinson who narrowly focused on original order, provenance, and custodianship, Schellenberg focused on the archival functions of appraisal and selection. Covering more ground than his Dutch predecessors and his counterpart across the Atlantic through his extensive discussions on principles and techniques, Schellenberg argued for an interventionist strategy in shaping and managing the archival record. He was particularly vocal in his criticism of Jenkinson's view on the question of appraisal and found his theories incompatible in meeting the archival needs in the United States. In Schellenberg's formulation of appraisal, the archivist, in consultation with record managers and subject specialists, actively shaped the future of the archival record. While Schellenberg has done much to advance archival discourse, there are a few problematic issues to his theory. According to Cook, one of the challenges of Schellenberg's theory is the concept of "user-defined archives."[118] The danger of following a "user-based approach" that is determined by trends in historiography and the expectations of users "removes records from their organic context within activities of their creator and imposes criteria on both appraisal and description that are external to the record and its provenance."[119] Gerald Ham also argued that user-based approaches to the archive would result in "a selection process so random, so fragmented, so uncoordinated, and even so accidental [that it] […] too often reflect[s] narrow research interests rather than the broad spectrum of human experience."[120]

Whether still rooted in a 19th-century positivist paradigm which viewed the archivist within Jenkinsonian terms as passive, invisible, and neutral,[121] or because of administrative tasks and technical duties, it is glaringly obvious that save for a few archivists, the archival profession is largely absent from theoretical and disciplinary debates about the impact of the archive, the power it imbibes, and it how it shapes and is in turn being reshaped by society, culture, and politics.[122] One must ask whether the archival profession has become too insular, with an almost exclusive preoccupation with answering the political, managerial, and professional demands placed upon them. This cursory perusal of the underpinnings of 'practical' archival theory that have permeated much of the last century has revealed the richness of the thinking around the archive. Much has changed over the last century, with technological advancements and shifts in historiography, but despite these developments, the archival profession has, for the most part, remained rooted in a 19th-century positivistic approach where records are inert and innocent, and archivists are passive guardians and custodians of history. As Cook argued:

> ... archival theoretical discourse is shifting from product to process, from structure to function, from archives to archiving, from the record to the recording context, from [...] the passive by-product of administrative activity to the consciously constructed and actively mediated 'archivalisation' of social memory.[123]

Reiterating Cook's argument, Ridener cautioned that "theory is not a monolithic series of 'scientific' laws objectively true in all times and places, but rather an on-going, open-ended quest for meaning about our documentary heritage that itself is ever evolving."[124] This open-ended, mediated, indeterminate, and uncertain nature of the archive lies at the heart of the necessity to transform the archive and to argue for a fundamental paradigm shift in archival thinking. It is in this regard then that the next chapter will argue that one of the ways the archive can be transformed is for the archivist to adapt to the ever-changing environment of the archive by becoming a scholar and an activist who is actively engaged in the production of knowledge.

Endnotes

1. A. Farge. 2013. *The Allure of the Archives*, translated by T. Scott-Railton. London: Yale University Press, 31. https://doi.org/10.12987/yale/9780300176735.001.0001
2. J.M. Panitch. 1996. 'Liberty, Equality, Posterity? Some Archival Lessons from the Case of the French Revolution'. *The American Archivist*, 59(1):47. https://doi.org/10.17723/aarc.59.1.an67076131u104kj;

    Also see S. Timcke. 2015. 'Discourse, Memory, and Post-Apartheid South African Archives'. *SSRN Electronic Journal*. https://doi.org/10.2139/ssrn.2630403
3. C. Hamilton, V. Harris, M. Pickover, G. Reid, R. Saleh & J. Taylor (eds.). 2002. *Refiguring the Archive*. Cape Town: David Philip, 14-16. https://doi.org/10.1007/978-94-010-0570-8
4. H. Taylor, quoted in T. Cook & G. Dodds (eds.). 2003. *Imagining Archives: Essays and Reflections by Hugh Taylor*. Lanham, MD: Scarecrow Press, 15.
5. A. Buchanan. 2011. 'Strangely Unfamiliar: Ideas of the Archive from Outside the Discipline'. In: J. Hill (ed.), *The Future of Archives and Recordkeeping: A Reader*. London: Facet Publishing, 37.
6. J. Derrida. 1995. *Archive Fever: A Freudian Impression*, translated by E. Prenowitz. Chicago, IL: University of Chicago Press, 90. https://doi.org/10.2307/465144 In addition to Derrida's articulations of the archive, the formulations of Michel Foucault have also contributed much to the fervour and debates around archives. See M. Foucault. 1972. *The Archaeology of Knowledge*. New York, NY: Pantheon Books. There is also earlier work on the concept of the archive in which Walter Benjamin preceded Foucault and Derrida in terms of critically thinking about the archive. See W. Benjamin. 1989. 'Theses on the Philosophy of History'. In: S.E. Bronner (ed.), *Critical Theory and Society: A Reader*. New York, NY: Routledge, 257.
7. C. Hamilton. 2011. 'Why Archive Matters'. In: X. Mangcu (ed.), *Becoming Worthy Ancestors: Archive, Public Deliberation and Identity in South Africa*. Johannesburg: Wits University Press, 121. https://doi.org/10.18772/22011085324.11
8. H. Taylor, quoted in T. Cook & G. Dodds (eds.). 2003. *Imagining Archives: Essays and Reflections by Hugh Taylor*. Lanham: Scarecrow Press, 19.
9. T. Cook & J.M. Schwartz. 2002. 'Archives, Records and Power: From (Postmodern) Theory to (Archival) Performance'. *Archival Science*, 2:181. https://doi.org/10.1007/BF02435620
10. Ibid., 181.
11. J. Derrida. 1995. *Archive Fever: A Freudian Impression*, translated by E. Prenowitz. Chicago, IL: University of Chicago Press, 90. https://doi.org/10.2307/465144; Also see V. Harris. 2012. 'Genres of the Trace: Memory, Archives and Trouble'. *Archives and Manuscripts*, 40(3):147-157. https://doi.org/10.1080/01576895.2012.73582
12. H. Bradley. 1999. 'The Seductions of the Archive: Voices Lost and Found'. *History of the Human Sciences*, 12(2):119. https://doi.org/10.1177/09526959922120270
13. T.S. Eliot. 1936. *Burnt Norton*, http://bit.ly/3KdXweF [Accessed 18 November 2021].
14. I. Velody. 1998. 'The Archive and the Human Sciences: Notes towards a Theory of the Archive'. History of the Human Sciences, 11(4):1. https://doi.org/10.1177/095269519801100401
15. See T. Osborne. 1999. 'The Ordinariness of the Archive'. *History of the Human Sciences*, 12(2):58. https://doi.org/10.1177/09526959922120243

16. See H. Freshwater. 2003. 'The Allure of the Archive'. *Poetics Today*, 24(4):730. https://doi.org/10.1215/03335372-24-4-729;
    Also see F.X. Blouin & W.G. Rosenberg (eds.). 2011. *Processing the Past: Contesting Authority in History and the Archives*. Oxford: Oxford University Press, 23-28.
17. Farge. *The Allure of the Archives*, 46.
18. Ibid., 8.
19. Ibid., 4-71.
20. Ibid., 54.
21. Bradley. 'The Seductions of the Archive', 110;
    Also see Farge, *The Allure of the Archives*.
22. Ibid., 109.
23. Derrida. *Archive Fever*, 90.
24. Ibid., 91.
25. Ibid., 90.
26. Ibid., 91.
27. Freshwater. 'The Allure of the Archive', 738.
28. Ibid., 738.
29. Ibid., 745.
30. Ibid., 745.
31. Freshwater. 'The Allure of the Archive', 745; Also see J. Laplanche. 1976. *Life and Death in Psychoanalysis*. Baltimore, MD: Johns Hopkins University Press, 19-20.
    C. Steedman. 2002. *Dust: The Archive and Cultural History*. New Brunswick, NJ: Rutgers University Press, 77.
32. Steedman. *Dust: The Archive and Cultural History*, 77 (emphasis in the original).
33. Ibid., 81.
34. G. Bachelard. 1994. *The Poetics of Space*. Boston: Beacon Press, 8.
35. Steedman. *Dust: The Archive and Cultural History*, 80.
36. Ibid., 72.
37. For critical discussions on the archive see M. Foucault. 1972. *The Archaeology of Knowledge*. New York, NY: Pantheon Books;
    J. Derrida. 1995. *Archive Fever: A Freudian Impression*, translated by E. Prenowitz. Chicago, IL: University of Chicago Press. https://doi.org/10.2307/465144;
    C. Steedman. 2002. *Dust: The Archive and Cultural History*. New Brunswick, NJ: Rutgers University Press.;
    T. Richards. 1993. *The Imperial Archive: Knowledge and the Fantasy of Empire*. London: Verso.;
    T. Osborne. 1999. 'The Ordinariness of the Archive'. *History of the Human Sciences*, 12(2):51-64. https://doi.org/10.1177/095269599221202436
38. I. Velody. 1998. 'The Archive and the Human Sciences: Notes towards a Theory of the Archive'. *History of the Human Sciences*, 11(4):2. https://doi.org/10.1177/095269519801100401
39. T. Cook. 2009. 'The Archive(s) is a Foreign Country: Historians, Archivists and the Changing Archival Landscape'. *The Canadian Historical Review*, 90(3):524. https://doi.org/10.1353/can.0.0194
40. Derrida. *Archive Fever*, 4, note 1.

41 See R.H. Brown & B. Davis-Brown. 1998. 'The Making of Memory: The Politics of Archives, Libraries and Museums in the Construction of National Consciousness'. *History of the Human Sciences*, 11(4):20. https://doi.org/10.1177/095269519801100402

42 B. Brothman. 1993. 'The Limits of Limits: Derridean Deconstruction and the Archival Institution'. *Archivaria*, 36, 1993, 208.

43 Ibid., 208.

44 E. Ketelaar. 2002. 'Archival Temples, Archival Prisons: Modes of Power and Protection'. *Archival Science*, 2:221. https://doi.org/10.1007/BF02435623; Also see R.C. Jimerson. 2006. 'Embracing the Power of Archives'. *The American Archivist*, 69(1). https://doi.org/10.17723/aarc.69.1.r0p75n2084055418

45 See Velody. 'The Archive and the Human Sciences', 11.

46 Brothman. 'The Limits of Limits', 208.

47 V. Harris. 2011. 'Archons, Aliens and Angels: Power and Politics in the Archive'. In: J. Hill (ed.), *The Future of Archives and Recordkeeping: A Reader*. London: Facet Publishing, 105.

48 W. Benjamin. 1968. *The Work of Art in the Age of Mechanical Reproduction*. New York, NY: Schocken, 221, 224.

49 Ibid., 223.

50 Freshwater. 'The Allure of the Archive', 732.

51 T. Cook. 1994. 'Electronic Records, Paper Minds: The Revolution in Information Management and Archives in the Post-Custodial and Post-Modernist Era'. *Archives and Manuscripts*, 22(2):314.

52 W. Benjamin. 1968. 'Theses on the Philosophy of History'. In: H. Arendt (ed.), *Illuminations: Essays and Reflections*. New York, NY: Harcourt Brace Jovanovich, 256-257.

53 Ibid., 256-257.

54 See E. Hooper-Greenhill. 1992. *Museums and the Shaping of Knowledge*. New York, NY: Routledge. https://doi.org/10.4324/9780203415825
K. Walsh. 1992. *The Representation of the Past: Museums and Heritage in the Post-Modern World*. New York, NY: Routledge. https://doi.org/10.4324/9780203320570

55 Foucault. *The Archaeology of Knowledge*, 4-8.

56 Ibid., 139.

57 Ibid., 138-139.

58 Ibid., 129.

59 Ibid., 129.

60 Ibid., 130.

61 Derrida. *Archive Fever*, 1-2.

62 Ibid., 2.

63 Ibid., 2 (emphasis in the original).

64 Ibid., 2.

65 Ibid., 2.

66 Ibid., 2 (emphasis in the original).

67 Ibid., 2.

68 M. Lynch. 1999. 'Archives in Formation: Privileged Spaces, Popular Archives and Paper Trails'. *History of the Human Sciences*, 12(2):65, 67. https://doi.org/10.1177/09526959922120252

69 Ibid., 67.

70 This is often a point in his argument that is not taken up as most scholars or archivists writing on the archive only take up Derrida's literal view of the archive as a physical space. See Derrida. *Archive Fever*, 18.

71 Derrida. *Archive Fever*, 18;
Also see Arjun Appadurai's brief yet concise essay on archives where he makes a similar argument of the archive being an aspiration rather than a recollection. Appadurai argued, "Rather than being the tomb of the trace, the archive is more frequently the product of the anticipation of collective memory." In: A. Appadurai, *Archive and Aspiration*, 16. https://bit.ly/42Olhjy [Accessed 18 November 2021].

72 Derrida. *Archive Fever*, 68.

73 Ibid., 10.

74 Ibid., 11.

75 Ibid., 12.

76 Ibid., 11 & 19.

77 Derrida. *Archive Fever*, 17.; Foucault. *The Archaeology of Knowledge*, 130.

78 Derrida,. *Archive Fever*, 4.;
See also M. Marnoff. 2004. 'Theories of the Archive from Across the Disciplines'. *Libraries and the Academy*, 4(1):5. https://doi.org/10.1353/pla.2004.0015

79 H. Rapaport. 1998. 'Archive Trauma'. *Review Article, Diacritics*, 28(4):69. https://doi.org/10.1353/dia.1998.0030

80 C. Steedman. 2008 'Romance in the Archive'. *Presentation*, 5. https://bit.ly/40JmKXK [Accessed 14 November 2021].

81 Steedman. *Dust: The Archive and Cultural History*, 3.

82 Irving Velody shares a similar view in which he argued that *Mal d'Archive* might be better titled 'The Trouble with Archives' rather than 'Archive Fever'.
See Velody. 'The Archive and the Human Sciences', 1.

83 Steedman. *Dust: The Archive and Cultural History*, 22, 27.

84 Jules Michelet, quoted in Steedman. *Dust: The Archive and Cultural History*, 27.

85 T. Richards. 1993. *The Imperial Archive: Knowledge and the Fantasy of Empire*. London: Verso, 4-6.

86 Ibid., 11.

87 C. Hamilton, V. Harris, M. Pickover, G. Reid, R. Saleh & J. Taylor (eds.). 2002. *Refiguring the Archive*. Cape Town: David Philip, 14-16. https://doi.org/10.1007/978-94-010-0570-8

88 Hamilton et al. *Refiguring the Archive*, 11.

89 M. Garber. 2001. *Academic Instincts*. Princeton, NJ: Princeton University Press, 96.

90 J.M. Schwartz. 2007. 'Having New Eyes: Spaces of Archives, Landscapes of Power'. *Archives and Social Studies: A Journal of Interdisciplinary Research*, 1:362.

91 Freshwater. 'The Allure of the Archive', 754.;
Also see T. Cook & J.M. Schwartz. 2002. 'Archives, Records and Power: The Making of Modern Memory'. *Archival Science*, 2:19. https://doi.org/10.1007/BF02435620

92 See H. Foster. 2004. 'An Archival Impulse'. *October*, 110:3. https://doi.org/10.1162/0162287042379847

93 J. Roberts. 1987. 'Archival Theory: Much Ado About Shelving'. *The American Archivist*, 50(1):67. https://doi.org/10.17723/aarc.50.1.l357257455776g52

94 H. MacNeil. 2007. 'Archival Theory and Practice: Between Two Paradigms'. *Archives and Social Studies: A Journal of Interdisciplinary Research*, 1(1):519 (emphasis in the original).

95 Terry Cook argued that the impact of postmodernism has resulted in a crisis that calls into question the positivist concepts and methodologies on which the archive rests. To meet the challenges of postmodernism and various new technologies, Cook argued that a paradigm shift is required.
See T. Cook. 2001. 'Archival Science and Postmodernism: New Formulations for Old Concepts'. *Archival Science*, 1:3-4. https://doi.org/10.1007/BF02435636

96 MacNeil. 'Archival Theory and Practice', 519.

97 Cook. '*Archival Science and Postmodernism*', 4.

98 MacNeil. 'Archival Theory and Practice', 541-542.;
Also see B.L. Craig. 1992. 'Outward Visions, Inward Glance: Archives History and Professional Identity'. *Archival Issues*, 17(2):114-124. https://www.jstor.org/stable/41101829

99 See Barbara Craig's argument about the necessity for an understanding of the history of archives in relation to the study of archival records in Craig, *Outward Visions, Inward Glance*, 121.

100 Ibid., 121.

101 T. Cook. 1997. 'What Past is Prologue: A History of Archival Ideas Since 1898 and the Future Paradigm Shift'. *Archivaria*, 43:19.

102 F.G. Burke. 1981. 'The Future Course of Archival Theory in the United States'. *American Archivist*, 44(1):45. https://doi.org/10.17723/aarc.44.1.485380l307551286;
Also see F.G. Ham. 1975. 'Archival Edge'. *American Archivist*, 38(1):13. https://doi.org/10.17723/aarc.38.1.7400r86481128424

103 L. Cappon. 1982. 'What, Then, is There to Theorise About?'. *The American Archivist*, 45(1):21. https://doi.org/10.17723/aarc.45.1.q03v972668401056

104 Roberts. 'Archival Theory: Much Ado About Shelving', 74.

105 Ibid., 74.

106 Cook invoked Shakespeare's phrase to emphasise the point that archivists can only write their prologue for the next century if they are able to understand their past. See T. Cook. 1997. 'What Past is Prologue: A History of Archival Ideas Since 1898 and the Future Paradigm Shift'. *Archivaria*, 43:19.

107 J. Ridener. 2009. *From Polders to Postmodernism: A Concise History of Archival Theory*. Duluth, MN: Litwin Books, 21.

108 T.R. Schellenberg. 1956. *Modern Archives, Principles and Techniques*. Melbourne: Cheshire, 175.

109 According to Ridener, the concept of respect *des fonds* was already in place well before the publication of the *Manual* as the Dutch trio drew heavily from Josef Anton Oegg's *Ideen einer Theorie der Archivwissenschaft* (Ideas of a Theory of Archival Science) in 1804. See Ridener. *From Polders to Postmodernism*, 32-33 (emphasis in the original).

110 Ibid., 28.

111 Cook. 'What Past is Prologue', 22.
112 J. Hill (ed.). 2011. *The Future of Archives and Recordkeeping: A Reader*. London: Facet Publishing, 4. https://doi.org/10.29085/9781856048675;
Also see Cook. 'What Past is Prologue', 23.
J. O'Toole. 1990. *Understanding Archives and Manuscripts*. Chicago: Society of American Archivists, 71.
113 Ridener. *From Polders to Postmodernism*, 28-41.
114 Terry Cook quoted, in J. Hill (ed.). *The Future of Archives and Recordkeeping*, 4.
115 H. Jenkinson. 1937. *A Manual of Archive Administration*. London: Percy Lund, Humphries and Co Ltd, 12.
116 Ridener. *From Polders to Postmodernism*, 41.
117 Ibid., 68.
118 Cook. 'What Past is Prologue', 29.
119 Ibid., 29.
120 Gerald Ham, quoted in Cook. 'What Past is Prologue', 29.
121 See J.H. Hodson. 1972. *The Administration of Archives*. Oxford: Pergamon Press Ltd, 3;
Cook. 'What Past is Prologue', 23.;
T. Cook & J.M. Schwartz. 2002. 'Archives, Records and Power: The Making of Modern Memory'. *Archival Science*, 2:18. https://doi.org/10.1007/BF02435620
122 See T. Cook. 2009. 'The Archive(s) is a Foreign Country: Historians, Archivists, and the Changing Archival Landscape'. *The Canadian Historical Review*, 90(3):497-534. https://doi.org/10.1353/can.0.0194;
Schwartz. 'Having New Eyes', 326.
123 Cook. 'Archival Science and Postmodernism', 4.
124 Ridener. *From Polders to Postmodernism*, xix.

Transforming the Archive – Archivist as Historian/Historian as Archivist

> The work of the archivist is not simply a work of memory. It's a work of mourning. And a work of mourning [...] is a work of memory but also the best way just to forget the other, to keep the other in oneself, to keep it safe, in a safe – but when you put something in a safe it's just in order to be able to forget it [...]. When I handwrite something on a piece of paper, I put it in my pocket or in a safe. It's just in order to forget it [...]. So, suppose that one day South Africa would have accomplished a perfect, full archive of its whole history – not simply apartheid, but what came before apartheid [...] everyone in this country [...] would be eager to put this in such a safe that everyone could just forget it [...]. And perhaps [...] this is the unconfessed desire of the Truth and Reconciliation Commission. That as soon as possible the future generation may have simply forgotten it [...]. Having kept everything in the archive [...] let us forget it to go on, to survive.[1]

In a lecture delivered by Derrida as part of the *Refiguring the Archive* project at the University of the Witwatersrand in 1998, he poignantly reminded us that the work of the archivist is inextricably tied to the existence and dynamic forces of the archives. More explicitly for Derrida, the work of an archivist is a work of mourning that is ritualistically performed and reified. However, the work of an archivist is such that it also involves activism and scholarship. The archive not only asks for it but demands it. In transforming the archive, a fundamental paradigm shift of how archivists work within and with archives needs to occur.

Although the historical and the archival professions developed in tandem during the 19th century, historians have come to be the 'discoverers' and authors of the archival record while archivists are regarded as the guardians or keepers of records in their often accepted role as the 'handmaidens to history'.[2] This has created a widening fracture in the once productive partnership which characterises the symbiotic relationship between archivists and historians. As a way of negotiating the somewhat tenuous relationship between the archivist and historian, one of the aims of this chapter is to argue that archivists and scholars should become more self-aware of the mediation that takes place within archives. In the words of prominent Canadian archivist, Terry Cook, both archivists and researchers should become aware of the "mediated nature of archives as appraised and selected records, as curatorial institutions, as professional activity, or as a body of theoretical and practical knowledge."[3]

Through a self-reflexive enquiry of our own engagement with the archive, both as heritage practitioners and researchers who have worked with several archival collections and within a number of archives studying its records, this chapter will seek to bring to light the challenges and possibilities that frame this sometimes-complex engagement that underscores the process of transformation. More importantly, by locating archivists as central to and within the archiving process, we argue that it has become crucial for archivists to study the history of the archival records that they work with. This, in turn, will create a better understanding of the archival processes that these records are subject to. It is only then that archivists can start to imagine what a transformed archival landscape might look like. But how would archivists arrive at such a transformation and what would the new archivist look like? And why does the archival profession even need a paradigm shift?

Haunted by the spectre of positivism

In the popular imagination, archivists have long been imagined as "aged antiquarians stooped over piles of ledgers in dusty basements"[4] who have been entrusted with the sacred mission of guarding the past through upholding the dictums of truth and objectivity. This perception echoes Hilary Jenkinson's methodology which was informed by Darwinian evolutionary theory and positivist historiography. According to his positivist formulation of the archive, Jenkinson proposed a methodology which saw archives as "simply written memorials authenticated by the fact of their official preservation" in which "[t]he Archivist's career is one of service."[5] Jenkinson argued that "[h]e (the archivist) exists in order to make other people's work possible […]. His Creed, the Sanctity of Evidence; his task, the Conservation of […] Evidence […] the good Archivist is perhaps the most selfless devotee of truth the modern world produces."[6] The Jenkinsonian archivist does not mediate, interpret, or help construct archives. Instead, their professional career is a life of servitude where they unobtrusively work behind the scenes by bringing order to archives through arranging, describing, and preserving the archival record. However, in the habitual cleaning and storing of the archive, archivists inevitably leave very large and often permanent footprints behind.

Although there has been a shift away from positivism, archives and archivists, for the most part, have remained locked in a positivist Jenkinsonian discourse that has become naturalised and has found expression through an archival practice that continues to perpetuate this professional myth of neutrality, passivity, and objectivity.[7] Bringing this closer to home, Verne Harris takes this point further by arguing that much of the positivist archival thinking in South Africa has remained stubbornly resistant to transformation much like the embedded nature of apartheid patterns that are still very much prevalent within post-apartheid South African society.[8] Harris argued that in archives in South Africa, "many of our core ideas resist new realities, at most entertaining re-formation (rather than trans-formation)."[9] As a consequence, this both reinforces outmoded positivist archival ideas steeped in colonial and apartheid history and also continues to shape the way in which archivists imagine themselves and accept their scripted role as mere custodians of archives. This image of archivists as antiquarians has remained pervasive and has cast them in the role of passive, neutral, and often invisible keepers and caretakers of archives. Though this depiction is finally being challenged by some archivists and scholars across various academic disciplines, the reality is that archivists continue to be regarded as the "hewers of wood and drawers of water"[10] in historical knowledge production. Unfortunately, this is an image that has been actively cultivated and projected by archivists and accepted by scholars without much consideration of the mediation and continuous intervention that takes place during archival practices.

Drawing on W. Kaye Lamb's argument in which he took issue with the self-accepted and prescribed role of archivists as the invisible caretakers of the archives, Cook has argued that archivists have done very little to address this continued perception of the archivist as passive, curatorial, neutered and impartial.[11] According to Cook, Lamb argued that to many historians, the archivist:

> ... collects things, cleans them, catalogues them, puts them on shelves, and eventually takes them off shelves and puts them on a table when a historian wants them. All this is true enough, but it neglects entirely those aspects of the archivist's job that call for intelligence, knowledge and judgment [...].[12]

Cast within this light, archivists are not only regarded as passive but also as intellectually castrated as they perform the work of mere technicians who are preoccupied with managing and administering archives through digitisation, standardisation, and preservation. In his analysis of the relationship between the historian and the archivist, and how archives have, in a sense, become a foreign country to both archivists and historians, Cook made a compelling argument for the reinvention of archives. According to Cook, this approach should be centred upon the history of the record through a process where both archivists and scholars must reacquaint themselves with the archives by abandoning traditional approaches they previously engaged archives with.[13] For archivists, this should be through interrogating their own history, work methodology, and material practices. It should also be through acknowledging their intervention and subjectivities and finally recognising that their work is highly informed by institutional and societal dynamics and professional divisions.[14] For scholars, it should be to gain a better understanding of how archival practices, theory of the archival profession, and the subjectivities of the archivist might give shape, meaning, and context to the record that ultimately informs how the mediated and enriched record is read and interpreted.[15]

In addressing the neutered and self-deprecating image simultaneously nurtured and loathed by archivists and positively reinforced through a confluence of societal and political factors, we make the argument that archivists need to wake up from what Terry Cook calls their "comfortable state of complacent narcosis."[16] Indeed, following Michelle Pickover's argument:

> Archivists, through archival practices such as appraisal, selection, arrangement, and description are not passive guardians but gatekeepers, active participants and contextualisers who posit layers of interpretative frameworks. They therefore play an important proactive role in the production of knowledge and in creating, preserving, controlling, altering, reinventing and reinterpreting the fragments of personal identities and social memory.[17]

Moreover as "agents of social change",[18] archivists are entrusted with the responsibility to perform their work in the interests of social justice and activism rather than just acting as mere custodians. This has become pertinent, especially because archives are increasingly finding themselves on shifting ground in response to consistent epistemological, political, financial, and technological changes without a decisive strategy on how to chart a course through the foggy waters of the present to the future. One way of coming to terms with the ever-shifting ground underneath their feet is for archivists to reimagine themselves through a process of "philosophising, contextualising, self-reflection, self-disclosure, [and] self-deconstruction."[19] Put another way, archivists need to start questioning recalcitrant orthodox archival practices and rigid principles, and be creative and imaginative as they take up the call for social justice, activism, and scholarship through their work of documenting, interpreting and mediating the archive.

But what would it mean to transform a profession that has become imprisoned in scientific reductionism and bound up in the bureaucratic and technological constructions of the trade in response to the professional demands exercised on them? How would archives and archivists navigate their way through the webs of archival politics and the politics of archiving? How would archivists start to think themselves out of this predicament of being perceived as passive guardians towards becoming more engaged, imaginative activists and interpreters of archives? To answer these questions, it may be productive to consider the ways in which archives tend to shift between conditions of power and precariousness in response to increased competition between institutions for funding and resources, remaining relevant within society while negotiating its relationship to an existing political will.

Between power and precariousness

Until recently, archives were perceived "as a value-free site of document collection and historical inquiry, rather than a site for the contestation of power, memory, and identity."[20] Far from being disengaged, archives can never be neutral, sanitised, and passive repositories of inert and static objects gathering dust. Though archives might contain 'old stuff' or relics, archives are not passive storage vaults of raw, antiquated records as they sometimes engage quite vigorously in public policy debates around freedom of information, the protection of privacy, copyright and intellectual property, and issues around digitisation.²¹ It is in this sense that archives have and will always be about power. Recognising that power has always been central to archives, Terry Eastwood and Heather MacNeil have argued:

> When public archival institutions were first established, they were defined and defended as bastions of citizen and state rights and laboratories of history. The raison d'etre of both archives and archival repositories was to serve the needs and interests of law, administration, and history. Contemporary discussions link the purposes of archives and the role of archival institutions to more broadly defined societal needs and interests and revolve around issues of accountability, identity, inclusivity, and social justice. The notions of 'archives as arsenals' and as 'sites of collective memory' encapsulate this broader perspective.²²

While archives have evolved over the years from first being perceived as bastions of citizen rights and laboratories of history to sites of collective memory and arsenals of accountability and social justice, archives have remained the *loci* of power as they move between the intersection of the past, present, and future. The archive, according to Derrida's formulation, opens up into the future because the open archive "produces more archive, and that is why the archive is never closed. It opens out of the future."²³ George Orwell recognised the inherent power and importance of the archive when he wrote in his novel, *1984*:

> Who controls the past, controls the future; who control the present, controls the past […]. The mutability of the past is the central tenet of Ingsoc. Past events, it is argued, have no objective existence, but survive only in written records and in human experiences. The past is whatever the records and the memories agree upon. And since the Party is in full control of all records, and in equally full control of the minds of its members, it follows that the past is whatever the Party chooses to make it.²⁴

More than just reminding us that control of the archive is central to attaining and maintaining political power, it accentuates the importance of archives in society not only for the present but also for the future. Archives are implicated and entangled in complex webs of power relations which are underpinned by historical, political, and economic undercurrents within society. As sites of power, archives can protect and sanctify certain records while dismissing and destroying others. Additionally, they also control and determine the conditions of access which are enforced through a regime of archival practices, policies, and processes. Writing about the power of archives, Schwartz and Cook have argued that archives are "a product of society's need for information, and the abundance and circulation of documents reflects the importance placed on information in society."²⁵

Thus, according to Schwartz and Cook, the very nature of archives is such that they are "active sites where social power is negotiated, contested and confirmed."²⁶ More than this, Schwartz and Cook have asserted that archives validate our experiences, perceptions, and stories, and this in turn contributes to a sense of a shared past and cohesion among individuals and groups in society. Following the pair's argument, we argue that archives, as records, and archivists, through their professional responsibilities, wield power over how knowledge is produced. They also lend shape to collective memory and national identity while promoting accountability and social justice. However, as Schwartz and Cook reminded us, the power of archives and records is also unstable as it is responsive to changes both inside and outside of archives,[27] including archival practices, organisational dynamics, ideological differences, and violent conflicts among others. This makes the archives a contested terrain fraught with challenges where ideological, political, and fiscal battles are waged for the soul of the archives which can be bartered either as a tool of silence and oppression or of social justice and activism. Alluding to the perilous nature of archives as they shift between power and precariousness, Michelle Pickover argued that "archives are always about propaganda, rights, desires, lies, ownership, personal histories, trust, nationalism, freedoms, concealments, acquisitiveness and surveillance."[28]

As a consequence, this makes archives a highly sought-after commodity not so much for the information that they may contain but how this information can be deployed, interpreted, hidden, or destroyed by the public, researchers, archivists, and the state.[29] Despite the power that archives wield through archival objects and archivists, there still seems to be reluctance, on the part of archivists in particular, to accept the inherent power of archives and the power that archivists have in shaping the archive. We argue that this reluctance might be located in the way archivists have situated themselves primarily as technicians and custodians in relation to archives. Emphasising this, Pickover argued that:

> … many archivists do not see themselves in a social and political context or as documenting history but rather cocooned in the practical world of processing and storing material. Lost in the perceived practical banality of it all, archivists become immersed in their Sartrean selves […] and broader societal terrains are silenced […] and marginalised voices are *de facto* excluded."[30]

Echoing this argument, Harris argued that, "any attempt to be impartial, to stand above the power-plays, constitutes a choice, whether conscious or not, to replicate if not to reinforce prevailing relations of power."[31] Following Harris' argument, the archivist will unavoidably become engaged in politics even if it is not through their own active decision-making. Harris argued that:

> The archive […] is not a quiet retreat for professionals and scholars and craftsperson. It is a crucible of human experience. A battleground for meaning and significance. A babel of stories. A place and a space of complex and ever-shifting power plays. Here you cannot keep your hands clean. Here the very notions of profession and scholarship and craft must be reimagined.[32]

More than just calling attention to the archives as a place of memory, mediation, and contestation, Harris points out that the denial of the archives as a site of power can leave archives in a precarious position because the danger herein is that archives are presented as unproblematic and divorced from socio-economic and political fluctuations. Schwartz and Cook emphatically argued that archivists and users of the archive should realise that "power recognised becomes power that can be questioned, made accountable and opened to transparent dialogue and enriched understanding."[33] If archivists do not question, the archival myth of neutrality and objectivity continues to be perpetuated and worse yet, archivists will continue to privilege the official narratives of the state to the detriment of the personal and multiple narratives of the marginalised and silenced.

In transforming archives, it has become crucial to understand the underlying power of archives and the umbilical cord they share with scholarship, collective memory, and nationhood. In a sense, this understanding of archives as a site of power, veneration, and activism has become almost urgent, especially with political uncertainties and other operational challenges that are facing arts and culture projects at present in South Africa. Perhaps as a consequence of the perception of archives as passive storage facilities and the failure to understand the underlying power of archives, archives are marred by neglect and apathy.

The shifting ground of the South African archival system

The conceptualisation of the South African national archival system emerged alongside the negotiation process in the early 1990s as part of South Africa's transition to a democracy. In the wake of sweeping political changes, consultative processes were set up through which practitioners and other stakeholders could participate in developing policy and legislative frameworks for an archival system for the new dispensation. Equally important, these national dialogues and consultative processes provided a platform to discuss an archival strategy for the future that would address issues of redress and transformation. These processes culminated in the formulation of the *National Archives of South Africa Act No 43 of 1996*. The 1996 Archives Act held much promise, as was articulated by its optimistic and bold agenda, but this promise has not been realised as the initial energy and optimism around transformation waned in the absence of adequate resources, funding, and an understanding of the work of archives. According to a report prepared by UCT-based archive and heritage information and promotion agency, Archival Platform, "the optimism that marked the 1990s crumbled away as resources failed to materialise, backlogs in processing archives and records grew to unmanageable levels, training and opportunities for professional advancement became limited …"[34]

Currently, the vision of archives in the future seems dismal and unsettling at best, beset as archives are with epistemic and political uncertainties at the present. The crisis the national archival system finds themselves in was already flagged as early as 2007 in 'Archives at the Crossroads: Open Report to the Minister of Arts and Culture' following deliberations of the conference, National System, Public Interest, that considered the dismal state of archives in South Africa. The 'Open Report to the Minister of Arts and Culture' argued that the significance of archives is, for the most part, unacknowledged and concluded that the danger herein lies in the creation of an inadequate and strained archival system that is plagued by protracted under-funding and poor service delivery.[35] The stark reality is that after 28 years of transformation processes informed by the promissory note of democratic change, archives are still under siege from both within and from outside the archival realm. In their report, Archival Platform argued:

> Much good work was done systematically through the 1990s, but the hopes of that period have not been realised. Today the national archival system is in trouble. Good work is being done only in isolated pockets. There is no overarching policy framework for archives beyond that implicit in national and provincial legislation. The vision of the 1990s has evaporated. Chronic underfunding and a lack of resources is ubiquitous. The political will to change things is largely absent. The system, simply put is not delivering.[36]

Slightly predating this report, Carolyn Hamilton attributed the crisis facing the national archival system to a combination of fractures, uncertainties, changes, and ambiguities around archival inheritances of the colonial and apartheid periods. According to Hamilton, "the neglect of the official archival institutions also speaks to contemporary epistemic and political uncertainties, ambiguities and contradictions surrounding the formal archival inheritance and the many forms of material held in other custodial formations."[37] Although Hamilton conceded that the crisis in the national archival system is much more complex than bad management and being under-resourced, her argument was mostly concerned with how colonial and apartheid state archives were seemingly being relegated to the margins because they were tainted and dubious in nature, and therefore viewed with distrust.[38] While Hamilton mostly focused her attention on the swirling turmoil the national archival system found itself in by looking at public archives, the Archival Platform's report went beyond that. Their report, 'State of the Archives: An Analysis of South Africa's National Archival System' considered how this crisis had also filtered through to non-public archives. The report provided a brief analysis of non-public archives by highlighting challenges such as funding and sustainability which was often a cause of immense anxiety and insecurity for some archives. Their report also focused on issues of preservation, custodianship, and digitisation among the challenges experienced with the implementation of collection management strategies. To address these challenges, the report called for greater integration between public and non-public archives, the safeguarding of records, and promoting access and use of archives among some of the suggested interventions.[39]

Although we agree with most of these interventions, as suggested by Archival Platform, we argue that the challenges that archives are facing run deeper than issues of funding, custody, care, capacity, or lack of technical expertise. Although these issues can contribute to archives experiencing challenges, we believe this peripheral vision needs to be broadened by emphasising the need to transform archives.[40] By transforming archives, we argue that we need a new approach to the way we engage with archives by understanding its work in a democratic society and by escaping the straitjacket of positivist archival theory. Because archives are often surrounded by ambiguities and seemingly insurmountable challenges, archives often find themselves confronting a very uncertain future.

As a way of addressing this uncertain future, we argue that it is crucial for archivists to study their own history and the records that they work with as this would anchor archivists in a professional identity of their own. Hugh Taylor, a strong proponent of this view, advocated that central to the work of the archivist should be "a new form of 'social historiography' to make clear how and why records were created […]".[41] Echoing this sentiment, one of Canada's pre-eminent archival educators, Barbara L. Craig, argued that the archival profession has a broad outward view in relation to their relationship with other professionals and society but has neglected to direct the view inward which would invite a probing analysis of their own history and the records that they are preserving.[42] Craig whimsically argued that instead of being chefs, archivists are waiters who "serve up a sumptuous bill of fare, but they have very little understanding either of the current cuisine or of its history."[43] It is in this sense that she urged the archival profession to reverse their field of vision. As such, a reversal would enable a robust reorientation of the archival profession that would bring the practical, theoretical, and philosophical understanding to how archivists engage with archives.[44]

As archives are tethering on the edge of either remaining locked in their custodial cloisters or transforming themselves, archivists need to adopt a more critical approach to the way they work with and within archives. Within a similar vein as Craig, we argue that it is essential for archivists to both study archival history and the history of the archival record itself. The benefits of such an approach may place archivists in a better position to respond to present and future challenges that the archive may face. It may also enable archivists to make informed decisions regarding collections based on the history of the archival record. Though Craig provided archivists with a skeletal framework towards becoming transformed archivists, she acknowledged the difficulty herein as archivists are always being pulled between being philosophers or plumbers. Archivists are often criticised for their almost exclusive focus on the practicalities or technicalities of their work at the expense of theoretical issues which cannot be disaggregated from the archive, while conversely, they are also ridiculed by scholars and other archivists within the field for even having theoretical aspirations.[45]

The predicament of the archivist

Quoting Proust, Joan Schwartz asserted that "[t]he real voyage of discovery consists not in seeking new landscapes but in having new eyes."[46] She further argued:

> If archivists are to discover the new intellectual landscape of 'the archive' – to seek out, expose, and address the physical intellectual, procedural, metaphorical, and functional spaces where knowledge and power intersect, to recognize spaces of archives as landscapes of power – then it will be, not only by looking for that territory from within the profession, but also by seeking it through new eyes, including those on the 'outside' looking in.[47]

Following from Schwartz's argument, it has become pertinent for archivists to re-evaluate their craft with new eyes. One way of acquiring an alternate vision and to reimagine the profession is to reconsider the relationship of history to the archive. Although archivists have disengaged themselves from the historical profession for numerous reasons which are mostly tied up with the technicalities of archival work, historical research remains a crucial and central component of archival work. Despite the inherent importance of historical research to archival work, it seems that research which is undertaken by archivists is not encouraged within archives, especially if it is at the perceived expense of the technical duties of archiving. Restricted by the technical side of archiving that finds itself in an uneasy relationship with information science and knowledge management and limited by administrative policies and procedures, most archivists still perceive themselves as mere technicians or caretakers of archival collections.

It seems that archivists are firmly caught between this dichotomy of theory and practice which, in part, is of their own doing but in responding to this predicament, archivists need to explore ways of finding a balance as they move between the porous boundaries of the disciplines of archiving and history. In his reflections on the importance of historical knowledge in archival work, Tom Nesmith argued that "archival work is driven by an overriding historical imperative."[48] Nesmith argued that many archivists had an historical orientation towards their work from as early as the 19th century and thus saw themselves both as archivists and historical researchers. However, as the archival profession evolved over the 19th and early 20th centuries with the emergence of various archival manuals that advocated for a more contextual and practical application to archival work, most notably by Jenkinson, historical research eventually became side-lined and almost came to be regarded as a frivolous pursuit.

Although there were other leading figures such as Samuel Muller and Theodore Schellenberg who argued for an approach to archival work that encompassed history, archivists eventually established themselves as distinct from historians as the practical approach to archiving gained more ground. This resulted in an unfortunate distance between archivists and historians in a relationship that shares several communalities which can be traced back to the 19th century. In an attempt to address the emerging tensions in the fractious relationship between archivists and historians and more importantly, to advocate for a more historical or theoretical approach to archiving, Schellenberg proposed in his manual that the best preliminary training that an archivist can have is advanced training in history.[49] According to Schellenberg, this will provide the archivist "with a knowledge of the development of his country" and will provide the archivist with "training in research methodology, which is needed in all the work he does rationalising public records."[50]

Weighing in on the archivist/historian debate, George Bolotenko argued that "[t]he archivist and historian are in fact in symbiosis […]. [O]ne might say that even as a good archivist needs to be, in some part, an historian, to know the world which interprets the facts in his keeping, the good historian must also be […] an archivist, to understand the world which preserves […]".[51] Despite being two sides of the same coin, archivists remain in a predicament where they are compelled to choose between one of two paths: either become an archivist-historian focused on scholarly pursuits or an information technician focused on standardisation and administration. This begs the question: why does it have to be either this or either that? Bolotenko argued that in moving towards the new archivist, the archivist need not necessarily be an historian, but "he should always be an archivist-historian."[52] He argued that the new archivist should ideally be "a representative of the world of research in the world of administration – skilled in the trends, techniques, personalities, and developments of that world."[53]

Moving towards the new archivist

Central to the work of archives and archivists is the need to preserve, safeguard, and care for archives. However, in the face of crises and future uncertainties, archivists need to do a little bit more than just guarding archives. In transforming the archival landscape from "passive custodial to active interventionist",[54] it is imperative that archivists become visible both to themselves and to others. They should not hide and quite simply cannot indulge any longer in their constructed invisibility. Instead, through their archival work, archivists should become activists who engage with the public and pursue social justice as a way of fostering social transformation and diversity. In moving towards the new archivist who, in part, is an advocate and activist for social justice issues, and very importantly, also a scholar, archivists will have to abandon their comfortable traditional antiquarian approach. The new archivist should interrogate their work methodology, acknowledge their intervention and subjectivities, and recognise that their work is highly informed by institutional and societal dynamics. We strongly argue that the archivist has an obligation to focus on the technical side of their work as much as recognising that archives are spaces of "knowledge, memory, nourishment and power"[55] in which the archivist is entrusted with the responsibility to also interpret the records they work with. In this way, archivists should also actively engage in the production of knowledge.

Having identified the ideal characteristics of the new archivist as an activist and a scholar, we have an outline of what the transformed archivist should look like. Yet, the question that remains is: how would we transform the archival landscape to facilitate this move towards the new archivist? One of the first things to consider in transforming the archival landscape is for archives to adopt an institutional policy that makes provision for archival scholarship whereby archival staff are encouraged to write, present, and publish based on research within their own institutions and also other archives and collections. Although archival scholarship exists in some institutions and in others it exists on a voluntary basis, archives need to implement it as an institutional policy. Walter Rundell argued that "[t]he scholarly curator is a better curator because of the deepened understanding that research and publication bring to his task. Thus, he is better able to serve the needs of history, as well as his own institution."[56] Reiterating this, David Mycue has also made an argument for archival scholarship to become a priority within archives along with creating inventories, indexing, and preservation. According to Mycue, "[a] research program in institutional history would provide training for archivists, generate favourable publicity for their institutions, and demonstrate that their collection offered varied services for government officials, academics, or other citizens."[57] Moreover, archival scholarship will also provide a solid foundation from which archivists can approach other archival practices such as appraisal, provenance, and description. For example, archival scholarship might assist the archivist in making more informed decisions regarding what is deemed important for research and preservation based on research trends and their own research background.

Verne Harris has reminded us earlier that in the pursuit of activism and social justice, archives should never be a quiet retreat for archivists, scholars, and the public.[58] Instead, they should be spaces of vigorous debate, contestation, and public engagement as it is constituted and continues to be reconstituted by archivists, record creators, donors, institutional dynamics, knowledge production, and political undercurrents. In this intricate nexus, through their archival work, archivists have a significant mission as active memory workers in which they give meaning and shape to memory. In this tumultuous time of archives being under siege, archivists need to take up the call to arms whereby they transform themselves from hoarders of ruins and relics to becoming active participants where they can be activists of social justice and scholars who contribute towards knowledge production.

Endnotes

1. J. Derrida. 2002. 'Archive Fever'. Transcript of seminar, University of the Witwatersrand, August 1998. In: C. Hamilton, V. Harris, M. Pickover, G. Reid, R. Saleh & J. Taylor (eds.), *Refiguring the Archive*. Cape Town: David Philip, 54.
2. H. Taylor. 2003. 'The Discipline of History and the Education of the Archivist'. In: T. Cook & G. Dodds (eds.), *Imagining Archives: Essays and Reflections by Hugh A. Taylor*. Metuchen, MD: Scarecrow, 52.
3. T. Cook. 2009. 'The Archive(s) is a Foreign Country: Historians, Archivists, and the Changing Archival Landscape'. *The Canadian Historical Review*, 90(3):509. https://doi.org/10.1353/can.0.0194
4. Cook. 'The Archive(s) is a Foreign Country', 505.
5. H. Jenkinson. 1937. *A Manual of Archive Administration*. London: Percy Lund, Humphries and Co Ltd, 12.
6. Ibid., 12.
7. T. Cook & J.M. Schwartz. 2002. 'Archives, Records and Power: The Making of Modern Memory'. *Archival Science*, 2:5. https://doi.org/10.1007/BF02435628
8. V. Harris. 1997. 'Claiming Less, Delivering More: A Critique of Positivist Formulations on Archives in South Africa'. *Archivaria*, 44:132.
9. Ibid., 132.
10. Cook. 'The Archive(s) is a Foreign Country', 507.
11. Ibid., 516.
12. Ibid., 507.
13. Ibid., 497.
14. V. Harris. 2000. *Exploring Archives: An Introduction to the Archival Ideas and Practice in South Africa*. Pretoria: National Archives of South Africa, 3.
15. J.M. Schwartz. 2007. 'Having New Eyes: Spaces of Archives, Landscapes of Power'. *Archives & Social Studies: A Journal of Interdisciplinary Research*, 1:331.
16. Taylor. 'The Discipline of History and the Education of the Archivist', 18.
17. M. Pickover. 2005. 'Negotiations, Contestations and Fabrications: The Politics of Archives in South Africa Ten Years After Democracy'. *Innovation*, 30:2. https://doi.org/10.4314/innovation.v30i1.26493
18. Ibid., 2.
19. Harris. 'Claiming Less, Delivering More', 140.
20. Cook & Schwartz. 'Archives, Records and Power'. https://doi.org/10.1007/BF02435628
21. Ibid., 1.
22. T. Eastwood & H. MacNeil (eds.). 2010. *Currents of Archival Thinking*. Santa Barbara, CA: ABC-CLIO, viii.
23. J. Derrida. 1995. *Archive Fever: A Freudian Impression*, translated by E. Prenowitz. Chicago: University of Chicago Press, 68. https://doi.org/10.2307/465144
24. G. Orwell. [1949] 2013. *Nineteen Eighty-Four*. London: Penguin, 35, 213.
25. Cook & Schwartz. 'Archives, Records and Power', 13. https://doi.org/10.1007/BF02435628
26. Ibid., 1.
27. Ibid., 13.

28 Pickover. 'Negotiations, Contestations and Fabrications', 6.
29 Ibid., 6.
30 Ibid., 3 (emphasis in the original).
31 V. Harris. 2007. *Archives and Justice: A South African Perspective*. Chicago, IL: Society of American Archivists, 248.
32 V. Harris. 2003. 'Freedom of Information in South Africa and Archives for Justice'. *Transactions of Public Culture Workshop*. University of the Western Cape, Cape Town, 11 January.
33 Cook & Schwartz. 'Archives, Records and Power', 2. https://doi.org/10.1007/BF02435628
34 Archival Platform. 2015. *State of the Archives: An Analysis of South Africa's National Archival System*. https://bit.ly/40JmKXK [Accessed 21 November 2021].
35 'Archives at the Crossroads 2007: Open Report to the Minister of Arts and Culture' from the Archival Conference 'National System, Public Interest', April 2007. https://bit.ly/3ZCcVKe [Accessed 22 March 2014].
36 Archival Platform. 2015. Executive Summary. *State of the Archives: An Analysis of South Africa's National Archival System*. https://bit.ly/42ZeWmy [Accessed 21 November 2021].
37 C. Hamilton. 2013. 'Forged and Continually Refashioned in the Crucible of Ongoing Social and Political Life: Archives and Custodial Practices as Subjects of Enquiry'. *South African Historical Journal*, 65(1):21. https://doi.org/10.1080/02582473.2013.763400
38 Ibid., 20.
39 For a glance at the set of interventions which were proposed to address the crisis of the national archival system see Archival Platform. 2015. *State of the Archives: An Analysis of South Africa's National Archival System*, 150-151. https://bit.ly/40JmKXK [Accessed 21 November 2021].
40 The report argues that one of the interventions into the crisis should be to fundamentally review the archival system to address the deep systemic flaws and structural challenges.
41 H. Taylor quoted in Taylor. 'The Discipline of History and the Education of the Archivist', 23.
42 B.L. Craig. 1992. 'Outward Visions, Inward Glance: Archives History and Professional Identity'. *Archival Issues*, 17(2):113. https://www.jstor.org/stable/41101829
43 Ibid., 115.
44 Ibid., 113-124.
45 Ibid., 116.
46 J.M. Schwartz. 2007. 'Having New Eyes: Spaces of Archives, Landscapes of Power'. *Archives and Social Studies: A Journal of Interdisciplinary Research*, 1:362.
47 Ibid., 362.
48 T. Nesmith. 2004. 'What's History Got to Do With It: Reconsidering the Place of Historical Knowledge in Archival Work'. *Archivaria*, 57:5.
49 T.R. Schellenberg. 1956. *Modern Archives, Principles and Techniques*. Melbourne: Cheshire, 131.
50 Ibid., 131.
51 G. Bolotenko. 1983. 'Archivists and Historians: Keepers of the Well'. *Archivaria*, 16:20.

52 Ibid., 20.
53 Ibid., 20.
54 Cook. 'The Archive(s) is Foreign Country', 530.
55 R.C. Jimerson. 2006. 'Embracing the Power of Archives'. *The American Archivist*, 69(1):20. https://doi.org/10.17723/aarc.69.1.r0p75n2084055418
56 W. Rundell & C. Herbert Finch. 1977. 'The State of Historical Records: A Summary'. *American Archivist*, 40(3):344. https://doi.org/10.17723/aarc.40.3.fm4qj3613841k014
57 D. Mycue. 1979. 'The Archivist as Scholar: A Case for Research by Archivists'. *Georgia Archive*, 7(2):13.
58 Harris. 'Freedom of Information in South Africa and Archives for Justice', 11.

The Configuration of Archives in Post-apartheid South Africa 3

> Archives keep the secrets of the state; novels keep the secrets of culture, and the secret of these secrets.[1]

As has been argued in the preceding chapters, the archive, both as an institution and episteme, has been at the fulcrum of an intense debate for several years. More than just reminding us that the archive is a site of struggle shrouded in contestation and ambiguity, these debates have brought into sharp focus the indeterminate and opaque nature of the archive in the way it refuses to be fully laid bare and calls attention to the fragility of the archive. With the transition from apartheid to democracy, the new South African state inherited the documentary traces of apartheid and colonialism. Having to contend with this legacy, the early 1990s saw a proliferation of post-apartheid archives and memory institutions. Conceived as one of the ways to redress "apartheid-fashioned gaps in social memory",[2] the formation of post-apartheid archives and the augmentation of existing collecting institutions with anti-apartheid and liberation struggle material were about "bringing the hidden, the marginalised, the exiled, the 'other' archive, into the 'mainstream'."[3] Repatriated from exile, and consisting of the material of previously banned organisations, as well as the records of solidarity organisations, and those of activists who had fought in the struggle against apartheid, liberation struggle and anti-apartheid materials were unceremoniously thrust into a national process of heritage and archival transformation in the service of promoting the principles of democracy and reconciliation. Highly controversial because of its enduring contemporary significance and mired in continued secrecy because of the conditions they were constituted in, some post-apartheid archives have been at the forefront of intense debates regarding issues of ownership, commodification, competition, marginalisation, silencing, and collective amnesia.

To understand some of these complex issues, especially when placed within the greater crisis of the national archival system, this chapter will argue that while the formation of post-apartheid archives held a promise of transformation and "of unlocking the past, of lifting the veils of secrecy and of transparency",[4] in effect, this did not happen. Disillusionment has gradually set in because post-apartheid archives have increasingly become caught up in the politics of identity, heritage, and memory pervasive within the larger project of memorialisation and nation-building. This chapter will argue that to understand how post-apartheid archives were deployed and for what purposes, one can begin to understand the challenges and limitations that framed the transformation process of the archival system in South Africa. As a way of situating the central question of the transformation process of post-apartheid archives in South Africa, this chapter will explore the ideology and discourses that underpinned the configuration of what could be broadly termed as liberation and solidarity archives. By focusing on the ways and purposes post-apartheid archives have been deployed, such as the National Heritage and Cultural Studies Centre (NAHECS) and the University of the Western Cape Robben Island Museum Mayibuye Archives, this chapter will argue that because of the politics of transformation in post-apartheid South Africa, some of these archives became caught in a nationalist liberation narrative that encourages selective amnesia while others have been hindered by a lack of resources. As much as collective amnesia has been nurtured as a condition of post-apartheid, there has also been a sustained and almost obsessive desire to possess, own, and control material related to the liberation struggle as this is considered politically fashionable and prestigious. This has disconcertingly led to increased rivalry between some post-apartheid archives, with the focus shifting to commodification and ownership which is often subject to political interference rather than focusing on the processes of archiving and knowledge production. However, it is important to place the formation of post-apartheid archives in relation to the historical developments of the South African archival system.

Traces of archives in South Africa

Although traces of archiving in the form of carvings, rock paintings, body scarification, and collective stories that were passed from one generation to the next can be found throughout South Africa today, and predates the arrival of European colonialism, it has habitually been ignored.[5] The arrival of European colonialism from the 17th century supplanted these forms of archiving, and by the 19th century, formal repositories came into being because of the centrality of the archive in the formation and creation of the nation as argued in Ann Laura Stoler's study on 19th-century Dutch colonial archives.[6] While most post-apartheid archives were forged in the shadows of the underground or in exile as subversive and counter to the archives of the apartheid state, following Stoler's argument, it can be argued that in post-apartheid South Africa, post-apartheid archives were deployed to help bolster the production of the new democratic state. However, as with all archives, post-apartheid archives also reveal as much as they conceal. Holding mere fragments of the past, they could only ever offer temporal and spatial incisions into a troubled past.

Stoler argued that colonial archives should be regarded as epistemological experiments and as sites of contested knowledge.[7] According to Stoler, "scholars should view archives not as sites of knowledge retrieval, but of knowledge production, as monuments of states, as well as sites of state ethnography."[8] Although Stoler's study exclusively focused on colonial archives, we argue that parts of her argument could also be productive in thinking through the questions of what constituted post-apartheid archives, how they were shaped, and how this rendering as post-apartheid archives influenced the way these archives were positioned between power, knowledge, and state. Following Stoler's argument of thinking of the archive as a site of knowledge production rather than as source, we argue that such a shift in thinking allows for the possibility of a more critical way of thinking through the notion of the post-apartheid archive and begs for a more critical approach of doing archival work not only in colonial archives but also in post-apartheid archives.

Apartheid was very successful in reaching into almost every aspect of the people's lives it governed by having control over the "racial classification, employment, movement, association, purchase of property, recreation and so on, all were documented by thousands of government offices."[9] In this sense, the apartheid regime produced a vast archive of its own activities of repression, control, and discrimination. However, while the apartheid regime might have been ardent record keepers, access to the records of the state archive were tightly controlled and shrouded in a culture of secrecy which has prevailed well into the present. Apart from the public records generated by the apartheid state, the apartheid archival system also encompassed records of the security police and intelligence services that documented their surveillance activities on those in opposition to apartheid. While these records constituted a significant part of the State Archives Service (SAS), large quantities of records that documented the struggle against apartheid were confiscated during raids from individuals and organisations opposed to apartheid as they also started keeping their own account of the struggle against apartheid. Often forced by the long reach of the apartheid system into informal spaces, liberation movements, solidarity organisations, and activists generated an expansive record of their activism and resistance work that documented the underground activities and exile experiences of those opposed to apartheid. This material, considered to be subversive by the apartheid state, would constitute the shadow archives of the liberation struggle and would later be deployed as the antithesis or counter archives to the state archives. These archives would remain in the shadows until apartheid was legislatively dismantled in the early 1990s.

Through a sustained campaign of resistance punctuated with protests, mass mobilisation, sanctions, and international solidarity which culminated during the 1980s to fever pitch as the apartheid state clamped down on its opponents, the National Party (NP) realised the need to engage with its opponents as the apartheid system would not be able to sustain the mounting pressure for reform calls. On 2 February 1990, then President F.W. de Klerk made an announcement in which he lifted the ban on political and solidarity organisations such as the Communist Party of South Africa (CPSA), African National Congress (ANC), and the Pan Africanist Congress (PAC), along with other political organisations, as well as the International Defence and Aid Fund (IDAF), an international solidarity organisation, and also announced that political exiles would be allowed to return and that all political prisoners would be released from prison.

After centuries of colonial oppression and four decades of experiencing the brutal force of apartheid, the revolution did not happen. Instead, apartheid was dismantled through a negotiated settlement between the liberation movement and the apartheid regime.[10]

The struggle for liberation in South Africa was a long and bitter battle in more ways than one. It is a fragmented story marked by violence, pain, loss, and suffering but equally, it is a story about memory erasure, silencing of oppositional voices, exclusion, and marginalisation. The remnants that remained bear testimony to a tumultuous, divisive, and painful past, some of which the apartheid regime managed to destroy in the last few feverish moments of apartheid in the early 1990s, just as the country was casting off the shackles of apartheid and emerging as a fledgling democracy. The archive as a site of struggle, contestation, and ambiguity, in particular the archives of the apartheid era, and after being shrouded in an imposed state of public amnesia for more than two decades following the democratic transition, has recently become prominent again in public discourse through a renewed call for justice for victims of apartheid era atrocities as the process inaugurated by the Truth and Reconciliation Commission (TRC) remains unfinished.[11]

The apartheid regime was built on secrecy and lack of transparency and as the pillars of apartheid's architecture started crumbling during the early 1990s, those in opposition to apartheid feared that the regime might be tempted to destroy public records revealing apartheid secrets and culpability in human rights violations as evidence suggested that the regime routinely destroyed public records during apartheid.[12] Engineered by the apartheid state, and designed in part to withhold perceived sensitive information from the future government under the cloak of the very vague and dubious *Protection of Information Act* (PIA) of 1982, the state undertook a comprehensive sanitisation exercise on its archival resources. While this operation involved various departmental structures within the regime, the focus of this large scale destruction of public records was the records of the security and intelligence arms of the state in particular.[13] According to the findings of an investigation that was launched by the TRC into the destruction of public records, huge volumes of public records were destroyed between 1990 and 1994 in an attempt to sanitise the official record and keep the secrets of the apartheid state buried.[14]

Equally disconcerting, especially when viewed against a background of deliberate practices of memory erasure, the silencing and marginalisation of oppositional voices during apartheid through exile, banning, detentions, torture, imprisonment, enforced disappearances, and deaths, was the destruction of records that went beyond the repressive activities of the state and included the records of those that were opposed to apartheid. As revealed by the TRC investigation into the destruction of apartheid era records, records encompassing material that were confiscated during raids, collected as evidence against individuals or organisations considered to be enemies of the state, were not spared from being destroyed. Sometimes these records were part of the collateral destruction caused by bombings and other violent acts against those opposed to apartheid, but unfortunately, most of these surviving non-public records that made it into the twilight of apartheid were subsequently also destroyed during the early 1990s in the hope of whitewashing the historical record.

Apart from the widespread destruction of public records whether through intentional destruction or through the confiscation of private records which eventually led to their destruction, it remains to be told how many private records were obliterated from social memory within the rigid conditions of apartheid for fear of imprisonment, torture, harassment, and even death. Hindered by a lack of resources, coupled with the state confiscation of material considered to be revolutionary and the possibility that individuals and organisations opposed to apartheid might have destroyed some of their own records to combat infiltration and prosecution by the apartheid state, this has resulted in an even more fragmented record of historical memory by the end of apartheid. Verne Harris, a former archivist at SAS commented in his detailed account of the destruction of public records by the South African state between 1990 to 1994, that "this was a struggle of remembering against forgetting, of oppositional memory fighting a life-and-death struggle against a systematic forgetting engineered by the state."[15]

Transition to democracy

With the negotiated transition from apartheid to democracy, the new South African state was shaped around the notion of a unified rainbow nation focused on fostering transformation, reconciliation, and nation-building as the central tenets of building a democracy. Although the negotiated settlement facilitated a Government of National Unity after the sweeping victory of the ANC in the 1994 general elections, the new democracy tentatively emerged in the post-apartheid setting burdened by the deeply entrenched psychological scars and documentary inheritances left behind by apartheid and colonialism. These sometimes deeply etched traces have left an indelible imprint on South African society as they continue to operate in very pervasive and often subversive ways.

With the apartheid system being disassembled, the early 1990s saw a flowering of new heritage institutions, national museums, community museums, memorial projects, monuments, archival institutions, and heritage training programmes. This included the South African History Archive (SAHA), the Mayibuye Centre for History and Culture which was later absorbed into the Robben Island Museum and became known as the University of the Western Cape Robben Island Museum Mayibuye Archives, the District Six Museum, the Gay and Lesbian Memory in Action Archive (GALA), and the National Heritage and Cultural Studies Centre (NAHECS) at the University of Fort Hare (UFH) among a host of heritage and archival institutions and heritage training programmes that came to be at the forefront of change by offering alternative histories and practices. The creation of these counter archives and the augmentation of existing collecting institutions with anti-apartheid and liberation struggle material were about showcasing and creating access to the marginalised and exiled archive. Moreover, these post-apartheid heritage institutions allowed for the other, the marginalised, the exiled, and the hidden to be brought into the mainstream as a means of challenging conceptualisations of the mainstream. In addition, these institutions also played a key role in the transformation discourse that emerged alongside the political transformation that South Africa was undergoing both by leading discussions in heritage transformation and through their archival practices premised on activism and social justice.

The transition to a democratic form of government held the promise of a new beginning in which people could imagine better lives for themselves, but more than this, a new democracy carried with it the hopes of social justice, equity, and accountability. Amidst the palpable excitement of the changing political situation within South Africa, with the unbanning of political and solidarity organisations and the return of political activists from exile in the early 1990s, the records of the liberation struggle also underwent a shift from exile to freedom. Returning triumphantly from exile and crafting a prestigious position within a changing political landscape whose agenda, among other things, was concerned with the remembering, recuperating, and rewriting of history, the records of the liberation movements, solidarity organisations, and records from anti-apartheid activists that documented different aspects of the liberation struggle came to be known as post-apartheid archives and coalesced around a transformation discourse, informed by the assumption that archives in South Africa required a reimagining or a refiguring.[16] Constitutive of the 'hidden, exiled or counter' archives of the struggle against apartheid, post-apartheid archives were formally positioned in opposition to the state archives through the emergence of a transformation discourse during the early 1990s. A discourse on transformation, especially one that speaks to issues of memory, education, and culture can be traced back to as far as the 1970s with the emergence of resistance art and literature and the conceptualisation of a people's education during the 1980s as a means of countering apartheid.

Building on these projects of memory construction and oppositional historiography which emerged from the 1970s, the transformation discourse of the 1990s was primarily informed by the need for reconciliation, redress, and equality. Reflecting on this period, Verne Harris observed that:

> ... [t]he nature of the transition to democracy meant that there would be no dramatic dismantling and reconstruction of the apartheid archival system. Rather, the new would be built out of the old through a process of transformation.[17]

Cognisant of the limitations and omissions within colonial and apartheid era archives, it can be argued that post-apartheid archives aimed to play a significant role in the narration of a new nation-in-the-making, both by filling the gaps in the official record and by potentially serving as "instruments of empowerment and liberation."[18] Following

Richard Harvey Brown and Beth Davis-Brown's argument that archives, libraries, and museums "help to preserve a collective national memory and thence, to constitute a collective national identity",[19] we want to make the argument that post-apartheid archives were configured as one of the ways to create modern 'imagined communities'[20] and to "contribute to the social stability and solidarity amid rapid and otherwise more centrifugal change."[21] In sharp contrast to colonial archives that racially excluded, omitted, and elided, post-apartheid archives held the promise of "archives for the people, by the people"[22] in which the colonial subject could be reconstituted as an equal citizen of the new nation in the making. As the SAS was clambering to reinvent and reassert itself within a rapidly changing environment of political and social transformation, various post-apartheid archives started to emerge as records were repatriated to South Africa with the hope of redressing past imbalances.[23] Among these post-apartheid archival repositories that mushroomed as a result of the influx of these collections were existing ones like the Historical Papers Research Archive at the University of the Witwatersrand and emerging ones like the Mayibuye Centre for History and Culture at UWC, NAHECS at the UFH, the Nelson Mandela Foundation's Centre of Memory, SAHA and the South Africa History Online (SAHO) to name but a few. By briefly discussing the emergence of two institutions in historically and politically specific ways, we hope it will better shape our understanding of them as sites of memory, power, and contestations, and the processes through which these institutions have been crafted as post-apartheid archives within the transformation discourse. Some of these institutions have their antecedents in memory projects such as the collection of oral history and arts and culture projects which can be traced back further than the 1990s.[24]

Liberation archives and the University of Fort Hare: Power and politics of the archive

Demonstrating the configuration of post-apartheid archives and the deeply contested terms which sometimes framed their existence was one that played itself out in a small university town located in the Amathole district in the Eastern Cape. Established in 1916 in the small rural town of Alice in the Eastern Cape, the South African Native College, which was later renamed the University College of Fort Hare, for many years remained one of the only academic institutions that provided for the higher education of Africans, and for the early phase of its history, for other blacks as well.[25] The University of Fort Hare (UFH), as it is known today, has a long and illustrious history of providing one of the training grounds where resistance struggle figures such as Oliver Tambo, Robert Sobukwe, Govan Mbeki, and Chris Hani and scholars like I.B. Tabata and Z.K. Matthews were nurtured. Given the UFH's involvement in cultivating the minds of some of the luminary figures in the struggle for independence on the African continent and its close association with the liberation movements in South Africa, it was decided that the university would become the archival repository of the liberation movements' material in the early 1990s. Amidst intense debate and disappointment for some who had hoped that the material would be deposited with them, Nelson Mandela announced that the ANC archives would be lodged at Fort Hare in recognition that the history of the ANC is interwoven with the history of UFH.[26]

There was some opposition to this decision as some in the ANC felt that Fort Hare would be inaccessible for researchers because of the remote and isolated location of the university. Others such as Nelson Mandela, Oliver Tambo, and Govan Mbeki (who at the time were highly placed within the ANC) were in favour of Fort Hare to be the designated archival site of the ANC's repatriated struggle material. Revitalised by the prospect of hosting the archives of one of the liberation movements, UFH went on a proactive and vigorous acquisitions drive whereby they approached the Pan Africanist Congress (PAC), the Azanian People's Organisation (AZAPO), the Unity Movement, and the Black Consciousness Movement (BCM) to become the premier archival destination of all the liberation movements in South Africa. The decision to lodge the ANC material at UFH simultaneously placed two historically black universities, namely UFH and UWC, directly into a conversation and competitive struggle with each other, with both institutions vying for the prized archives of the liberation struggle.[27] This is a point which has also been argued by Michelle Pickover as she observed that many institutions became engaged in an intense scramble for liberation struggle collections in the quest for prestige.[28] According to Pickover, "[c]ollections and collecting then reflect possession rather than process, access or preservation."[29] Although the emergence of the Mayibuye Centre for History and Culture at UWC, which was configured in anticipation of the end of apartheid and initially built on some of the visual and documentary materials of the International Defence and Aid Fund's (IDAF) research programme, predated the development of the liberation archives project at UFH, it was the latter that eventually won the struggle over the archives of the liberation movements.

While the historical development of the Mayibuye Centre at UWC will be discussed later in the chapter, it is important to note that the Mayibuye Centre and the liberation archives project at UFH were conceptualised along similar lines with both institutions having proposed a museum and an archival component documenting the struggle for liberation in South Africa.[30] Beyond the similarities and contentions between these two institutions, this period saw the installation of diverse, yet equally significant collections pertaining to the liberation struggle at UFH and UWC. The positioning of these respective archives at universities located on the margins as conceptualised through the consequences of spatial apartheid, effectively placed this material in seclusion, where they are unable to stir up trouble in the new society. Despite controversy and unhappiness regarding the decision to lodge the ANC material at UFH, other organisations such as the Unity Movement, PAC, AZAPO, and the BCM followed the ANC's lead by also signing agreements with UFH at a momentous event held in Johannesburg on 26 October 1992 which allowed for the depositing of their material at the Centre for Cultural Studies (CCS) at the university.[31] Being a historically black university with an illustrious past that had produced a number of black intellectuals and prominent political figures across Africa such as Robert Sobukwe, I.B. Tabata, Robert Mugabe, and Govan Mbeki, among others, it seemed a fitting choice, particularly against the background of a fast-evolving political landscape in which it seemed likely that the ANC would become the new ruling party in South Africa.

Offering a detailed account of the politics and challenges surrounding the formation of NAHECS and by looking at the challenges of constructing an archive with the explicit purpose of housing struggle material of the liberation movements, Bavusile Maaba studied the emergence of NAHECS by focusing on the politics around the repatriation of the material of the ANC, PAC, and the BCM to the archive. Maaba's study traced the idea of an archive which came to house the material of the liberation movements at UFH back to 1990. While this idea of a liberation archive germinated following preliminary discussions between the ANC and UFH about the future of the ANC material in 1990, Maaba's study suggested that the ANC's archival imperative went as far back as their days in exile. Maaba argued that the ANC's archival imperative was evident from the construction of an archive at the Solomon Mahlangu Freedom College (SOMAFCO) in Tanzania which was used to house the records and artefacts generated from the ANC's educational and cultural activities. In addition to the construction of a building that served as the repository for the material, some SOMAFCO students were also sent for archival training.[32] Symbolically, some of these students from SOMAFCO would later become the future archivists of some of the most prominent archives housing material pertaining to the liberation struggle in South Africa.[33]

Framed within national debates regarding transformation and various consultative processes which started to emerge during the early 1990s, the ANC's Arts and Culture Desk set up a Commission for Museums, Monuments and Heraldry (CMMH) in 1991 as a vehicle for the formulation of a national policy on museums, monuments archives, heraldry, and national symbols that would both safeguard and educate people about the heritage of South Africa. Chaired by Wally Serote, head of the ANC's Arts and Culture Desk and coordinated by Professor Themba Sirayi, director of CCS at UFH, the objective of the CMMH was to work towards "a common integrated and integrating cultural framework that [would help] to promote the shared cultural identity and to put such identity at the centre of the development paradigm."[34] Criticising heritage institutions that were created under apartheid, the CMMH castigated these institutions for being "otiose, monuments of privilege, waste of money, institutionalised proof of white hegemony and abuse of the environment and culture."[35] Having recognised that there was no coherent national policy for the management of heritage resources, the CMMH sought to advance a national policy through which heritage institutions and structures could "foster national unity, reconciliation and democratic values and be accessible to and preserved for the education, benefit and development of all South Africans."[36] In the ANC's proposed national policy, archives were positioned "at the nexus of cultural and civil rights", their role was accentuated as one in which they "should collaborate with cultural and heritage institutions in a people's history programme aimed at empowering the voiceless, and [where] archival centres [are] positioned as community resources, not simply repositories."[37]

Framed against this background, the CMMH convened a workshop near Bloemfontein in March 1992 with the objective of discussing the development of heritage policies. Drawn together from a wide range of experts and activists, the workshop expressed both disquiet over the wholesale destruction of state records dealing with the liberation struggle and a growing concern regarding the status of records that were confiscated by the state from liberation organisations at the height of apartheid.[38] As a result of these concerns, it was suggested that a moratorium should be placed on the destruction of such records and that records that were seized should be returned to the place or individual where they were taken from. Following the workshop, the ANC appointed an archives subcommittee which was tasked with examining the state of archival management in the country, formulating a draft archival policy document, and making recommendations regarding the transformation, popularisation, and democratisation of existing archives.[39]

Shortly after the ANC returned from exile, the new government in waiting established new headquarters in 1991 at Shell House in Johannesburg. In another move, the ANC further emphasised their commitment towards transforming existing cultural and heritage institutions and structures, as well as developing new ones by establishing an archives unit. Responsible for the repatriation of material from 33 ANC missions from different parts of the world, the ANC's Archives Division had an enormous task which was often plagued by organisational and logistical challenges that were deepened by a lack of capacity and human resources.[40]

The challenges inherent in repatriating evidentiary material from across the globe surfaced through the arrival of the SOMAFCO material that arrived directly from Tanzania, unchecked and unprocessed at UFH in 1992. This prompted the ANC in becoming more cautious about the repatriated material, with Shell House, in a sense, becoming a holding area in which subsequent repatriated material from other missions were quarantined, sorted, and sequestered from public memory. There they waited to be sifted and sanitised. Analysing the state of archives and access to information in 2004, Seán Morrow and Luvuyo Wotshela argued that "this episode does reveal a shift in balance within the governing party, with a moment of openness between exile and office, a utopian pause between the old regime and the new realities, regrettably if predictably giving way to a more secretive mode."[41]

The developments around the formulation of heritage and cultural policies and other heritage initiatives laid the foundation for the configuration of a liberation archive at UFH. Being regarded as "singularly fitted to be the repository of the records of the liberation movement because its chequered history [was], in itself, a mirror of the struggle of the oppressed people", UFH was tasked with driving the establishment of the liberation archives project focused on "two structures of national importance, namely the Archives and the Museum of Resistance."[42] Divided into three categories, the university's archival holdings consisted of liberation archives, cultural heritage archives, and university records which were housed between the spaces of the CCS and the University Library. In particular, the objectives of the archives were to support research on the liberation struggle in South Africa, serve as a community resource, support tertiary and school curriculum development, establish links with similar archives of the South African liberation struggle, be recognised as a national treasure, and be consolidated into a specially designed archival building which will also be representative of a monument to the struggle.[43]

Initially installed at the CCS, it seemed that the Centre was "destined to become the Mecca of the history of the struggle for liberation and the champion of the cultural dimension of development."[44] Established in 1981 and formerly known as the Centre for Xhosa Literature that focused on collecting and preserving oral and written Xhosa material, it was transformed in 1991 into the CCS in the spirit of the changing political tide.[45] Under the leadership of Prof Themba Sirayi, who was actively involved in formulating policies for the management of heritage resources through his strategic deployment as national coordinator within the ANC's CMMH, we would argue that this, perhaps, gave the CCS a strategic political advantage when it came to a decision regarding the placement of the archives of the liberation movements. Framed within new terms of reference, the CCS was charged with being the repository and custodian of archival material pertaining to arts, oral, and literary materials, to serve as an educational resource for the academic community and wider public and to preserve this material.[46] However, similar to most historically black tertiary institutions in South Africa, UFH also bore the burden of apartheid's discriminatory laws which divided universities along ethnic and racial lines. While the legacy of apartheid left an indelible scar on the very fabric of life in South Africa, it also left institutions such as UFH with serious challenges that needed to be addressed. It is, in this sense, that the archives of the liberation movements soon found their development plagued by various challenges. Describing these challenges as crisis flashpoints in the Institutional Plan of the Liberation Archives Project, several concerns were identified regarding capacity building, funding, resources, and preservation stemming from the challenges incurred in the implementation of the liberation archives project.[47]

Having not been able to escape unscathed from apartheid's grip, UFH started picking up the pieces in the 1990s by starting a process where issues such as sub-standard education and crumbling or lacking of infrastructure and academic staff could be addressed. Added to this headache was the development of the archives of the liberation movements which the university was not primed for as the archives required financial resources, infrastructure, and staffing. According to Maaba, this placed the archives at "risk of not being properly managed and not meeting certain archival standards."[48] Although several measures such as the recruitment of archival specialists were put in place as a means of addressing the challenges of the development of the archives,[49] there were some at the university and within the ANC who felt that the CCS could be doing more in relation to the research and preservation of the ANC archives. It was also the consensus among some at the university that the CCS was not doing enough to procure more struggle material as some of this was lost to rival institutions.[50] Additionally, the CCS also required a sustained source of financial assistance to repatriate some of the material and for the remuneration of archival work.[51]

The other vexing issue that troubled the liberation archives project was the question of a proper archival facility. This prompted the ANC into action by having a series of meetings to ascertain the status of acquiring a suitable site for their archival records. In a confluence of increasingly troubling meetings between the CCS and ANC, the contentious decision to transfer the ANC archives from the CCS to the University Library was taken at a meeting on 3 May 1994.[52] Although the reasons cited for this decision were based on the failure of the CCS to adhere to the strategic plan of the liberation archives project in appropriately accommodating, preserving, and researching the ANC collection, we would argue that this relocation was mostly tied to what seemed to resemble misunderstandings, personal politics, and party alignment.

With the ANC archives transferred to the University Library in 1995 under the direction of head librarian, Manileo Tau, the CCS barely survived the battle for the ANC archives. Left with the archives of the other liberation movements, the CCS started to regroup by building partnerships with universities such the University of Michigan and by re-engaging in negotiations with De Beers regarding the building of an archives complex.[53] After years of delay, the CCS which was then subsequently renamed NAHECS, finally got a new building fully equipped in terms of archival regulations and the preservation needs of the archival collections. NAHECS opened on 19 September 1998. Ironically, as Maaba observed, the ANC material was returned to NAHECS in January 2010 after plans of the university and the library to "extend the building for [the] proper storage of the ANC archives did not materialise."[54] The fluctuations experienced by NAHECS points to what Michelle Pickover described as "[a]rchives, whether as spaces or as records, are continually transforming and shifting in meaning" as "they are fundamentally political in nature and as such are mediated sites of power, ideology and memory."[55] The ideological agendas and battles which underpinned the development of NAHECS also played itself out in the contested archival terrain of the Mayibuye Centre for History and Culture.

Anti-apartheid archives and the university of the left: Activism and Public History

As noted earlier, the tussle over archival collections placed UFH and UWC in conversation with each other. Resonating with the peripheral positioning of UFH in Alice, UWC is also located on the margins of Cape Town and secluded alongside the ecological sanctuary that the Cape Flats Nature Reserve offers. More than just being alongside a sanctuary for fauna and flora, UWC also offered itself as a political and academic refuge where students and staff could partake in political activities during the 1980s in the last stages of the struggle for liberation in South Africa. Against the background of the political ferment of mass political mobilisation and student radicalisation of the 1980s, UWC sought to reinvent itself as the 'university of the left'. Under the leadership of then rector Jakes Gerwel, UWC embarked on a process of applying an open admissions policy and started to employ more radical scholars in an attempt to reconstitute itself as the 'university of the left'.[56]

As the political barometer reached critical and feverish points due to P.W. Botha's reforms which was shortly followed by a State of Emergency in 1985, the Department of History at UWC initiated a People's History Project in 1986 in an attempt to "institutionalise the demands of the mass-based democratic movement for people's education."[57] More importantly, as Gary Minkley and Ciraj Rassool argued, "[p]eople's history produced a politics of history as weapon, tool, and vehicle for empowerment, as part of 'a broad project to develop an education for a post-apartheid South Africa'."[58] Working towards much of the same aims as the History Workshop at Wits and the Western Cape Oral History Project at UCT, the People's History Project sought to teach students how to do research before sending them into their communities to write the 'hidden' or marginalised histories of these oppressed communities.[59] In a sense, it can be argued that the People's History Project was a forerunner to the Mayibuye Centre although, of course, there were other factors that also contributed to the creation of the Centre.

In the spring of late 1986, following a suggestion by UWC economics professor Lieb Loots, Loots and Gerwel had a meeting to discuss the possibility of creating an apartheid museum under the auspices of UWC. On receiving a positive response from Gerwel, Loots proceeded to formalise these ideas into a formal proposal to the rector. In this proposal, Loots outlined in detail the motivations, activities, launching strategy, and financial implications for such an undertaking. Loots furthermore stated the need to establish an institution such as an apartheid museum that could "assist in the portrayal and study of apartheid in its historical and current dimensions" and for this material to be "collected under one roof and be presented in an accessible and dynamic manner."[60] Given the political and social changes that were taking place and a gradual shift towards thinking of the possibilities of a post-apartheid South Africa, Loots argued that the creation of an apartheid museum was imperative as it would serve an educational, commemorative, and historical purpose.

Loots' proposal was followed up by a memorandum which was submitted in November 1987 by an ad hoc committee set up by Gerwel. Their task was to investigate the establishment of an apartheid museum at UWC. The ad hoc committee consisted of Lieb Loots, André Odendaal (educationist), Brian O'Connell (literary historian), and Goolam Aboobaker (adviser and strategist). In this memorandum, the ad hoc committee made several recommendations regarding the steps that should be taken towards the implementation of an apartheid museum, the appropriate institutional arrangement during the initial phase of the project, the level of the university's commitment towards this project, community involvement, and how the proposed museum could be employed as an instrument of the struggle. Beyond the recommendations made by the ad hoc committee, the memorandum also underlined the importance of UWC being appropriately and strategically placed to develop an apartheid museum.[61]

Finally, it was decided that UWC would "embark on a project on the history of resistance in South Africa."[62] André Odendaal, a lecturer from the Department of History, who was also a member of the ad hoc committee was tasked with determining the feasibility of setting up an apartheid museum, and was granted sabbatical leave by UWC for the duration of 1988 to go to England for research. Odendaal was also tasked with exploring opportunities and possibilities around the collection and the preservation of the history of resistance in South Africa. At the outset, Odendaal's journey was based on a two-pronged research agenda which was firstly to build up a photographic collection and secondly to write an illustrated overview of the history of resistance politics from the 1880s to the 1980s.[63] Initially, Odendaal was affiliated to the Institute of Commonwealth Studies (ICS) at the University of London and to the Centre for Research in Ethnic Relations (CER) at Warwick University where he presented papers at the seminar programmes of the respective centres. Odendaal's research gradually took him outside the formal structures of the ICS and CER and brought him closer into the ambit of the work of the anti-apartheid movement. Extending the original concept of an apartheid museum, as proposed by Lieb Loots and Jakes Gerwel, Odendaal proposed in a brief to Gerwel that an historical archive should also form part of the idea for an apartheid museum.[64] With a promising relationship developing between IDAF and UWC, and with IDAF's commitment of donating 8 000 photographs and approximately 250 videos to UWC for this project, Odendaal applied for further study leave to further the objectives of the project on the history of resistance.[65] Having acquired invaluable, primarily visual material about the liberation struggle in South Africa that would have been previously unseen by most South Africans, this material re-energised the idea of the apartheid museum project and would later serve as the foundation on which the Mayibuye Centre for History and Culture was created. This prompted Gerwel to request that Odendaal draw up a formal proposal for him to table at a meeting of the Academic Planning Committee.[66]

At a meeting convened by Gerwel on 26 March 1990, Odendaal presented the draft proposal for the UWC "Mayibuye" History Project which he had drafted the year before towards the end of his sabbatical. Building upon the original concept of Loots and Gerwel, Odendaal's proposal envisaged that the museum should include an area for historical exhibitions, an archive on the history of resistance and black social and political life in South Africa, a theatre, a space for workshops, offices for community groups, and a photographic and film collection. In addition, he proposed that a distinct physical location in a building be constructed for this purpose.[67] In what Odendaal referred to as UWC's "Mayibuye" History and Cultural Centre, he emphasised that the museum should function both as a repository for historical material and as a living community centre. With specific emphasis on the archival component of the project, Odendaal outlined what was envisioned for the creation of a new archive on liberation at UWC. He proposed that the archive initially focus on political resistance, as well as black economic life, literature, sport, religion, and other general categories.[68] In concluding the stages for the archival component of the project, Odendaal proposed the launch of a publishing unit, Mayibuye Books. Through this unit, the Mayibuye Centre would make publications available that had previously been banned, censored, or were unknown. As the flagship of the Mayibuye History Project, Mayibuye Books would focus on the reprinting of series, publishing new titles, and publishing popular histories and photographic books through the Mayibuye History and Literature series, The Mayibuye Library, and The Mayibuye Centre Occasional Papers. It was also envisaged that the Mayibuye History and Literature Series would assist in institutionalising an intellectual and historical tradition, which that had not been adequately represented in South African universities.[69]

In an unintended, though serendipitous, turn of events with the closure of IDAF in 1991, the Mayibuye Centre's publication series became crucial to the workings of the history project as it took over where IDAF left off. Continuing IDAF's tradition which started in the late 1960s, the Mayibuye Centre now began to publish new documentary, autobiographical, and creative writing in addition to re-issuing previously banned or censored titles under the Centre's imprint.[70] Going beyond the parameters of a traditional archive, we would argue that the energy generated from this endeavour was significant and contributed to the vibrancy that surrounded the history project in its initial stages. It was this energy that made the Mayibuye project come alive. Amidst intense political developments such as the release of political prisoners and the unbanning of political and solidarity organisations such as IDAF, the stage was set for an exciting period for the further development and implementation of the Mayibuye History Project. Also more broadly, this historic moment heralded a new political and transformative beginning for the country. UWC proceeded with their project by seconding André Odendaal from the Department of History to "develop and to begin implementing plans towards a Historical/Cultural Centre at UWC."[71]

Mayibuye i Afrika! (Let it return to Africa!)

With the changing political situation in South Africa and their unbanning, and after many discussions with the ANC and various other institutions, IDAF decided to close its operations in London. The niggling issue which needed to be resolved was the question of the material that they had accumulated during the course of their work and how their work could be continued through other emerging organisations in South Africa. Having already established a relationship with UWC through their representative, André Odendaal, during his sabbatical in London which saw IDAF donating a substantial amount of visual material to the fledgling Mayibuye Centre, UWC had put forward a strong proposal for the relocation of the entire IDAF archive. With the impending closure of IDAF in mind, employees of IDAF, Barry Feinberg and Gordon Metz, undertook a fact-finding mission to South Africa to assess issues relating to the relocation of the film, video, audio, and photographic archive and to the development and continuation of the work of the publications and audio-visual departments of IDAF. After a whirlwind trip to South Africa in November 1990 which included meetings with the ANC, COSATU, SACP, SAHA, the History Workshop at Wits, UWC, and other organisations, it was recommended that the film, video, photographic and audio material be relocated to the Mayibuye Centre for History and Culture.[72] The legal and welfare archival material would eventually join the rest of the material as soon as it was deemed appropriate.[73]

In the Publications and Audio-Visual Department's report on their trip to South Africa, IDAF employees, Feinberg and Metz, recommended that the proposed UWC Museum of Liberation and Cultural Centre would be the most appropriate institution to receive the IDAF archives in their entirety, subject to the fulfilment of certain conditions.[74] According to the report, "[i]t [was] proposed that the archive remain intact for historical reasons and the practical purposes of centralised distribution and be located in one institution, identified specifically as the IDAF collection […] subject to certain conditions".[75] The first condition was "that the institution in question has an on-going working relationship with the liberation movement." The second condition was "that there [should] be an accountable and representative structure in place to ensure that the aims and objectives of the relocation of the resources are implemented." The last conditions specifically spoke to the responsibilities of the institution as it stipulated that:

> … [t]he institution commits itself to making the resources available and accessible to the democratic movement and its related organisations inside South Africa nationally; that the institution demonstrates that it has the commitment and capability to manage, conserve and protect the collection and that the institution commits itself to activating the material within a political context for the benefit of all South Africans.[76]

Another element that strengthened the recommendation was that UWC was one of the foremost institutions that was involved in anti-apartheid activities and enjoyed close ties with the liberation movements. The relocation of the IDAF material to UWC, which included the photographic material, audio and video recordings, books and publications, as well as equipment consisting of computers, cinematographic projectors, magnetic tape sound recorders and reproducers, television monitors, viewing equipment, and camera and darkroom equipment be relocated to UWC, gave the Mayibuye History Project a critical advantage.[77] Besides providing the Centre with technical equipment that enabled them to become fully operational, it was also envisaged that the IDAF material would be reactivated and developed as a tool in the informing and educating of people about the struggle against apartheid as this material had previously been banned and had thus been inaccessible to most people in South Africa.

With prospects looking favourable for the project, the History and Culture Centre set up an office at the Old Library at the end of March 1991, where the Institute for Historical Research (IHR) was housed. However, they quickly expanded their operations from two to four rooms as the project gained momentum with more material streaming in from various individuals and organisations. With the promise of even more material being donated to the Centre such as the archive of the International Anti-Apartheid Movement (IAAM) and the South African Non-Racial Olympic Committee (SANROC) among others, the Centre would soon outgrow the space that was allocated for it in the IHR and eventually, it was moved to the first level of the main library. With the affirmation for the project from the ANC, reinforced by a historically close relationship with the liberation movements, as well as the relocation of the IDAF archival collection, UWC's Mayibuye History and Culture Centre was set to become one of the premier destinations for the collection and preservation of material of the liberation struggle.

Though the Mayibuye Centre intended to become the primary repository of the liberation movement, the Centre had to contend with other emerging archival institutions such as NAHECS and SAHA and existing ones like Historical Papers at Wits that were all engaged in the pursuit of liberation struggle material. In fact, the struggle for the ANC material later intensified when the ANC demanded that their material from the London and Lusaka missions be returned to them at their headquarters in Johannesburg, upon which it was later shipped to UFH after the removal of seemingly sensitive documents.[78] A fragmented copy of the ANC material was later returned to the Mayibuye Centre. Whereas the Mayibuye Centre previously led the development of liberation struggle initiatives and was also used as a model for the creation of other institutions, in a move that shows how archives can become a means of empire-building, the Mayibuye Centre was surpassed in its efforts of being regarded as the premier destination of liberation struggle material.

As UFH was positioning itself to become the foremost custodian of the material of the liberation movements, the Mayibuye Centre was left mainly with the corpus of the IDAF administrative and organisational records, records from trade unions, anti-apartheid and solidarity organisations, NGO's, and individual archives of prominent struggle veterans, activists, as well as lesser-known struggle veterans and activists involved in the liberation struggle. Barry Feinberg, Gordon Metz, and Norman Kaplan, all former employees of IDAF, arrived just after the IDAF material reached South Africa to take up their respective positions in the various departments of the Centre. The material was packed into two massive shipping containers and arrived at the university towards the end of 1991. Held within the shipping containers were the:

> … residual stocks of its [IDAF's] two publishing projects, amounting to about 150 000 copies of nearly 100 titles, none of which had been openly distributed in South Africa before; a research library of books, documents and cuttings on southern Africa; a photographic library of roughly 100 000 images; and a film collection of over 800 cans of film material, including at least 1 000 documentary productions together with a vast video reference library.[79]

As a result of the on-going political turmoil in South Africa at the time, the classified material that related to IDAF's clandestine legal and welfare support for victims of apartheid were transferred to a security vault in London; however, they also later become part of the Centre.[80] In many ways, these materials constituted a ready-made archive on which the Mayibuye Centre could build its work.

With the emphasis on its cultural component through the numerous activities hosted by the Centre such as conferences, workshops, film events, performances, exhibitions, publications, and campus and community outreach programmes, the Mayibuye Centre intended to become a 'living', community-oriented resource and a space focused on recovering and re-interpreting all aspects of apartheid and resistance. "Far from being a dead archive, the multi-purpose centre host[ed] exhibitions, workshops and research programmes", and in this way, it ensured that it was "not just trapped in the past."[81] Though the Mayibuye Centre's focus was primarily on the dissemination of Public History, it also embarked on a vigorous programme of conferences and workshops as a way to stimulate critical debate and produce knowledge. In that way, the Centre contributed much to the post-liberation discussions in South Africa by serving as a platform for much of these debates inside and outside the university framework of academic work. As some of the Centre's staff also became involved in the national debates around the transformation of museums and heritage institutions through their respective appointments to serve on the Arts and Culture Task Group (ACTAG) and the Western Province Task Group (WESTAG), the Centre became even more integral as "a catalyst for change in the historical and cultural spheres in South Africa."[82] Reiterating this point, Gordon Metz noted in his interview that "the Mayibuye Centre became a point of reference, a reference point for so-called critical and progressive thinking around archival and museum practice."[83] Taking this point further in his brief exploration of the early beginnings of the Mayibuye Centre, Ciraj Rassool argued that the Centre became one of the central institutions that mediated the production of Public History in the imagining of a new nation in South Africa in the early nineties.[84] Rassool stated:

> [T]he Mayibuye Centre was a key and influential agency of historical production in South Africa and an 'active shaping force' for the production of memory. It was central in both the creation and management of historical images and narratives. The histories produced took shape in different mediums, each seeking to recover hidden pasts and resistance histories for the new nation. The Mayibuye Centre was not merely a conduit for the reversal of amnesia. Instead it was a 'theatre of memory' with its own 'patterns of constructing and forgetting', through which history was revised and revisioned.[85]

Publicised as the 'birthplace for culture' in Cape Town and 'a resting place of history' in the early 90s, which was in contrast to the Centre's intention to become a living museum, the Mayibuye Centre quickly became the centrepiece of UWC.[86] After it was formally incorporated into the university management structures as a component of the IHR in 1992, albeit with its own distinct identity, the Mayibuye Centre consisted of five units or departments. This included the units of historical papers, photographic, film and video, and oral history archives, and the visual arts and publishing unit whose activities and resources fed into the projects and programmes of the Centre. Its expanding archival holdings consisted of collections such the Eli Weinberg photographic collection, the documentary material of activists such as Brian Bunting, Wolfie Kodesh, Desmond Tutu, Kader and Louise Asmal, Albie Sachs, and Ahmed Kathrada, among some of the more prominent collections. In addition, it held the archival records of the anti-apartheid movements and other solidarity organisations. The Mayibuye Centre was "positioned as a magnet in order to draw the interest of other individuals and organisations in locating their archives at the Mayibuye Centre."[87] Through its activist work in the historical and cultural fields, the Mayibuye Centre became a progressive and vibrant manifestation of what was envisaged for a post-apartheid South Africa.

Growing pains

Having realised the dream of becoming a centre focused on highlighting issues of apartheid and resistance through workshops, publications, and exhibitions, among others, the Mayibuye Centre now also had to contend with other issues such as the realities of institutional competition on campus and inadequate infrastructure and resources. As a component of the IHR, a functional working relationship came to exist between the IHR and the Mayibuye Centre. Apart from physically sharing the same space in the Old Library building which could also have been a source of tension because of space constraints, the Mayibuye Centre quickly became the cultural showcase of the university as they played host to various exhibitions, workshops, and conferences. In addition, the Centre also played a prominent role in the shaping of policies and legislation in the museum and heritage sector and operated a vibrant publications department. Although they complemented each other in certain ways, the objectives of the two institutions were sometimes at odds with each other and where their interests overlapped, this sometimes, caused tension. While Odendaal alluded to this tension through correspondence in respect of the reporting structure of Mayibuye Centre, the tension between the two institutions became more pronounced, as was apparent from various discussions that started from as early as 1996 around the future of the Mayibuye Centre and its recommended incorporation into the newly formed Robben Island Museum. This is a point we will return to later in the discussion.

Institutional rivalry was not the only challenge faced by the Mayibuye Centre. From the earliest conceptualisations of the apartheid museum, there seemed to have been challenges already around securing a suitable site for the centre, as summed up in a progress report of the coordinator of the Mayibuye Centre to the Academic Planning Committee Working Group in 1991. Although a suitable site was identified on the UWC campus that could potentially be the location of a multi-purpose historical and cultural centre, this idea was later abandoned due to lack of funding. In his progress report Odendaal wrote:

> … [t]he Vice Rector has made it clear that the university has no funds to contribute to a building – and indeed, the Centre would not feature on UWC's building priority list for at least seven years … This is our biggest challenge: how do we get the money to build a major building complex, when the university cannot or will not contribute and when funders are extremely reluctant to support building projects generally?[88]

Although the Centre was dependent on a slight grant from the university, the university itself also experienced ongoing financial difficulties. The Centre thus had to look for financial support from other local and international funders such as the Swedish International Development Authority (SIDA), the Norwegian Foreign Ministry, the Ford Foundation, and the Equal Opportunities Foundation, among others, by the end of 1992.[89] A part of this funding also came from the Mayibuye Centre's own income which was generated from the publications it produced and the usage of photographic, film, and audio material for commercial purposes. Despite the difficulty in securing a space to house this vision for a multi-purpose historical and cultural complex and the challenges of financial support, the Mayibuye Centre still managed to raise funds of over R1 million and in this way, they could sustain themselves between 1991 and 1992. According to Odendaal, resources, or rather the lack thereof, are crucial in understanding where the Mayibuye Centre went and where it ended up. Odendaal revealed that from 1991 to 1999, "SIDA put about R9 million in. The University put very little in terms of making it an institution […]. But in terms of resources, they paid my salary [and] they paid for a few student assistants […] And how do you run a dynamic cultural institution without resources?"[90] Odendaal argued that "[y]ou can't create an institution without the institutional capacity in terms of funding and staff. So we were kind of a community project on campus […] that didn't always work according to formal university patterns […]."[91]

While being regarded as a community project might have had its benefits, a cursory glance at the finances of the centre, as illustrated in the Annual Reports from 1992 to 1999, suggests that there was a definite tension between securing the institutional capacity and running a dynamic centre. Amid the challenges of securing a suitable site at the university, the Centre's collections expanded rapidly, with more material streaming in from various organisations and individuals, so that the issue of infrastructure and human resources soon became a matter of great concern. The Centre had a small permanent staff component and thus depended heavily on a handful of visiting fellows, student assistants, volunteers, and trainees. The latter came through the Gender and Affirmative Action programme "through which the Centre sought to offer further study and career-focused opportunities to promising post-graduate students."[92] Although the Centre's small staff component still managed to produce countless exhibitions, publications, workshops, and conferences and made progress with rapidly expanding archival collections within the different departments of the Centre, making this material accessible was a cause of concern. This situation of understaffing was exacerbated by a lack of space, access control, and adverse environmental factors such as climate control that began to affect the historical material. These concerns raised in the 1993 Annual Report have continued to be issues for the Centre.

Undeterred by these challenges, the Mayibuye Centre moved ahead with limited resources which often translated into a feverish, proactive style of working and conducting projects. Framed against the backdrop of the transition to a democratic dispensation in South Africa, the remainder of the IDAF records arrived in 1995 for use by the TRC. The remaining IDAF records that joined the rest of the archive consisted of the legal and welfare records that had been stored in a secured vault in London until it was appropriate for them to join the rest of the material that had already been relocated to the Mayibuye Centre in 1991. Within a rapidly changing political landscape, and despite a frenetic workload compounded by inadequate funding and resources, the Mayibuye Centre navigated through financial and organisational difficulties. While this energetic approach might have been one of its strengths as this resulted in countless exhibitions, film projects, and publications, we would argue this may have been one of the Centre's organisational weaknesses in its desire to build an archive. Although this was the distinctiveness of the Centre at that time in its drive to 'make things happen', this style of working left a lasting impression on the future work of the Mayibuye Centre, particularly when it was taken into RIM and became formally inscribed as an archive of the struggle against apartheid.

Showcasing the new nation

The latter part of the 1990s was a time of considerable shift in how the Mayibuye Centre functioned. In addition to the organisational difficulties that the Centre continued to experience, the mid-1990s were also characterised by limited funding for projects of

NGOs as funding was channelled to infrastructure and other developmental programmes. Alongside funding constraints, and as a prelude to its future involvement with Robben Island, the Mayibuye Centre was commissioned by the ANC's CMMH in 1993 to draft proposals for the future development and management of Robben Island. The Mayibuye Centre found itself at the coalface of the transformation of museum and heritage policies and legislation through ACTAG and various other committees. The political developments and intensive transformation process which followed allowed for a proverbial 'clearing in the bush' with new museums being constructed and old museums being reconstructed.

These developments saw the emergence of various post-apartheid institutions such as community museums like the District Six Museum and the Lwandle Migrant Labour Museum, and national museums such as Robben Island Museum (RIM), the Nelson Mandela Museum, and Freedom Park. It is within this framework that the Cabinet of the Government of National Unity established the Future of Robben Island Committee in August 1995 to decide on the future of Robben Island.

While there were various developments that contributed to this shift, we argue that the recommendation from Cabinet for the Mayibuye Centre to be incorporated into RIM in 1996 is critical in understanding the subsequent trajectory of the Centre. This recommendation resulted in an extensive process of negotiations between the university, RIM, and the Mayibuye Centre. A joint UWC/RIM Working Group was established in this regard on 10 June 1998 which was mandated to ascertain the feasibility of this recommendation from Cabinet and to explore possible ways for its implementation. The Working Group consisted of Henry Bredenkamp, Colin Johnson, Gary Minkley, Ben Martins, Carolyn Hamilton and André Odendaal. Following intensive and exhaustive discussions, the Working Group recommended that the Mayibuye Centre should be incorporated into RIM in a way that would be beneficial to both institutions and that the incorporation of the Mayibuye centre should be accompanied by a long-term co-operation and partnership agreement between UWC and RIM.[93] According to Odendaal:

> The goal was always going to make sure that this incredible archive that we collected was preserved properly and that the project could get security and the way for that, besides the idea of the apartheid museum, after 1991, Robben Island being the logical space for it.[94]

The nexus between the Mayibuye Centre, the Robben Island Museum and UWC

Walter Sisulu, ANC stalwart during the liberation struggle and incarcerated in the Robben Island maximum prison for more than 20 years, stated that "Robben Island is a source of enlightenment and education on the dangers of myopic philosophies."[95] This statement by Sisulu was based on Robben Island's role as the Gulag of the apartheid system, and its centrality in the narratives of resistance and the ultimate collapse of apartheid, which cemented its iconic status as a symbol of resistance, struggle, hope, and reconciliation.

In a sense, Robben Island also epitomised the deliberate refusal especially by political prisoners to respond to hatred with hatred and it is in this 'refusal' that the "Robben Island Museum has been and is being designed to exhibit; and through this, to celebrate a 'way of being' worthy of South Africans".[96] The establishment of RIM was one of the major initiatives of the new, democratic South African government to facilitate political transition from apartheid to a "fully established, inclusive, and prosperous democracy."[97]

In their study of the Robben Island Museum as a museum of hope, Shearing and Kempa argued that:

> Like most museums, Robben Island is a site for the preservation and exhibition of objects thought to be of lasting value. But as a site designed to promote a hope sensibility; it is also more than that. It belongs to a class that we might think of as 'governance museums' – that is, museums that are concerned with promoting sensibilities rather than with simply exhibiting valued objects."[98]

Within a similar vein as Shearing and Kempa, we also argue that the RIM was conceived as a museum of consciousness through which sensibilities could be shaped. Significantly in delineating the specificity of RIM as a museum of consciousness, hence as an ideological apparatus of the democratic South Africa, Shearing and Kempa argued that:

> If we think beyond museums to symbolic sites more generally, we might think of Robben Island as a site of 'figurative governance'. That is, as an instance of figurative sites designed to shape sensibilities that it is hoped will promote a desired future by promoting certain ways of thinking and therefore acting across the population to shape the identities of South Africans as part of 'citizenship education'.[99]

Writing about the history and challenges of museums in post-apartheid South Africa in 2010, Leslie Witz noted that Robben Island was re-envisioned as the birthplace of the new nation and the quest for national reconciliation. This, as he argued, was because no other museum in South Africa "encompass[es] the narrative of assertions of an indigenous precolonial nationhood, a paradigm that continually couples apartheid and resistance, with centrality given to the 'emergence' and 'triumph' of the ANC in the anti-apartheid struggle, and a narrative of ascending and descending troughs of despair and crests of hope, ultimately carried through to 'victory' by iconic figures, primarily Nelson Mandela, culminating in the emergence of a multicultural South Africa" more than the Robben Island Museum.[100]

To understand how RIM became a museum of consciousness, hence the transformative importance of its role in the Robben Island Training Programme (RITP), it is necessary to appreciate the political and socio-cultural climate within which the South African Cabinet established the 'Future of Robben Island Committee' in August 1995.[101] The committee was headed by Ahmed Kathrada, an ex-political prisoner of Robben Island and confidante of Nelson Mandela, and its objective was to decide the future use of the Island. As expected, especially for a significant site with a long contentious and dissonant history, there were over two hundred public submissions to the committee proposing different uses for the island which ranged from proposals of a holiday resort on the island to housing a casino. After some deliberations, the committee decided that the site should be developed into a national museum that would serve as a symbolic reminder of the struggle against apartheid and emblematic of understanding and reconciliation.[102] Having cultivated an intimate relationship with the liberation movements in the past and having continued this relationship by establishing the Robben Island Gateway, a Section 21 Company whose aim was to build a major cultural centre at the Victoria and Alfred Waterfront in Cape Town in 1994,[103] the Mayibuye Centre submitted a proposal to Cabinet in 1996 along with the other public submissions on the proposed uses for the island. In the 'Suggested Robben Island Action Plan for the Department of Arts, Culture, Science and Technology', prepared by André Odendaal, dated 4 March 1996, it was envisaged that:

> The island should become a lasting memorial to the struggle for freedom and democracy in South Africa. It should be developed as a dynamic 'living' heritage project, which can inspire and unite people in the process of nation building in South Africa, helping also to highlight the role of the Department of Arts, Culture, Science and Technology in the broader process of reconstruction in this country.[104]

The 'Robben Island Action Plan' submitted to the Minister of Department of Arts, Culture, Science and Technology (DACST), Lionel Mtshali, stated that Robben Island occupies a unique place in South African history and is perhaps the most symbolically important historical site in South Africa, therefore its recommended vision for Robben Island consisted of four points:

- The island should become a lasting memorial to the struggle for freedom and democracy in South Africa.
- It should be developed as a dynamic 'living' heritage project, which can inspire and unite people in the process of nation-building in South Africa, helping also to highlight the role of the Department of Arts, Culture, Science and Technology in the broader process of reconstruction in this country.
- This development should be based on a holistic and sustainable development and management plan involving the widest possible range of interest groups.
- The universal symbolism of Robben Island must be retained, inter alia by it becoming an internationally trend-setting historical and cultural heritage project for the 21st century from South Africa.[105]

To realise these objectives, the proposal suggested 'a three-pronged strategy' for Robben Island, which included:

- The formal declaration of Robben Island as a National Monument.
- An application to UNESCO for Robben Island to be declared a World Heritage Site.

- The declaration of Robben Island as a declared Cultural Institution (i.e. a national flagship museum, which will become part of the proposed Cape Town Flagship Museum umbrella structure). This model will entail running the island as a site museum, conserving the total environment (*a la Tswaing*), as well as converting the political prison into a 'Museum of Resistance'.[106]

The 'three-pronged strategy', according to Odendaal, was to "ensure a heritage-driven approach to Robben Island as a 'Museum of Resistance', under the auspices of DACST, with the island being managed and subject to national (National Monument Council) and the International (World Heritage Convention) conservation guidelines."[107] In response, then Minister of Arts, Culture, Science and Technology, in a direct endorsement of proposed Robben Island Action Plan by Odendaal, stated that:

- Robben Island should be developed as a World Heritage Site, a National Monument, and National Museum, which can become a cultural and conservation showcase for the new South African democracy, while at the same time maximise the economic, tourism, and educational potential of the island and so encourage its multi-purpose usage.
- With regard to the museum functions mentioned above, Robben Island should be run as a site museum, where the total environment is conserved in an integrated way, in line with modern international conservation approaches; and that the ex-political prison be converted into a Museum of the Freedom Struggle in South Africa.[108]

The main, official mandate of RIM, as contained in the ministerial statement, thus focused on four key aspects:

- The need to commemorate and conserve the historical and political importance of the island;
- Tourism as a means of generating income;
- The natural environment; and
- Ensuring Robben Island's ongoing relevance as an inspiration and educational 'living memorial'.[109]

A major recommendation of the Minister that had a direct effect on the origin of the RITP Diploma in Museum and Heritage Studies in the Mayibuye Centre, and Research in Public History at the Department of History at UWC, was the Minister's request that "the University of the Western Cape agree to the incorporation of the Mayibuye Centre and the non-profit Robben Island Gateway project in the Robben Island institution."[110] This injunction was crucial because it was through the acquisition of the Mayibuye collections that the Robben Island project became a museum with tangible archival collections. In furtherance of the ministerial mandate, the interim management authority of the new Robben Island Museum requested André Odendaal, in his capacity as RIM interim director, to "start negotiation with UWC about implementing the Cabinet resolution as soon as possible."[111]

To this effect, Odendaal circulated a 'Discussion Document on Future Possibilities for the Mayibuye Centre, the Institute for Historical Research (IHR), and the University of the Western Cape in Relation to the Development of the Robben Island Museum'.[112] A proposal contained in the 'Discussion Document' includes that RIM jointly sponsors a Chair in Public History in the Department of History at UWC for 5 years; and that RIM sponsors the 'Robben Island Research Project' to run in conjunction with the department, providing for three doctoral students per year to study at the university (from different departments if necessary), as well as a joint annual conference or activity.[113] As can be seen in these last two points in the proposal, especially the fourth, the origin and development of RIM was linked right from the very beginning to the Public History research at UWC's Department of History, which tied the merger of the Mayibuye Centre and the IHR to RIM sponsoring a research Chair in Public History at UWC. More importantly, the centrality of the Department of History to the origin of the RITP was further confirmed in the immediate actions suggested in the proposal, which requested other departments to start becoming involved in RIM developments,[114] for example introducing courses related to Robben Island (as the Department of History has done at postgraduate level).[115]

Odendaal argued for the incorporation of the IHR/Mayibuye Centre and the involvement of the Department of History in the Robben Island Museum institution, in terms of research, teaching, and learning. According to him, this arrangement would help develop capacity and promote UWC as a place for international research, which would attract scholars from throughout South Africa and abroad, and provide an opportunity for multi-disciplinary co-operation, encourage the involvement and training of postgraduate students, and lead to joint projects and publications.[116] In conclusion, he argued in the proposal that:

> There was a moral issue; though UWC is the legal owner of the Mayibuye collections, they should be seen as part of the national heritage and not the narrow property of UWC. It was in this spirit that the ANC recommended that the massive, core IDAF collection, which enabled the Centre to be started, be donated to UWC in 1991 […].[117]

One crucial point which clearly shows the intricate relationship of RIM as an institution to Public History research, the Department of History, and the RITP, was item 2.6 of the Proposal, which stated that "RIM seeks accreditation from UWC for its National Heritage Training Programme, and discusses ways of linking it to the proposed post-graduate diploma being suggested as an accompaniment to the new chair in Public History."[118] As seen in these proposals, RIM has its roots in the public historical scholarship nexus between the Mayibuye Centre, IHR, and Public History research in the Department of History at UWC. More importantly, the proposals showed how a programme of Museum and Heritage Studies from a Public History perspective is constitutive of Robben Island as a museum. This grounding of its museumness in RITP was reflected in the 'immediate action' of the updated 'Discussion document', which reiterated "introducing courses relating to Robben Island (as the History Department has done at post-graduate level) and pursuing the possibility of giving accreditation to Robben Island National Heritage Training Programme."[119] Based on the stated objectives, which were within the framework of Odendaal's proposal, the RITP approached UWC's Department of History with a proposal to co-convene a programme in Museum and Heritage Studies, which was accepted. In a seminal moment in the history of the Mayibuye Centre that would irrevocably change its future course, Cabinet also recommended that the Mayibuye Centre's collections and other components be incorporated into the newly formed Robben Island Museum.[120] The Robben Island Museum opened on 1 January 1997 as a related institution of the DACST and was later formally launched by then president Nelson Mandela on 26 September 1997.

With the Mayibuye Centre considering its incorporation into RIM, the Centre also embarked on its own process of introspection. While this recommendation for its incorporation into RIM might have seemed liked a fitting and well-timed opportunity, for the first time since their inception, there was a decline in the number of exhibitions and public activities. According to the fifth Annual Report of the Mayibuye Centre in 1996, the process of looking inward meant that the Centre had to start planning its future around Robben Island and to consolidate its archival collections and administration for incorporation into the Museum.[121] This resulted in an improvement of the historical papers archive and closer attention being paid to issues of conservation in the archive.[122] From this process of planning and consolidation around the archive, it is apparent that the Mayibuye Centre gradually shifted from the pioneering activist axis it occupied through its public activities to becoming a passive repository of inactive, silenced material as it became embedded in a process of memorialisation.

The Mayibuye Centre trudged along despite the secondment of Gordon Metz to the DACST, in which he was tasked with the responsibility to oversee the restructuring of 18 national museums in 1996, followed by Odendaal's secondment to act as administrator and head of the interim management of RIM in 1997. Norman Kaplan and Metz who had made up part of the original IDAF staff who joined the Centre both left, leaving Barry Feinberg who assumed the leadership role at the Mayibuye Centre when Odendaal was appointed as the Chief Director of the Robben Island Museum in 1998. After the Centre's incorporation into RIM, Feinberg also left. The symbolic link of continuity to the work of IDAF was effectively severed with the departure of the original IDAF members from the Mayibuye project to pursue other prospects. According to Gordon Metz, it was not only the link of continuity that was severed as he noted in his interview:

> People who put the IDAF collection together, who then relocated to the Mayibuye Centre knew that the collection was developed through activism. They were the catalysts by which this documentation came to be in the first place. And it was recognised that if you discontinue that activist dynamic, the collection would fossilise and die.[123]

The Centre's work continued, but the focus shifted to the development of RIM which inevitably started to overshadow some of the Centre's very important activities such as outreach and publications. The significance of the Centre's public and outreach activities was summarised in the seventh Annual Report of the Mayibuye Centre by Feinberg when he reported that the national profile of the Centre's archival collections can be attributed to its outreach activities and public programming which contributes to learning and access but also serves as an income stream.[124] Although much of its reputation was owed to its activist work through the deployment of archival material, the Centre notably shifted its focus from public activities such as conferences, workshops, and producing publications and exhibitions as it almost became fixated with the management of archival collections and the archive. As a result of the close working relationship that was being cultivated between the Mayibuye Centre and RIM, the Mayibuye Centre agreed to act as the collections manager for the museum in 1998.[125] By agreeing to act as collection management consultants to RIM, the Mayibuye Centre was tasked with developing a collections management system, establishing a resource centre and establishing an institutional archive among the objectives, as outlined in the project agreement between the Mayibuye Centre and RIM.[126]

After a few years of fostering a close working relationship and engaging in joint projects with RIM, the recommendations of the joint UWC/RIM Working Group were eventually formalised into a legal agreement between UWC and RIM, which stipulated the terms and conditions on which the co-operation and partnership would rest. According to the Memorandum of Agreement, the incorporation of the Mayibuye Centre into RIM entailed a 99-year agreement by which UWC agreed to the long-term loan of the IDAF/Mayibuye Collection to RIM. The Centre's incorporation also meant that RIM had to incorporate the staff of the Mayibuye Centre into its structure and take responsibility for the management and conservation of the collections.[127] Underlining the co-operation aspect of the agreement, it was stipulated that UWC and RIM should establish the new archives in a suitable facility on the UWC Campus through joint fundraising, working together on projects "to advance research and scholarship" and to "facilitate exhibitions and displays."[128] It was also stipulated that a joint Working Group should be established to review the agreement on a regular basis and also to "facilitate joint projects in respect of the archives."[129]

One of the reasons for the final agreement was because of a belated intervention by younger members of the Department of History, who had been concerned about the loss of the collections to the university and the potential dangers involved in removing them from an academic environment. Similar concerns had been expressed from within the RIM council. In the end, the ambiguities contained in the agreement ensured that UWC would retain a significant stake in the collection through its ownership and that the collection would continue to be housed at the university and not be removed to Robben Island or to the Waterfront.[130] After a long process of negotiation, an agreement for the incorporation was finally reached in December 1999 whereby the Centre and its staff would be incorporated into RIM on 1 April 2000.[131] In practice, this agreement increasingly gave rise to a set of complex and ambiguous issues around questions of responsibilities, ownership, and management between UWC and RIM. The Mayibuye Centre was formally and ceremoniously taken into RIM at the launch of the 'new' UWC Robben Island Mayibuye Archives which was opened by then deputy president Jacob Zuma on 13 June 2001. This moment inaugurated a new beginning yet also a very different future from what was envisaged for the Mayibuye Centre when it first started its pioneering work in the early 1990s.

Resting place of history

It has been argued by Rassool and Witz that "the Robben Island Museum, 'cultural showcase of the new South Africa', can be seen as the culmination of the cultural work of the Mayibuye Centre and its antecedent institutions such as IDAF and even the Treason Trial Defence Fund of the 1950s."[132] While it was intended that the incorporation of the Centre into a national museum of resistance would further enhance and stimulate the work of the Centre, we argue that the pioneering and activist work which marked the efforts of IDAF and the Mayibuye Centre were gradually displaced by a more intense focus on developing Robben Island as a site of reconciliation and triumphalism, which later was transplanted as a site of tourism consumption. Whereas before, the Mayibuye Centre pulsated with activities such as exhibitions, conferences, outreach work, and publications in which its leadership and staff contributed much towards the production of knowledge, these activities showed signs of slowing down in the latter part of the 1990s as the future of the Mayibuye Centre was being weighed up. Eventually, the publications, outreach work, and the production of exhibitions came to a halt partly because of shifting political sensibilities, financial considerations, and the changed focus of the Centre on collections management. In many ways, these were the very components of the Mayibuye's Centre's work that were transferred to and formalised within RIM, leaving only an archival collection to be managed. Inaugurated as the collections unit under the heritage division in RIM, charged with the responsibility to manage and preserve the archival collections of the museum, we argue that this exclusive focus on collections management left the once vibrant cultural and historical centre devoid of cultural work which had been integral in transforming the Centre into a vibrant hub of archival activism in the early period of the post-apartheid.

In his autobiography, *Time to Tell*, Barry Feinberg, a former employee of IDAF who had joined the Mayibuye Centre in 1991, lamented that "the Mayibuye Centre was reduced to an archive of political and cultural materials."[133] Feinberg's evocation of the diminishing of the Centre into an archive hint at his nostalgic yearning for what the Mayibuye Centre once espoused. More than just being nostalgic, we argue that Feinberg's words constituted a mourning of the loss of the cultural and activist work which was buried in the process of becoming immersed within the organisational structures of RIM. Instead of reactivating this 'living archive', these records were relegated to the obscure recesses of memory and history. The Mayibuye Centre was inserted into a national museum project of commemoration and nation-building, particularly focused on the monumentalisation of Robben Island as a site of resistance, survival, and triumph. Consequently, the archives became incorporated into a project of triumphalism while it became buried underneath the weight of ongoing political, financial, and organisational challenges of the museum as a whole. The archives also became buried as RIM had the additional pressure of attending to the status of Robben Island as a World Heritage Site. The Centre's incorporation into the museum gave rise to a problematic set of challenges which have continued to haunt the archive well into the present. Framed by the larger crisis that has engulfed the national archival system, archives, as we have argued, are haunted by epistemic and political uncertainty and increasingly find themselves on shifting ground as a result of a failure to understand and appreciate their significance in society. In the absence of a political will, hampered by chronic under-funding, a lack of resources and apathy, and caught between the two realms of RIM and UWC, the Mayibuye Archives would have continued to remain submerged because it signifies the remnants of a painful and divisive past, a past that seemingly has no place in post-apartheid South Africa, if not for the development of the African Programme in Museum and Heritage Studies (APMHS), a postgraduate diploma academically located within the Department of History at UWC and which formed the nexus of the next stage of the continuing relationship between UWC and RIM.

Having explored the challenges that NAHECS and the UWC Robben Island Museum Mayibuye Archives have faced and continue to face, we should not believe that the transformation to post-apartheid South Africa has been completed or has even happened. The effects of apartheid and colonialism continue to reverberate in post-apartheid South Africa and plays itself out through inequality, representation, education, skills, accessibility, and so forth. Cast within this light, it becomes even more pertinent that archives are urgently transformed and reconstituted as creative, political, and intellectual projects for the future.

Endnotes

1. R. González Echevarría. 1998. *Myth and Archive: A Theory of Latin American Narrative*. Durham and London: Duke University Press, 33.
2. V. Harris. 2000. *Exploring Archives: An Introduction to the Archival Ideas and Practice in South Africa*. Pretoria: National Archives of South Africa, 11.
3. Ibid., 11.
4. M. Pickover. 2014. *Patrimony, Power and Politics: Selecting, Constructing and Preserving Digital Heritage Content in South Africa and Africa*. Conference paper presented at IFLA, Lyon, 5.
5. One reason for early traces of archiving being overlooked is that the written record has always enjoyed more privilege at the expense of other modes of communication and recordkeeping such as the oral, visual, and other sensory forms.
For a discussion on the connections between orality and literacy see I. Hofmeyr. 1994. *We Spend Our Years as a Tale That is Told: Oral Historical Narrative in a South African Chiefdom*. Johannesburg: Wits University Press.;
Also see A. Portelli. 1998. 'What Makes Oral History Different'. In: R. Perks & A. Thomson (eds.), *The Oral History Reader*. London: Routledge. for his argument about the use and function of oral sources in creating meaning, content, and form;
For a discussion on how visuality has been subordinated to textuality, see P. Hayes, J. Silvester & W. Hartmann. 1998. 'Photography, History and Memory'. In: W. Hartmann, J. Silvester & P. Hayes (eds.), *The Colonising Camera: Photographs in the Making of Namibian History*. Athens: Ohio University Press, 2.
6. A.L. Stoler. 2002. 'Colonial Archives and the Arts of Governance'. *Archival Science*, 2:97-98. https://doi.org/10.1007/BF02435632
7. Ibid., 87.
8. Ibid., 90.
9. Harris. *Exploring Archives*, 8.
10. For a trajectory of the negotiated settlement see S. Friedman & D. Atkinson. 1994. *The Small Miracle: South Africa's Negotiated Settlement*. Randburg: Ravan Press.; W. Esterhuyse. 2012. *Endgame: Secret Talks and the End of Apartheid*. Cape Town: Tafelberg Publishers.
11. In the Final Report of the TRC, one of the recommendations was that at least 300 cases should be investigated and prosecuted, however only six cases have been reopened in the past two decades since the report was presented to the then President Nelson Mandela in 1998. Several family members of victims of human rights violations during apartheid have consistently called for justice and accountability but also equally, to provide them with the right to know what happened to their family members.
12. Although it is not clear when a policy on record destruction was implemented, it certainly came into effect in 1978 when "all government departments received guidelines for the protection of classified information, signed by the Prime Minister and empowering department heads to authorise destruction outside the ambit of the Archives Act." See V. Harris. 2000. 'They Should Have Destroyed More: The Destruction of Public Records by the South African State in the Final Years of Apartheid, 1990-1994'. *Transformation*, 42.
13. It is estimated that the National Intelligence Service headquarters destroyed 44 tons of paper-based and microfilm records in a 6-8 month period during 1993. See Harris, 'They Should Have Destroyed More', 39.

14 V. Harris. 2002. 'The Archival Sliver: Power, Memory and Archives in South Africa'. *Archival Science*, 2:64. https://doi.org/10.1007/BF02435631;
   Also see Harris. *Exploring Archives*, 9.
15 Harris. 'They Should Have Destroyed More', 29.
16 In their interrogation of the archive, the contributors to the volume Refiguring the Archive proposed a (re)figuring of the archive by investigating the ethnographies and histories of archives, how institutions such as archives are implicated in creating a particular vision of society and, very significantly, the conditions and processes of the record. See C. Hamilton, V. Harris, M. Pickover, G. Reid, R. Saleh & J. Taylor (eds.). 2002. *Refiguring the Archive*. Cape Town: David Philip, 7-16. https://doi.org/10.1007/978-94-010-0570-8
17 Harris. *Exploring Archives*, 10.;
   Harris. 'The Archival Sliver: Power, Memory and Archives in South Africa', 76.;
   Also see L. Witz. 2006. 'Transforming Museums on Post-apartheid Tourist Routes'. In: I. Karp, C. Kratz, L. Szwaja & T. Ybarro-Frausto with G. Buntix, B. Kirshenblatt-Gimblett, & C. Rassool (eds.), *Museum Frictions: Public Cultures/Global Transformations*. Durham: Duke University Press, 108. https://doi.org/10.2307/j.ctv11cw1hd.10
18 M. Pickover. 2005. 'Negotiations, Contestations and Fabrications: The Politics of Archives in South Africa Ten Years After Democracy'. *Innovation*, 30:5. https://doi.org/10.4314/innovation.v30i1.26493
19 R.H. Brown & B. Davis-Brown. 1998. 'The Making of Memory: The Politics of Archives, Libraries and Museums in the Construction of National Consciousness'. *History of the Human Sciences*, 11(4):19. https://doi.org/10.1177/095269519801100402
20 See B. Anderson. 1991. *Imagined Communities*. London: Verso.
21 Brown & Davis-Brown. 'The Making of Memory: The Politics of Archives, Libraries and Museums in the Construction of National Consciousness', 19.
22 R.C. Jimerson. 2006. 'Embracing the Power of Archives'. *The American Archivist*, 69(1):32. https://doi.org/10.17723/aarc.69.1.r0p75n2084055418
23 The State Archives Service reinvented itself as the National Archives in terms of the National Archives of South Africa Act in 1997.
24 Harris. *Exploring Archives*, 11.
25 For a history of the University of Fort Hare see D. Williams. 2001. *A History of the University College of Fort Hare, South Africa – the 1950s: The Waiting Years*. New York, NY: Mellen Press.;
   Also see D. Massey. 2010. *Under Protest: The Rise of Student Resistance at the University of Fort Hare*. Pretoria: Unisa Press, for the university's involvement in the liberation struggle.
26 Nelson Mandela quoted in B. Maaba. 2013. 'The History and Politics of Liberation Archives at Fort Hare'. Unpublished PhD Dissertation. Cape Town: University of Cape Town, 63.
27 This point was raised by Helena Pohlandt-McCormick in her brief discussion of the liberation archives at UFH and UWC in which she argued that it is interesting that liberation struggle material was relocated to these two historically black universities, both historically disadvantaged by their location at the margins of development in geographical terms and their hierarchy in relation to other tertiary institutions.
   See H. Pohlandt-McCormick. 2013. 'Taking Risks in the Post-Colonial Archive: Towards a Post-Colonial Thinking of the Archive'. Unpublished seminar paper presented at the South African Contemporary History and Humanities Seminar, Centre for Humanities Research. UWC (16 April 2013), 11, (Permission to cite obtained from author).

28 Pickover. 'Negotiations, Contestations and Fabrications', 5-7.
29 Ibid., 5.
30 'Liberation Archives Project: An Institutional Plan'. Alice: University of Fort Hare: NAHECS.
31 'Preparatory Project: Archives and Museum of Resistance'. Alice: University of Fort Hare: NAHECS (Cultural Studies), 1.;
Also see 'Agreement of Deposit: Memorandum of Agreement entered into by and between the African National Congress and the University of Fort Hare'. Alice: University of Fort Hare: NAHECS.
32 Maaba. 'The History and Politics of Liberation Archives at Fort Hare', 39-40.
33 Ike Maamoe and Andre Mohammed, both former students at SOMAFCO, studied and later became archivists. Both Maamoe and Mohammed respectively continue to work at NAHECS at UFH and the UWC Robben Island Mayibuye Archives at UWC.
34 ANC Policy for Transformation and Development of Heritage Resources (Museums, Monuments, Archives and National Symbols) for a Democratic South Africa. Discussion paper presented on behalf of the ANC Commission for Museums, Monuments and Heraldry to the ANC Culture and Development Conference, Civic Theatre, Johannesburg, May 1993. Alice: University of Fort Hare: NAHECS, 1.
35 Ibid.
36 Ibid., 2.
37 Archival Platform. 2015. *State of the Archives: An Analysis of South Africa's National Archival System*, 28. https://bit.ly/42ZeWmy [Accessed 21 November 2021].
38 G. Dominy. 1993. 'Archives in a Democratic South Africa'. *S.A. Archives Journal*, 35:67.
39 Ibid., 67.
40 For a longer discussion on the challenges of the ANC's archives unit see Maaba. 'The History and Politics of Liberation Archives at Fort Hare', 48-57.
41 S. Morrow & L. Wotshela. 2005. 'The State of the Archives and Access to Information'. In: J. Daniel, R. Southall & J. Lutchman (eds.), *State of the Nation: South Africa 2004-2005*. Pretoria: HSRC Press, 329.
42 'Preparatory Project: Archives and Museum of Resistance'. Alice: University of Fort Hare: NAHECS (Centre for Cultural Studies), 1.
43 'Liberation Archives Project: An Institutional Plan'
44 'Preparatory Project: Archives and Museums of Resistance'. Alice: University of Fort Hare: NAHECS (Centre for Cultural Studies), 1.
45 'Highlights: 1981-1994'. Alice: University of Fort Hare: NAHECS (Centre for Cultural Studies).
46 Ibid.
47 'Liberation Archives Project: An Institutional Plan'.
48 Maaba. 'The History and Politics of Liberation Archives at Fort Hare', 95.
49 Ibid., 96-106.
50 Ibid., 111.
51 'Liberation Archives Project: An Institutional Plan'.

52 'ANC Archives Project: An Update'. Alice: University of Fort Hare: NAHECS (Centre for Cultural Studies.;
Also see Maaba's chapter three, 'The Battle for the ANC Archives: The CCS versus the University Library', in Maaba. 'The History and Politics of Liberation Archives at Fort Hare', 107-146, for a more detailed discussion on the confluence of events which led to the relocation of the ANC archives to the university library.

53 'Liberation Archives Project: An Institutional Plan'.

54 Maaba. 'The History and Politics of Liberation Archives at Fort Hare', 197.

55 Pickover. 'Negotiations, Contestations and Fabrications', 1. https://doi.org/10.4314/innovation.v30i1.26493

56 For a historical trajectory and reflections of the shaping of UWC as an academic institution at the coalface of resistance against apartheid, see P. Lalu & N. Murray (eds.). 2012. *Becoming UWC: Reflections, Pathways and Unmaking Apartheid's Legacy*. Cape Town: Centre for Humanities Research.

57 A. Odendaal. 1991. 'Developments in Popular History in the Western Cape in the 1980s'. In: J. Brown (ed.), *History from South Africa: Alternative Visions and Practices*. Philadelphia, PA: Temple University Press, 366.

58 G. Minkley & C. Rassool. 1998. 'Orality, Memory and Social History in South Africa'. In: S. Nuttall & C. Coetzee (eds.), *Negotiating the Past: The Making of Memory in South Africa*. Cape Town: Oxford University Press, 93.

59 Minkley & Rassool. 'Orality, Memory and Social History in South Africa', 91-94.; Odendaal. 'Developments in Popular History in the Western Cape in the 1980s', 366.

60 'Proposal: Apartheid Museum under the auspices of UWC, 1 January 1987', 2. Confidential Memorandum from Lieb Loots to the Rector, University of the Western Cape. In: Academic Planning Committee Working Group re Establishment of Historical and Cultural Centre including an Apartheid Museum at UWC. Background Documents, Volume 1, 1986-1987 (André Odendaal private collection).

61 'Confidential Memorandum: Apartheid Museum at the University of the Western Cape', 5. In: Academic Planning Committee Working Group re Establishment of Historical and Cultural Centre including an Apartheid Museum at UWC. Background Documents, Volume 1, 1986-1987 (André Odendaal private collection).

62 'Study Leave Report by Andre Odendaal, Department of History (1990)', 1. In: Fakulteit Lettere en Wysbegeerte. Verslae: Studieverlof, Konferensie/Kongresse Bygewoon (Ciraj Rassool private collection).

63 Ibid., 1.

64 'Briefing for Jakes, London, 4 June 1988'. In: Academic Planning Committee Working Group re Establishment of Historical and Cultural Centre including an Apartheid Museum at UWC. Background Documents, Vol. 2, 1988-1990 (André Odendaal private collection).

65 'Letter from Barry Feinberg to André Odendaal dated 10 October 1989'. In Academic Planning Committee Working Group re Establishment of Historical and Cultural Centre including an Apartheid Museum at UWC. Background Documents, Vol. 2, 1988-1990 (André Odendaal private collection).

66 'Letter from Jakes Gerwel to André Odendaal dated 8 February 1990'. In Academic Planning Committee Working Group re Establishment of Historical and Cultural Centre including an Apartheid Museum at UWC. Background Documents, Vol. 2, 1988-1990 (André Odendaal private collection).

67 'Letter from André Odendaal dated 21 March 1990'. In: Academic Planning Committee Working Group re Establishment of Historical and Cultural Centre including an Apartheid Museum at UWC. Background Documents, Vol. 2, 1988-1990 (André Odendaal private collection).;
'Memorandum from Rector to Executive Committee of Council, 27 March 1990'. In: Academic Planning Committee Working Group re Establishment of Historical and Cultural Centre including an Apartheid Museum at UWC. Background Documents, Vol. 2, 1988-1990 (André Odendaal private collection).

68 'Letter from André Odendaal to Rector and others dated 21 March 1990'. In: Academic Planning Committee Working Group re Establishment of Historical and Cultural Centre including an Apartheid Museum at UWC. Background Documents, Vol. 2, 1988-1990 (André Odendaal private collection).

69 'Mayibuye book launch'. *Campus Bulletin*, 24 July 1991 in the Mayibuye Centre for History and Culture, First Annual Report 1992, Bellville.

70 K. Williams. 1992. 'Closed Chapter for SA's Book Publishers'. *Southside 15* in the Mayibuye Centre for History and Culture, First Annual Report 1992, Bellville.

71 'Progress Report from Working Group re UWC Historical and Cultural Centre to Academic Planning Committee, 4 March 1991' (André Odendaal private collection).

72 'IDAF Publications and Audio-Visual Department Report on Trip to South Africa'. 26 November-3 December 1990 in Barry Feinberg collection, MCH 89, Box 19, Historical Papers. Bellville: UWC Robben Island Mayibuye Archives.

73 B. Feinberg. 2009. *Time to Tell: An Activist's Story*. Newtown: STE Publishers, 126.

74 'IDAF Publications and Audio-Visual Department Report on trip to South Africa'.

75 Ibid.

76 Ibid.

77 For a complete list of goods donated from the International Defence and Aid Fund to the Historical and Cultural Centre of UWC, see 'Draft Progress Report by Co-Ordinator'. UWC Historical and Cultural Centre project, for meeting of Academic Planning Committee Working Group, Wednesday 26 June 1991, Annexure A: Appendices (André Odendaal private collection).

78 For an account of the removal of the ANC collection at UWC see T. April. 2012. 'Theorising Women: The Intellectual Inputs of Charlotte Maxeke to the Discourse of the Liberation Struggle in South Africa'. Unpublished PhD. Dissertation. Bellville: University of the Western Cape, 224-225.

79 See Feinberg. *Time to Tell*, 133-4.

80 Ibid., 128.

81 J. Viljoen. 'Legacy of Apartheid'. *The Argus*, Monday, 12 October 1992. 4 in Mayibuye Centre for History and Culture First Annual Report, 1992, Bellville (André Odendaal private collection).

82 The Mayibuye Centre played an active role in the national debates on history and culture through the respective appointments of the Centre's director to ACTAG and Gordon Metz's appointment as the vice-chair of WESTAG in 1994. See Mayibuye. *Centre for History and Culture Third Annual Report*, Bellville (1994), 2.

83 Interview with G. Metz, 27 May 2014.

84 C. Rassool. 2004. 'The Individual, Auto/Biography and History in South Africa'. Unpublished PhD Dissertation. Bellville: University of the Western Cape, 201.

85 Ibid., 201.

86 ADA magazine quoted in the Mayibuye Centre for History and Culture. Second Annual Report, 1993, Bellville.
87 Interview with G. Metz, 27 May 2014.
88 'Draft Progress Report by the Coordinator, UWC Historical and Cultural Centre project, for meeting of Academic Planning Committee Working Group', 26 June 1991 (André Odendaal private collection).
89 'Finances Section'. In: the Mayibuye Centre for History and Culture, First Annual Report 1992 (André Odendaal private collection).
90 Interview with A. Odendaal, 28 May 2014.
91 Ibid.
92 'Mayibuye Centre for History and Culture Fourth Annual Report', 1995, 8 (André Odendaal private collection).
93 See 'Discussion Document of the Joint UWC/RIM Working Group re Proposals for a Co-Operation Agreement Between the University of the Western Cape and Robben Island Museum Relating to the Mayibuye Centre and Other Joint Arrangements dated 8 July 1998' in Box 32. Bellville: UWC Archives.
94 Interview with A. Odendaal, 28 May 2014.
95 W. Sisulu. 1999. *Robben Island – Nomination file for World Heritage Status*. Pretoria: Government of South Africa, 4.
96 C. Shearing & M. Kempa. 2004. 'A Museum of Hope: A Story of Robben Island'. *Annals of the American Academy of Political and Social Science*, 592(1):68. https://doi.org/10.2139/ssrn.2720241
97 Ibid., 62-78, 65.
98 Ibid., 65.
99 Ibid., 65.
100 L. Witz. 2010. 'Museums, Histories and the Dilemmas of Change in Post-Apartheid South Africa'. *University of Michigan Working Papers in Museum Studies*, 3:4.
101 The Cabinet established the Future of Robben Island Committee in August 1995 to deliberate and come up with acceptable proposals for the future of Robben Island, given its history and links to the biography of the most prominent leaders of the post-apartheid government, notably Nelson Mandela.
102 See 'Robben Island Business Plan' in Box 35, Robben Island Gateway. Bellville: UWC Archives.
103 'Director's Annual Report 1995' (Executive Summary): In: File 'Mayibuye Centre', Box 258. Bellville: UWC Robben Island Archives, Bellville.
104 A. Odendaal. 'Suggested Robben Island Action Plan for the Department of Arts, Culture, Science and Technology', 4 March 1996. In: Mayibuye Centre, Box 258. Bellville: UWC Archives.
105 Ibid., 4.
106 Ibid.
107 Ibid.
108 Media Statement by the Minister of Arts, Culture, Science and Technology, Mr Lionel Mtshali dated 4 September 1996 regarding the Future Management and Development of Robben Island' in Robben Island and Gateway, Box 35. Bellville: UWC Archives.
109 Ibid.

110 Ibid.
111 The Working Group consisted of Prof. Cecil Abrahams (UWC Rector), H.C Bredekamp (Director of IHR), Prof Carolyn Hamilton (Wits University), Ahmed Kathrada (RIM interim Board Chairman), Benedict Martins and Prof Gary Minkley (UWC Department of History), Prof André Odendaal (Robben Island interim, CEO), Mr Steytler (UWC Community Law Centre), and Mr G Thomas (Chairperson of UWC Council). Bellville: CHR archives, UWC.
112 'Discussion Document on Future Possibilities for Mayibuye Centre, The Institute for Historical Research (IHR), and the University of the Western Cape in Relation to the Development of the Robben Island Museum'. Prepared by A. Odendaal on 9 June 1997.
113 Ibid.
114 Odendaal. 'Discussion Document'.
115 Odendaal. 'Discussion Document'. According to Odendaal, of benefit to UWC, apart from the "prestige and recognition" synonymous with an association with Robben Island, which highlighted "the relevancy of a previously disadvantaged HBU in national life and the process of reconstruction" would be: 'Another benefit is that this arrangement will do away with past overlaps and tensions between the three historical interest groups on campus. With the IHR/Mayibuye disappearing in their current form, rigid old distinctions between research and teaching centres, for example, will be done away with, and the History Department will become the central locus of integrated activity in terms of historical theory and practice at UWC. The new Robben Island Archives will serve as collections and research base for the Department, and the RIM will encourage and fund certain History Department-based projects'.
116 Odendaal. 'Discussion Document'.
117 Ibid.
118 Odendaal. 'Discussion Document. 16 June 1997'.
119 Ibid.
120 'Media Statement by the Minister of Arts, Culture, Science and Technology'.
121 'Mayibuye Centre for History and Culture, Fifth Annual Report', 1996, 1 (André Odendaal private collection).
122 Ibid, 1.
123 Interview with G. Metz, 27 May 2014.
124 'Mayibuye Centre for History and Culture, Seventh Annual Report', 1998.
125 See 'Project Agreement between the Mayibuye Centre and the Robben Island Museum'. In: Mayibuye Centre, MCH 253, Box 26. Bellville: UWC Robben Island Mayibuye Archives.
126 'Project Agreement between the Mayibuye Centre and the Robben Island Museum'.
127 'Memorandum of Agreement between RIM and UWC in respect of The UWC Robben Island Museum Mayibuye Archives'. In: 4, in Box 32. Bellville: UWC Archives.
128 Ibid, 4.
129 Ibid, 7.
130 C. Rassool, personal communication, 9 November 2015.

131 See 'Mayibuye Centre for History and Culture, Seventh Annual Report' for an account of the uncertainties that were caused by the impending incorporation or rather absorption of the Mayibuye Centre into the Robben Island Museum. The impending incorporation of the Mayibuye Centre into RIM and the ambiguity around it seemed to have only exacerbated an already discontented relationship between staff and management regarding long-term contracts and salary discrepancies as was suggested by a memorandum in which the staff noted their dissatisfaction with their working conditions at the Mayibuye Centre. See 'Memorandum: Working Conditions'. Dated 19 January 1996 to the Director in Barry Feinberg collection, MCH 89, Box 6. Bellville: UWC Robben Island Mayibuye Archives.

132 C. Rassool & L. Witz. 2001. 'Transforming Heritage Education in South Africa: A Partnership Between the Academy and the Museum'. SAMP 2001: Strengthening the Network: A Meeting of African Museums of the Swedish African Museum Programme, 22-27 August 1999.

133 Feinberg. *Time to Tell*, 150.

A History of Museum and Heritage Studies in Africa

4

> The impact of any museum training for Africans should be noticeable in the way their museums function and are run [...] the way they interpret their collections and in the way they organise their educational programmes for the collective good of the public.[1]

Part of the outcome of the UWC Robben Island Mayibuye Archives' incorporation into the Robben Island Museum (RIM) was the Robben Island Training Programme (RITP), jointly convened by the University of the Western Cape (UWC), University of Cape Town (UCT) and RIM in 1998. This was the pilot initiative to transform the South African Museum and Heritage Studies and training from its colonial and apartheid legacy into an inclusive democratic orientation through fast-track training in museum and heritage skills geared towards social justice. One of the distinctions between this programme and others was the programme's rejection of concentrating on the acquisition of technical museum skills as the focus of Museum and Heritage Studies. The RITP distinguished itself as a programme that challenged and criticised the orientation of existing Museum and Heritage Studies programmes on the African continent as mostly focused on conservation management and archival technological training with an emphasis on the acquisition of technical skills to conserve artefacts and develop collections. As noted by Ciraj Rassool, the director of the African Programme in Museums and Heritage Studies (APMHS) and Professor of History at UWC:

> The education of African museum professionals has very often been limited to technical aspects, with the intellectual effort of conceptualising and leading museum work seen to be the prerogative of outside consultants. This contradiction between technical training and intellectual education has marked almost all African museum and heritage training and education initiatives, which have often been confined to the technical terms set by international agencies and partners.[2]

Redressing this deplorable state of African Museum and Heritage Studies (AMHS) was the impetus for establishing the RITP, which later evolved into APMHS, as a course of study rooted in critical Museology and museum debates. This aspiration Rassool argued "lay at the centre of the work of the APMHS that sought to build a core of African museum leaders through a critical, intellectual programme grounded in the cultural politics of museums, rather than exclusive focus on technical training in preservation and care."[3]

Despite the importance of training in scientific technology of museum and archival practice to recover and reconstruct African history through museums, it is also important for African Museum and Heritage Studies to be affirmed as a "locus of social theory and critical debate on the major questions of our time",[4] especially from the perspective of decolonising African Museum and Heritage Studies. This is because the exclusive focus on technical training has resulted not only in conceptual, theoretical, and practical limitations on the nature, orientation, and objectives of Museum and Heritage Studies and training programmes in Africa, but it has also greatly inhibited its transformative potential as a terrain of critical decolonial public scholarship. The problem with an over-emphasis on technical training for AMHS students, without any grounding in critical theories of the cultural politics of Museum and Heritage Studies, is comparable to the position of African students' introduction to Western philosophy without consciencism, as argued by Kwame Nkrumah in his seminal book of the same title.[5] The argument is that by over-focusing on a technical programme of Museum and Heritage Studies, or abstractions of philosophy in the case of Nkrumah, opportunities are lost to critically examine legacies of colonialism, apartheid, and current issues around historical, social, and epistemic justice, which the technologies and philosophy sustains. To better understand and appreciate the ideological, political, theoretical, and practical implications of RITP-APMHS distinctiveness on the critical issues of decolonisation of AMHS, an expository and comparative historical analysis of the Museum and Heritage Studies and training programmes on the continent is necessary as a background.

Issues in the history of African Museum and Heritage Studies in Africa (AMHS)

The literature on the origin, history, and development of AMHS in Africa is increasing, a positive and encouraging sign for the development of the field.[6] But as it is arguably the case with all other facets of knowledge production in or about Africa,[7] this literature is premised on the Authorised Heritage Discourse (AHD) European models of Museum and Heritage Studies.[8] The AHD, according to Laurajane Smith, is the hegemonic notion of heritage derived from Europe's specific history of modernity that is constitutive and legitimating of what is heritage, and who has the ability to speak for and about the nature and meaning of heritage.[9] Since AHD "is also a professional discourse that regulates professional heritage practices",[10] it has a defining and enduring influence of AMHS. Hence the starting point of most reflections on the origin, history, and development of Museum and Heritage Studies is the recognition of the colonial legacy of AMHS, and the need to decolonise and transform the sector into a vehicle for *Uhuru* (freedom), socio-economic-cultural-political objectives through appropriate training of professionals.

Emmanuel Arinze, George Abungu, Terry Little, and Webber Ndoro, along with Galia Saouma-Ferero, among others[11] addressed the colonial legacy of museums and the development of Museum and Heritage Studies, which provides a point of departure for understanding the origin and development of AMHS on the African continent. Significantly, the literature revealed the expansion of the field of Museum Studies to incorporate Heritage Studies. Beginning around the early 1990s and more prominently post-1994, Museum Studies became associated with Heritage Studies as part of the process of incorporating the discourses of intangible heritage, Public History, and other domains of heritage practice in museums. More importantly, the literature revealed that international institutions such as the United Nations Educational, Scientific and Cultural Organisation (UNESCO), International Council of Museums (ICOM), and International Committee for the Training of Personnel (ICTOP) were instrumental in the establishment and sustaining of Museum and Heritage Studies in Africa.

As with the rest of the continent, the basic defining feature of the origin of Museum and Heritage Studies in Africa, including South Africa, was their pedigree in European museum and heritage training initiatives. This rootedness in European epistemologies initiated, sponsored, and directed initiatives around the orientation and focus on the acquisition of "technologies of heritage",[12] with the objective of including African heritage as an "add-on"[13] to the World Heritage List as the ultimate purpose of AMHS. Given the exclusion of South Africa from the rest of the continent due to its policies of apartheid, the origin and history of AMHS presented by Arinze and other literature on the history of museum and heritage excludes the development and advancement of this field in South Africa, although it has a longer history of Museum and Heritage Studies. Archival records documented the history of formal Museum and Heritage Studies and training in South Africa since 1935 as we discuss in the next chapter, with the beginning of formal Museum Studies on the continent in 1963 at the Jos Institute in Nigeria.

The grounding assumption which informed the planning of Museum and Heritage Studies in Africa as revealed by Terry Little, a 'Rock art specialist' and leading figure of AMHS and one of the leading experts of heritage conservation training in Africa, was:

> In sub-Saharan Africa, since there was no conservation training in the region at that time, we worked with the universities in London and Paris to create courses and curricula. Since there were no conservators to train, we had to work with all existing museum categories to create the vocation. Since the museum directors were themselves part of the problem, we have to motivate them and involve them in the training of their personnel. Since many of the museums we were involved with seemed foreign or dead to their communities, we worked with the community leaders and the media to create awareness.[14]

To understand the implications of the assumptions contained in this statement, which seem to suggest that Africa is *tabula rasa* when it comes to managing the conservation of its heritage, we need to appreciate that key to this rhetoric is the idea that "non-European countries make less sophisticated stewards of their past on account of their lack of resources, training, general preservation and Museology traditions, and/or their endemic conflict."[15] These are 'Orientalist tendencies' which depicts Africa as a region endowed with historic resources, but suffering from substandard expertise, in other words, a territory in need of conservatorship. Problematically, this was the AHD perspective that informed the origin and development of Museum and Heritage Studies in Africa.

For us to trace the development of Museum and Heritage Studies on the African continent compared to the orientation of Museum and Heritage Studies which developed in post-1994 South Africa, the next section deals with the development of Museum and Heritage Studies as a specialised academic discipline in Europe and it's colonial and post-colonial transplanting and appropriation in Africa. This is done through a brief discussion of the roles of international Museum and Heritage Studies bodies, specifically: ICTOP,[16] ICOM, the International Centre for the Study of the Preservation and Restoration of Cultural Property (ICCROM), and UNESCO, all of which have historically defined the parameters and discourses of Museum and Heritage Studies in Africa and are crucial to understanding the history, development, and limitations of technical training as solely the focus of Museum and Heritage Studies in Africa.

International Museum and Heritage Studies

The broader origin, history, and development of Museum and Heritage Studies programmes as a specialised field of study can be located in the changed role of museums in the 19th century from "a repository for private collections to a place of study and research. This development obviously necessitated organised training designed to produce a new type of museum professionals."[17] The renowned Raymond Singleton, first Chairperson of ICTOP from 1968 to 1974, who in 1972 conducted training for museum professionals in South Africa, traced the origin of Museum Studies to the practices of acquiring training in museum professional skills through "on-the-job apprenticeship."[18] This, according to him, allowed existing staff in the museum to acquire ideas and skills in an informal manner from more experienced museum staff. The limitation of this training method was that "while the system permitted established techniques and procedures to be transmitted from one generation to the next, it left little room for initiative, innovation or progress because it failed to consider any of the basic fundamentals of museum purpose or functions beyond the limited focus of a particular museum."[19]

Another very important issue in the development of Museum Studies as a formal programme of study discussed by Singleton was the appropriate location for such programmes. Singleton criticised the initial mistaken assumption that "since ready access to museum collections, staff and facilities was desirable for training purposes, the museum was the obvious place in which to establish training courses."[20] He argued that the inherent weakness of 'on-the-job apprenticeship' was replicated in training located in museums, which provided little opportunity for wider exposure to broader museum dynamics. He concluded that locating museum training programmes solely in museums resulted in a deficiency of preparing museum professionals for the extraordinary variety of institutional challenges in the changing museum environment. This, he argued, was because "the attention and focus of training programmes located in the museums are usually the policies, methods and challenges pertaining to a single institution with little opportunity for a wider appraisal of the general museum scene."[21]

The alternative location for the Museum Studies programmes discussed by Singleton was the University of Buenos Aires' pioneered programme in Museum Studies in the 1920s. In contrast to the risk of locating museum training programmes in museums, the risk of locating a Museum and Heritage Studies programme exclusively in the university is that it would be too remote from the actual museum scene. As Singleton noted:

> ... the fear, indeed the suspicion, among senior museum staff was that such training would be so remote from the everyday problems and situations prevailing in museums as to be of little value; it would at best provide only a second-hand impression and would also probably be apt to concentrate on theoretical consideration only.[22]

However, Singleton suggested that in recognising these risks, "the university department which offers training in Museum Studies is well placed to avoid them."[23] Singleton argued, "not being museums and lacking in the numerous specialists which will be required to cover all aspects of the broad training syllabus, university departments are forced to look to museum colleagues for assistance."[24] As we observed in the history of the RITP-APMHS:

> ... it has been relatively easy for the university to provide students with the opportunity to visit, work in and meet the staff of many different types of museums, thus avoiding the main weakness of narrow focus of museum-based training programmes.[25]

This collaborative arrangement, helped not only to dispel the charges against museums of remoteness from the real world, but also provided students with opportunities to meet and exchange knowledge with museum specialists.[26] The APMHS, as we show in this study, is an example of Museum Studies in the last decades that has confirmed the university as the most appropriate location for Museum and Heritage Studies, because of the transdisciplinary intellectual environment it provides and the symbiotic collaborative historical connection of the museum and the university intrinsic to their origins, operations, and activities.

The International Council of Museums (ICOM)

Since its first Interim Conference in Mexico in 1947, ICOM had been "the professional and by definition the non-governmental world body for museums and the museum profession."[27] Apart from aspiring towards "coordinating their teaching programmes, diplomas and teaching methods, the meeting in its decision aspired to a basic standard syllabus which might be adopted for both the existing training courses and for any new museum staff training programmes."[28] Crucially, the meeting advocated:

> (a) that Museology should be recognised as a true discipline in its own right – and that (b) it was necessary to place as much importance on teaching of Museology as on museography, and distinguish between training for future heads of museums, who it was felt must receive a complete training, museological, as well as museographical, in contrast with future museum technicians whose training could be strictly museographical in content.[29]

The creation of ICTOP, in 1968 with Raymond Singleton as chairperson, has a direct impact on development of AMHS as the commissioning of ICOM's triennial programme for 1967-1971 included a series of regional museum training surveys and teaching visits by George-Henri Riverie to North Africa, Yvonne Oddon to West Africa, and Singleton to South Africa in 1972.[30] Significantly, an enduring result of the creation of ICTOP was the adoption of an ICOM Basic Syllabus, authored by Yvonne Oddon in 1971 at the 9th ICOM general conference, which set out the minimum elements that must be included in any basic professional museum training, whether at a university or in less formal training programmes. These principal curriculum elements for Museum Studies were:

1. Introduction to Museology: history and purpose of museums.
2. Organisation, operation, and management of museums.
3. Museum architecture, layout, and equipment.
4. Collections: origin, related records setting-up, and movement.
5. Scientific activities and research.
6. Preservation and care of collections.
7. Presentation: Exhibition.
8. The public (including public facilities).
9. Cultural and educational activities of museums.[31]

This was the curriculum transported to Africa, which continues to form the basis of Museum and Heritage Studies. The question of the appropriateness of this Eurocentric curriculum for AMHS is still definitive of the knowledge production problems in the field of Museum and Heritage Studies in Africa. The critical question posed by Martin Segger, ICTOP chairperson in 1996, was:

> How relevant is the traditional western museological model to the other half of the world? Do we [the West] have the moral or intellectual authority to go on exporting expertise or even training to the rest of the world? Is the now revered ICOM curriculum a crutch, a hindrance or in the worst case, yet another example of exploitative neo-colonialism?[32]

To answer these questions, it is necessary to briefly examine the origin, features, and characteristics of some of the different ICTOP/ICCROM/UNESCO programmes in museum training in Africa since the 1960s, starting with the Centre for Museum Studies, Jos, Nigeria, which was established in 1963.

Centre for Museum Studies, Jos, Nigeria

In contrast to Terry Little's arguments regarding the lack of heritage conservation professionals in Africa as something inherently deficient about Africans in their aptitude of museum and heritage management, the reason for the low numbers of African museum professionals in Africa, according to Arinze, ex-Principal of the Centre for Museum Studies, Jos, Nigeria was:

> In the beginning Africans were not given solid professional training that would empower them, nor were they encouraged to make the museums profession their career. What generally emerged was a situation where Africans served as attendants and cleaners. A few were taught how to operate a camera and move objects within the museum and in the field but were denied the hard-core professional training essential for the profession.[33]

This colonial-imposed situation, according to Arinze, resulted in a virtual lack of 'hard-core professionals' to respond to the needs of the newly independent states "for the museum to develop a vision or a mission consistent with the national goals and objectives."[34] It was this absence of African museum professionals in the immediate post-independence period that inevitably "entrenched the Western model of the museum training"[35] in post-colonial Africa. In a 2002 research paper for the ICOM/ICTOP study series, Arinze sketched a condensed history of the origin and development of Museum and Heritage Studies and training in Africa, which provides a framework for charting the history of Museum and Heritage Studies in Africa. According to him:

> In the last 25 years, various steps were taken to address the training issues affecting African museums, first in 1963, the Jos Centre was established by UNESCO in Nigeria; later in the 70's UNESCO established the Niamey Training Centre. Much later in the 1980's ICCROM established the PREMA programmes, which ran from 1990-2000 (Prevention in Museum in Africa). In 2001-2002, ICCROM, at the end of its PREMA programme, established two special training centres, EPA in Porto Novo, Republic of Benin and PDMA in Mombasa, Kenya.[36]

Expressing the problematics of transformation without decolonisation in museums, Arinze lamented that apart from slight variations, the idea of museums in post-colonial independent African countries was the same as in the colonial period. He therefore argued for what we now described as an 'Afrocentric turn'[37] when he advocated for the need to create 'African-based museums' through a combination of scholarship and practical, hands-on experience in the training of African museum professionals.[38] Further anticipating critical Heritage Studies and the Afrocentric turn, Arinze in addition argued that African museum professionals should be trained to use their expertise to help Africans clearly understand both their cultural and natural heritage and how it can be used to deal with the vital issues of peace, democracy, and economic development grounded in cultural realism within an African context.[39] This aspiration of an Afrocentric perspective as articulated by Arinze was however not behind the orientation of the Jos Centre for Museum Studies.[40]

The Jos Centre sought to provide "the much-needed training facilities for the conservation and preservation of museum objects, monuments, and the cultural and natural heritage in an African context."[41] The Centre, consisting of a museum exhibition gallery, zoo, and botanical garden, as well as an open-air museum "where the best examples of traditional Nigerian architectural designs and building techniques have been reconstructed" was, as stated by Arinze, an ideal environment for the training of African museum personnel for a broad-based approach that focuses on the specific needs of African museums.[42] The pedagogy and curriculum of the centre exposed students to theories of Museology through "various concepts of the museum and its historical development and evolution, as well as the scientology of museums, which deals with the ethos of museum philosophy and work."[43] Courses offered at the centre included an internship engagement, which entailed working with museum staff and doing practical conservation work on artefacts and formed part of the curriculum of the programme.

The specific courses it offered were based on the ICTOP curriculum:
- Museum Administration
- Museology: Museum Documentation
- Introduction to Ethnography
- Museum Education
- Museum Exhibition and Graphic
- Conservation of Natural and Cultural Heritage
- Archaeology and History of Africa
- Audio-Visual Techniques
- Maintenance of Monuments; Museum Security
- Photography; Library Science
- Ethnomusicology[44]

Like the impact of the RITP-APMHS on transformation of the museum and heritage sector in South Africa, post-1994 and its reverberation globally which we discuss at length in the next chapter as the harbinger of the Afrocentric turn in African Museum and Heritage Studies. The "well-defined training policy" of the Jos Centre, according to Arinze, benefited "a corps of skilled museum professionals who helped in shaping a new focus for museums across the continent" post-independence in the 1960s.[45] These trained professionals that benefited from the Jos Centre developed capacity to challenge the stereotypical Western models of museums they had inherited by "launching the heritage of Africa to a global audience in a manner that brought pride and dignity to Africa."[46] Notwithstanding the limitations of the colonial legacy, Arinze nonetheless noted that due to the African focused orientation of training offered at the Jos centre, a 'striking phenomenon' occurred in post-independence museums of Africa as they became "symbols of *Uhuru* and effective vehicles for nationalism and for fostering national consciousness and political unity to the newly independent countries."[47]

Regrettably, although African museums developed through adequate training programmes provided by the Jos Institute, in the late 1980s however, with few exceptions, the training initiatives ceased to evolve and became stagnant and confused.[48] This era of decay exposed the risk of dependence on international funding for AMHS typified by the decline of the Jos centre, Nigeria.[49] As stated in the ICOM's Secretary General Report for 1980-1983:

> The lack of financial resources has necessitated the gradual handing
> over of responsibility for countries in which training centres are located
> and consequently many more centres are now operating far below the
> minimum level of funding. They are unable to retain personnel and the
> quality of training courses has obviously decreased. Furthermore, by
> placing responsibilities with the host country the training centre has been
> hindered by purely domestic, political and administrative factors.[50]

The 1980s was the era of the International Monetary Fund's (IMF) imposed Structural Adjustment Programme (SAP) and its attendant destruction of African political economics, which had dire consequences especially for its social cultural infrastructure specifically education, health, and arts and cultural sectors. The solution to these problems of funding for museum training was ICCROM, which in 1984 started training courses at various levels to address the specific problem of Prevention Conservation in Museums in Africa (PREMA).[51]

Prevention Conservation in Museums in Africa (PREMA)

PREMA was a training initiative developed in 1984 by ICCROM to provide training and technical assistance to museum professionals from sub-Saharan African countries. Its stated aim was to establish a network of African professionals capable of taking charge of the conservation of collections and the training of colleagues, thereby giving sub-Saharan African museums tools for long-lasting development.[52] PREMA was established to mitigate against the unsuitability of African museum professionals who had received training in Europe or North America according to the specific needs and requirements of those countries, which are inappropriate to the African conditions.[53] Its rationale was to provide conservation training tailored to Africa. It therefore introduced a 'tailor-made' training programme for Africa. Commendable as the good intention of ICCROM was to provide Africa a tailor-made programme of museum training through PREMA, the question is how fitting the tailor-made programme was, because it continued to be manufactured in Europe and exported to Africa. This is because its flagship project, the International University Course, was based in Rome from its inception in 1987 until 1993, when it was moved – first to Jos, Nigeria, then to other countries in Africa.[54]

Nonetheless, George Abungu highlighted its advantages to the development of AMHS. Abungu noted that among PREMA's strengths was its flexibility to meet the specific needs of sub-Saharan African museums and he lauded the project as "a huge contribution to saving African heritage for future generations."[55] He explained that among the successful outcomes of PREMA was the 'training of trainers' project because the programme "not only addressed the condition of material culture but also helped to train a generation of African professionals who would ensure the practice of good conservation for a long time to come." This training of trainers, he maintained, "exemplified ICCROM's commitment to preserving and protecting sub-Saharan Africa's movable heritage."[56] However, despite Abungu complimentary comments, Terry Little acknowledged the colonial problem of the geo-cultural politics of knowledge production inherent in a situation where "mainly European and American professionals based in Rome"[57] were formulating and directing museum and heritage training programmes in Africa for Africans as a fundamental challenge of the PREMA programme. Nonetheless, PREMA seemed to have succeeded in achieving its principal objectives of the programme: "to establish by the year 2000, a network of African heritage professionals who can assume the responsibility of conservation of movable property and create a network of museum professionals trained in conservation and capable of training others in the future."[58]

This was achieved, as Abungu suggested, because PREMA was developed as:

> ... a long-term programme to arrest decay and prevent the deterioration of collections in the museums of sub-Saharan Africa. Its two objectives were (a) to ensure the conservation of sub-Saharan African museum collections and (b) to establish a network of African professionals who could assume responsibility for the conservation of movable property and for future training."[59]

These objectives of the programme, according to Little, were in response to an assessment of the conservation problems and training needs of the African museum and heritage sector. This assessment, as seen in Little's argument discussed earlier in the chapter, highlighted "the lack of trained personnel, the lack of possibilities of training, the lack of tools, the lack of motivation and a great sense of alienation by museum professionals"[60] in Africa.

The structure of the PREMA programme consisted of an International University Course, which provided specialised theoretical training in conservation management, with the award of a Diploma in Conservation Management for Museums of sub-Saharan Africa from the University College of London, Institute of Archaeology, and the Universite de Paris I *Pantheon-Sorbonne*. The programme was an intensive nine-month training course, alternating each year between English and French,[61] and supplemented by an auxiliary national/sub-regional course, which offered basic training in preventive conservation for all levels of museum workers, including technicians, conservators, archivists, keepers, and assistant keepers, with an emphasis on training trainers for future PREMA courses.[62]

The regional\national courses were organised in collaboration with host museums and based on an agreement to implement a preventive conservation programme. For example, the sixth PREMA National/Sub-Regional course in Zimbabwe from November 1995-1996 for Southern African countries, consisted of participants from Zimbabwe, Malawi, Lesotho, Swaziland, and Namibia. The nine-week course covered: an introduction to preventive conservation, identifying risk to collections, coping with main risks, caring for collections, and exhibition.[63] Tied to this was a one-week seminar for museum directors, aimed at integrating preventive conservation consciousness into all spheres of museum development.[64]

According to Little, the measure of the success of this programme was the subsequent expansion by the establishment of two formal training centres: EPA (l'Ecole du Patrimoine Africain), based in Porto Novo, Benin Republic for French-speaking African countries and PMDA (Programme for Museum Development in Africa), based in Mombasa, Kenya for English-speaking countries.[65] This was the outcome of the sixth (1998) PREMA review meeting in Benin Republic, which recommended "a new five-year programme from 2000 to support museums in sub-Saharan Africa".[66] The recommendation stated that such a programme should be coordinated from two bases, Benin and Kenya. The basis for the two institutions, according to Little, was the success of PREMA in correcting the then-current, pitiful state of museum/heritage training in Africa, and creating the imperative for its sustainability. PREMA programmes, he argued, highlighted the fact that "there appears to be a need for more technical training including workshops and seminars for technical and mid-level staff, as well as attendants, custodians and guides who have the most contact with the public."[67]

Programme for Museum Development in Africa (PDMA) – Centre for Heritage Development in Africa (CHDA)

The Programme for Museum Development in Africa (PDMA), based in Mombasa, Kenya was launched in 2000 as part of the outcome of the ICCROM PREMA 1990-2000 programme in collaboration with the National Museums of Kenya, and evolved into the Centre for Heritage Development in Africa (CHDA) in November 2004. According to the official website, CHDA is "an international Non-Governmental Organisation (NGO) dedicated to the preservation, management and promotion of cultural heritage in Africa through a programme of training and development support services. Its core focus is on the preservation of immovable, movable and intangible cultural heritage in Africa and its vision is to be a centre of excellence for heritage development in Africa."[68]

CHDA's notion of 'heritage' regards "heritage as both one's inheritance (language, culture, a way of seeing the world, for example) and objects or qualities that reflect one's culture: cultural traditions, historic buildings, World Heritage sites, even a birth right."[69] This notion of heritage as inherited birth right (which can also be a World Heritage Site) informed the approach to Heritage Studies reflected in CHDA training courses, seminars, publications, and advisory services. CHDA courses which include "both technical and hard skills and people-related or soft skills, promotes the use of heritage conservation, first, for sustainable development in Africa, and second, to deliver on the Millennium Development Goals."[70]

Africa 2009

The Africa 2009 programme, as a partnership of African heritage organisations, ICCROM, UNESCO, and CRATerre-EAG, was launched in 1998 and became operational in 1999. The stated aim of the project was to bring together a group of African heritage professionals to build a greater awareness of the most important issues in conservation planning and management, especially as it relates to African immovable heritage. The programme was conducted in two nodes of operation – CHDA in Mombasa, Kenya for the English-speaking countries, and EPA, in Port Novo, Benin Republic, for the French-speaking countries.[71] Over the course of its existence, both centres hosted 11 regional courses and 11 directors' seminars and contributed to the activities by providing staff and infrastructure in close collaboration with national institutions in Project Cadre. During the last phase of the programme, EPA and CHDA also took the lead in the coordination of some regional Projects Situés.[72]

Abungu stated that ICCROM "should be further commended for initiating the Africa 2009 programme to address conservation of immovable heritage in sub-Saharan Africa."[73] This, as he went on to explain, was because the programme recognised that "the problems facing conservation in African heritage were technical in nature and that solutions must integrate conservation into the larger environmental, social, cultural and economic development framework."[74] This problematic acceptance that the basic requirement of Museum and Heritage Studies in Africa is technical conservation skills acquisition is a position condemned by the critical Heritage Studies of the RITP-APMHS, which we discuss in the next chapter. Nonetheless, Abungu argued that the technical training strategy focus of Africa 2009 was based on the result of a 'preliminary needs assessment' by ICCROM of the state of conservation of immovable cultural heritage in Africa, which identified (among other challenges) the lack of qualified human resources capability in the technical conservation of Africa's immovable cultural resources. Africa 2009 was thus conceptualised and developed[75] to address these challenges by focusing on four main areas:

   (a) Organised training through seminars, workshops, and three-month training courses.
   (b) Promotion of networking and exchange of information and expertise through thematic seminars (directors' seminars, research, establishment of database of resource persons, etc.).
   (c) Resource and support mobilisation through increased awareness among wider audiences.
   (d) Project Cadre and Project Situés, aimed at improving conditions for conservation at specific sites.[76]

As revealed in the 'Final Report of the Africa 2009 First Regional course, held in Mombasa, Kenya from July to September 1999',[77] the course brought together a group of approximately 20 African heritage professionals to work towards the creation of a greater awareness of the most important issues in the area of conservation planning and management. The course also aimed at deriving a deepening of knowledge of the problems and challenges that are faced in carrying out conservation work in African contexts.[78] The nine-week course was divided into two main areas dealing with policy and practice at the national level, and with site planning and management.[79] According to the recruitment advertisement for the course: "participants must be professionals (architects, planners, archaeologists, managers) with a university degree and a minimum of three to five years' experience in heritage conservation." It was further outlined that "[t]hey must either be in charge of management/conservation of a major site or region within their countries; or have a significant decision-making role in regard to management/conservation of immovable cultural heritage within the central structure of their organisation."[80] Topics covered in the course were: Introduction to African Immovable Cultural Heritage and Heritage Conservation; Stakeholder Participation in Conservation of Cultural Heritage; Management Planning Exercise; Legal and Administrative Frameworks and Urban Conservation; Tourism and Inventory and Documentation; Partnership, Fundraising, and Advocacy.[81]

The last Africa 2009 course was the 11th regional course on the conservation and management of immovable cultural heritage in Africa, in Mombasa, Kenya, from July to October 2009. Compared to the first course presented in 1999, this was a 12-week course divided into two main parts:

> The first part deals with theoretical and policy framework of immovable heritage at international and local level, as well as current issues in immovable heritage conservation. The second part involves practical, hands-on exercise and lectures on the management planning process as applicable to conservation and management of immovable heritage.[82]

The two operative components of the Africa 2009 programme are Project Cadre and Project Situés. According to Abungu, "Project Cadre acted as the overall framework for the programme, offering a range of regional training and gathering and exchange of information and Project Situés was engaged in the improving of conservation at different sites by building awareness in the course of actual conservation projects."[83] As stated in the 2010 final report of the 11th Africa 2009 regional seminar, Project Situés ensured that Africa 2009 was deeply rooted in the realities of the field while responding to the specific needs of selected sites in terms of training and implementation of conservation activities. This was because Project Situés wase designed with an emphasis on a 'planned intervention' philosophy rather than the implementation of 'emergency works'.[84]

Project Cadre on the other hand was "developed at the regional level as the overall framework for the programme."[85] The report stated that 'Project Cadre' called for reflection and the progressive development of ideas, guaranteeing continuity within individual activities, and allowing for the dissemination of results obtained by the programme. Courses, seminars, research projects, and the improvement of networking were implemented, based on the realisation that the best way to treat problems is to work together, share ideas, and develop common frameworks, which can be adapted to specific local needs.[86]

Abungu applauded ICCROM for showing commitment to both movable and immovable cultural heritage in Africa, and for dealing "realistically with clear-cut issues concerning the conservation and management of the cultural heritage of the continent, which has added tremendous value to heritage protection and has made them an outstanding example of best practice emulated elsewhere in the world."[87] This, he argued, was because "the programme has been able to address the problems facing conservation through technical solutions, and to promote the successful integration of immovable cultural heritage within its social, environmental and economic environment."[88] As argued further by Abungu, a reason for the success of PREMA's technical conservation approach in African Museum and Heritage Studies was its 'participatory methods' and tangible results. According to him, this provided:

> A networking model for the sector, reinforced capacities in various areas and, above all, renewed confidence and enhanced skills among African heritage professionals. The participation of African heritage professionals and institutions gave rise to an awareness of responsibility for African heritage stemming from a new sense of ownership.[89]

Against the background of the funding crisis which befell the African cultural sector which reduced and, in most cases, dried up funding for Museum and Heritage Studies and training, as the case of the Jos centre attested, Abungu justifiably commended ICCROM for its commitment to Africa 2009 as "the only programme which has consistently, over a period of ten years, invested substantially in the preservation and management of immovable cultural heritage, an area in which", according to him, "African governments have not invested, even as custodians."[90] The return on this investment was the implementation of the UNESCO Global Strategy to 'add-on' African heritage to the World Heritage List (WHL).[91]

The Global Strategy was launched in 1994 by the World Heritage Committee for a representative, balanced, and credible World Heritage List with the aim to ensure that the List reflects the world's cultural and natural diversity of outstanding universal value.[92] It was further stated that by "adopting the Global Strategy, the World Heritage Committee wanted to broaden the definition of World Heritage to better reflect the full spectrum of our world's cultural and natural treasures and to provide a comprehensive framework and operational methodology for implementing the World Heritage Convention."[93] "This new vision", as it stated, "goes beyond the narrow definitions of heritage and strives to recognise and protect sites that are outstanding demonstrations of human co-existence with the land, as well as of human interactions, cultural co-existence, spirituality and creative expression."[94] Pivotal to the Global Strategy are efforts to encourage countries to become State Parties to the Convention, to prepare Tentative Lists and to prepare nominations of properties from categories and regions currently not well-represented on the World Heritage List.[95]

As noted by Abungu, it was thus "through Africa 2009, that it was realised that there was a need, not only to assist state parties in ratifying the 1972 Convention, but also to collaborate in the implementation of the Global Strategy to increase the representation of African heritage on the World Heritage List."[96] The Africa 2009 programme thus aimed to contribute to increase African representation on the World Heritage List by assisting to prepare files for the World Heritage List, encouraging the identification of Projects Situés to prepare management and conservation plans for sites identified on tentative national lists, and assisting to prepare international assistance requests to the African World Heritage Fund.[97]

The focus of AMHS from the training offered under the platform of Africa 2009 thus centred on the implementation of the Global Strategy. This included training to prepare or update 'Tentative Lists' and to nominate new sites through the 'Preparatory Assistance' programme that included both regional meetings and provision of technical and/or financial assistance.[98] As stated in the Africa 2009-2010 report: "in line with the Global Strategy, Africa 2009 has favoured the recognition of a broad spectrum of heritage properties, which are being prepared by African heritage institutions that can potentially be inscribed on the World Heritage List."[99]

Nonetheless, in a paper analysing the efficacy of the Global Strategy to remedy the inherent imbalance in the World Heritage System, Lasse Steiner and Bruno S. Frey traced the origin of the Global Strategy initiative to "the highly unequal distribution of Sites according to countries and continents."[100] They revealed that 46% of the Sites are in Europe, while only 9% are in Africa. This imbalance of World Heritage Sites according to continents and countries, they argued, has "been present from the beginning, and it has become a subject of major concern within the World Heritage Commission and the World Heritage Centre, UNESCO, and beyond."[101] Some scholars have questioned the legitimacy of the List and argued that "the concept of World Heritage is flawed by the fact that it privileges an idea originating in the West, which requires an attitude toward material culture that is distinctly European in origin."[102] Steiner and Frey therefore concluded that "the imbalance did not decrease and perhaps increased over time, thus reflecting the inability of the Global Strategy to achieve a more balanced distribution of Sites."[103]

The argument that the World Heritage List "was conceived, supported and nurtured by the industrially developed societies, reflecting concern for a type of heritage that was highly valued in those countries",[104] is a common criticism of the World Heritage System, especially in relation to African heritage and the World Heritage List. As Francesco Bandarin, the Director of the World Heritage Centre, acknowledged: "inscription has become a political issue. It is about prestige, publicity and economic development."[105] The World Heritage System is thus "highly politicised, as many political and bureaucratic representatives of countries consider it a worthwhile goal from which they personally profit."[106]

As seen in all the training of EPA-CHDA, PREMA, and Africa 2009, the focus and ultimate objective of heritage training in Africa became "the preparation of nomination dossiers for the World Heritage Committee[107] to increase the representation of African Heritage on the World Heritage List."[108] Notwithstanding claims that it "is concerned with a broad holistic development of African Heritage", its origin in conservation management and the focus on technical skills acquisition training for the preparation of dossiers and Conservation Management plans for application to be added to the World Heritage List continues to be the focus of its museum and heritage training programmes and activities.[109]

The African World Heritage Fund (AWHF) was launched in 2006 to support African State parties to implement the UNESCO Global Strategy of ensuring a geo-cultural balance on the World Heritage List. Towards this objective, AWHF put in place training programmes to build up competence of African heritage professionals in the development of nomination dossiers and management plans required by the World Heritage Committee when considering sites for listing on the World Heritage List.[110] This stated objective allows us to understand how the PREMA/CHDA/Africa 2009 approach to African Museum and Heritage Studies is a process of acquiring "technologies of heritage" to be added as an appendage to what Laurajane Smith referred to as the Authorised Heritage Discourse (AHD) through inscription on the World Heritage List.[111]

Towards critical African Museum and Heritage Studies

According to Corinne Kratz and Ivan Karp, ICOM, ICCROM, the Swedish International Development Cooperation Agency (SIDA), and the Swedish-African Museum Programme (SAMP) have been among the most important sustaining organisations for training African museums professionals, yet no one has considered the effects, both positive and negative, of these organisations on the work of museum professionals, especially in Africa.[112] Given this apt injunction by Kratz and Karp, it is necessary to understand the implications of these AHD-dictated, European-initiated AMHS in this brief overview of the history of museum and heritage training on the continent.

Notwithstanding the merits of UNESCO/PREMA/ICOM/ICCROM and other agencies' interventions in African museum training programmes, there are considerable problems in the orientations to Museum and Heritage Studies it advocated. As seen in the pedigree and orientation to Museum and Heritage Studies in these agencies' sponsored initiatives in Africa, they remain deeply Eurocentric in their ideological foundation, theoretical basis, and objectives. This includes the imposition, adoption, appropriation, and replication of European AHD as definitive of the orientation of AMHS. The peculiar, distinctive history of museums in Europe, which necessitated a specific training orientation and focus for European museum and heritage professionals, was universalised in Africa through uncritical appropriation, as seen in the AMHS in Africa.

Although the International Council of African Museums (AFRICOM), the central body for museums and heritage professionals in Africa, claimed the rationale for its existence in rather provocative language: "to kill the Western model of the museum in Africa so that new methods for the preservation and promotion of Africa's cultural heritage can be allowed to flourish,"[113] it continued to hold onto the apron strings of ICOM, which promised "to maintain close and privileged links with AFRICOM", which unfortunately is now defunct.[114] The implications of this orientation for AMHS is exemplified in the global strategy training designed to effect the 'add-on' of African heritage to the World Heritage List, without a critical engagement with the cultural politics implicit in this process. For example, as seen in the origin, history, development, and curricula of AMHS on the continent, the notion of African heritage as sub-Saharan without Egypt is taken for granted, as seen in the PREMA 'African' focus limited to sub-Saharan countries. Notwithstanding, Saouma-Ferero's still cautioned that it would be a 'non-achievement' if African experts did not "explore ways of understanding, defining and presenting their heritage from their own perspective rather than from the prevailing Eurocentric view."[115] However, the philosophy and pedagogical orientation of museums and heritage in Africa continues to depend on European models of heritage training, which dictated technical skills as definitive of AMHS. This is what dictated an Afrocentric turn, which would empower Africans "to present and define their heritage in ways that highlighted the specificity of African heritage in their own terms without necessarily referring to European categories of appreciation."[116] The problem is that this "highlighted specificity of African heritage" was construed in these training programmes as traditional, ethnic sub-Saharan. The feature of specificity of African heritage was defined by the lack of distinction between nature and culture, and beliefs in importance of sacred sites and the intrinsic relationship between tangible and intangible. These features of African heritage, including the role of traditional rulers and indigenous knowledge marked by oral tradition, risked not only essentialising the notion of African heritage as a distinct human experience shared only by a distinct breed of humanity, but also of relegating African heritage to a confined, marginalised exteriority, based on its supposedly specific African features.

As can be seen in numerous writings, African heritage is defined and conceptualised in these UNESCO/ICCROM/ICOM-sponsored training programmes as limited to inherited birth rights[117] of sub-Saharan Africa, consisting mainly of natural sites and pre-colonial cultural artefacts in intangible form, which were destroyed through colonialism and risk disappearing in the post-colonial present. The approach to Heritage Studies, according to this notion of African heritage, is thus the acquisition of technical skills of heritage conservation to retrieve and preserve the remnants of these inherited, destroyed, and neglected pre-colonial heritages, deemed to be at risk of disappearing through decay.[118]

It is the argument of this chapter that the emphasis on technical skills acquisition without questioning the power dynamics and cultural politics and epistemic hegemony inherent in museum and heritage as concepts and practices, with a specific history and geo-cultural political agenda places it on a first-order level of AMHS at best. While all the training initiatives laid emphasis on socio-economic development as a desired outcome of Heritage Studies through engagement with state parties in implementing UNESCO guidelines, one topic that is missing in all the training initiatives is lack of engagement with the cultural politics of heritage and its implications for Museum and Heritage Studies in Africa. Interestingly however, in 1998, when PREMA was inaugurating EPA Benin, and later PDMA in Mombasa, and Africa 2009 was beginning, a process was developing in South Africa between RIM, UWC, and UCT. These three institutions jointly convened a postgraduate diploma programme in Museum and Heritage Studies, which was renamed the African Programme in Museum and Heritage Studies (APMHS) in 2004. The programme was "distinctive in that the kind of Museum and Heritage Studies it offers is driven by an emphasis on conceptual understanding of the terrain of public culture and of the challenges of social and institutional transformation and of the work of representation."[119] This was "linked to new possibilities of developing significant layers of public intellectuals and fostering critical public scholarship as the central component of a democratic public sphere."[120]

In distinguishing itself from other heritage training initiatives in Africa, the programme stated that "through linking together theory with practice, the RITP-APMHS is able to challenge the emphasis of several African postcolonial AMHS which have tended to argue for creating mostly technically oriented museum professionals." The APMHS approach to Museum and Heritage Studies was therefore premised on the objective of avoiding the "danger that Heritage Studies will become a form of technical training and a 'new breed of heritage workers' will continue to be manual functionaries".[121] Notwithstanding this apparent rejection of a focus on technical training as an approach to Museum and Heritage Studies, the programme nonetheless incorporated technical training by offering courses in heritage conservation technologies of collections, conservation management, and Public Programming, as part of the electives offered by RIM. Despite this incorporation of training in conservation technologies, the next chapter will attempt an exploration of the fundamental distinction between the approach to Museum and Heritage Studies on the continent and the approach to AMHS in South Africa.

Endnotes

1. E.N. Arinze. 2002. 'Museum Training Issues in Africa'. *Research Paper for ICOM\ICTOP Study Series*, 10:4. http://bit.ly/3M8uHSg [Accessed 26 February 2010].
2. C. Rassool. 2018. 'Building a Critical Museology in Africa'. In: T. Laely, M. Meyer & R. Schwere (eds.), *Museum Cooperation Between Africa and Europe: A New Field for Museum Studies*, Bielefeld: transcript Verlag 2018, xxii- xxiii. https://doi.org/10.1515/9783839443811-005
3. C. Rassool. 2018. 'Building a Critical Museology in Africa'. In: T. Laely, M. Meyer & R. Schwere (eds.), *Museum Cooperation Between Africa and Europe: A New Field for Museum Studies*, Bielefeld: transcript Verlag, xxii-xxiii. https://doi.org/10.1515/9783839443811-005
4. Ibid.
5. K. Nkrumah. 1970. *Consciencism; Philosophy and Ideology for De-Colonization*. New York, NY: Monthly Review Press.
6. See for instance P. Abungu. 2011. *The Role of Heritage Training in Community Development: The Case of the Centre for Heritage Development in Africa (CHDA)*. London: Lambert Academic Publisher.
7. Publications on Museum and Heritage are mainly through ICCROM-UNESCO Publications. See for instance L. Abungu & G. Abungu (eds.). 2006. 'Africa: A Continent of Achievements'. *Museum International*, LVIII(1-2):229-230.
8. See L. Witz's review of A.B.A. Adande & E. Arinze (eds.). 2005. Museum and Urban Culture in West Africa. *International Journal of Heritage Studies*, 11(2):173-179.
9. L. Smith. 2006. *Uses of Heritage*. New York, NY: Routledge, 17. https://doi.org/10.4324/9780203602263
10. Ibid., 4.
11. E.N. Arinze. 1998. 'African Museums: The Challenge of Change'. *Museum International*, 50(1):31-37. https://doi.org/10.1111/1468-0033.00133; G. Abungu. 2009. 'ICCROM and Africa: Changing the Cultural Landscape in Museums and Immovable Heritage'. *Museum International*, 61(3):62-69. https://doi.org/10.1111/j.1468-0033.2009.01694.x; T. Little (ed.). 2001. *PREMA and the Preservation of Africa's Cultural Heritage: PREMA 1990-2000*. Rome: ICCROM.; G. Saouma-Ferero. 2006. 'Africa 2009: A Story of African Empowerment'. *Museum International*, 58(1-2):83-94. https://doi.org/10.1111/j.1468-0033.2006.00554_1.x
12. Technology of heritage – UNESCO promotion of archive, artefacts, ritual practices, performances, and material spaces as technologies for producing pasts and futures. F. de Jong & M. Rowlands (eds.). 2006. *Reclaiming Heritage: Alternative Imaginaries of Memory in West Africa*. Walnut Creek, CA: Life Coast Press Inc., 16.
13. See L. Witz. 'Towards a History of Post-Apartheid Pasts in South African Museums'. Paper at Re-Imagining Postcolonial Futures: Knowledge Transactions and Contest of Culture in African Present, UWC, 8-11 July 2009, on the concept of 'add-on' of African heritage.
14. T. Little. 2000. *The Future of Heritage in South Africa: Collaboration and Partnership*. www.sanch.org/colloquia/little.htm [Accessed 14 June 2010]; See also http://bit.ly/3nHnkHd
15. T. Rico. 2021. 'Heritage Studies After Said'. *Public Books*. http://bit.ly/3nErWhx [Accessed 21 November 2021].

16 ICTOP – International Committee for the Training of Personnel: ICTOP's primary aim is to promote training and professional development and establish standards for museum personnel throughout their careers. ICTOP works closely with other ICOM committees to achieve this aim. Its activities include the publication of a newsletter twice a year, the periodic publication of the International Directory of Museum Training, and the organisation of annual meetings/conferences. ICTOP also acts as an advisor for the establishment of syllabi for personnel training. It is a body of ICOM, the international organisation of museums and museum professionals, which is committed to the conservation, continuation, and communication to society of the world's natural and cultural heritage, present and future, tangible and intangible. Created in 1946, and based in Paris (France), ICOM is a non-governmental organisation (NGO) maintaining formal relations with UNESCO (http://www.unesco.org/) and having a consultative status with the United Nations' Economic and Social Council. http://bit.ly/3nuxx9U [Accessed 10 August 2010].

17 H.R. Singleton. 1987. 'Museum Training: Status and Development'. *Museum International*, XXXIX(4):221.

18 Ibid., 222.

19 Ibid.

20 Ibid., 223.

21 Ibid.

22 Ibid.

23 Ibid.

24 Ibid.

25 Ibid.

26 Ibid.

27 P.J. Boylan. 1987. 'Museum Training: A Central Concern of ICOM for Forty Years'. *Museum International*, XXXIX(4):225-230. https://doi.org/10.1111/j.1468-0033.1987.tb00698.x

28 Ibid., 226.

29 Ibid., 227. According to ICTOP Terminology, "Museology is the branch of knowledge concerned with the study of the theories, procedures, concepts, and organisation of museums. Museography is the application of that thinking in museum".
'ICTOP in Lubbock, Texas'. *ICTOP Annual Meeting Museums: Catalysts for Community Development Resolutions*, 14(1):11, 1996.

30 Ibid., 227.

31 Ibid., 228.

32 M. Segger. 1996. *Introductory Remarks, ICOM International Committee for the Training of Personnel*. Annual meeting, Lubbock, TX. http://bit.ly/3G9257U [Accessed 21 March 2021].

33 E.N. Arinze. 1998. 'African Museums: The Challenge of Change'. *Museum International*, 50(1):30. https://doi.org/10.1111/1468-0033.00133

34 Ibid., 31.

35 Ibid.

36 E.N. Arinze. 2002. 'Museum Training Issues in Africa'. *Research Paper for ICOM\ICTOP Study series*, 10:1. http://bit.ly/3zo2Ndt [Accessed 26 February 2010].

37 See L. Dondolo & O. Morakinyo. 2021. *Afrocentric Turn in African Heritage Studies*. Cape Town: Ace Publishers.

38 Arinze. 'African Museums: The Challenges of Change', 32.
39 Arinze. 'Museum Training Issues in Africa', 3.
40 E.N. Arinze. 1987. 'Training in African Museums: The Role of the Centre for Museum Studies Jos'. *Museum International*, XXXIX(4):278. https://doi.org/10.1111/j.1468-0033.1987.tb00711.x
41 Ibid., 278.
42 Ibid., 280.
43 Ibid., 279.
44 Ibid., 278.
45 Ibid.
46 Ibid.
47 Arinze. 'African Museums: The Challenges of Change', 31.
48 Ibid., 32.
49 Ibid. Arinze explained how after UNESCO withdrew their funding for the Jos programme, the Nigerian government was only able to sustain the programme for a limited period before it collapsed.
50 See F.T. Masao. 1987. 'The Balance Between Domestic Needs and International Aid in Museum Training'. *Museum International*, XXXIX(4):275-277. https://doi.org/10.1111/j.1468-0033.1987.tb00710.x
51 Arinze. 'African Museums: The Challenges of Change', 34.
52 'Preventive Conservation in Museums of Africa'. Special programme of ICCROM (International Centre for the Study of the Preservation and Restoration of Cultural Property) for African Museums South of the Sahara. https://bit.ly/42Yr1Zd [Accessed 20 April 2012].
53 Little. PREMA and the Preservation',10.
54 Ibid.,10.
55 Abungu. 'ICCROM and Africa', 63.
56 Ibid., 64.
57 Little. 'Collaborations and Partnership', 2.
58 Ibid., 5.
59 Abungu. 'ICCROM and Africa', 64.
60 Little. 'Collaborations and Partnerships', 10.
61 Little. PREMA and the Preservation', 10.
62 Ibid., 15.
63 Little. PREMA and the Preservation', 22.
64 Ibid., 16.
65 Ibid., 15, 49.
66 Ibid.
67 Little. 'Collaborations and Partnerships', 6.
68 'Centre for Heritage Development in Africa (CHDA)'. https://bit.ly/40AdPs1 [Accessed 23 June 2010].
69 'People are the Real Wealth of a Nation'. *Centre for Heritage Development in Africa (CHDA) Brochure*, 2011, 3. https://bit.ly/3M9dPe5 [Accessed 14 July 2010].
70 Ibid, 7.

71 Abungu. *ICCROM and Africa*, 66.
72 J. King. 1999. 'Final Report of the Africa 2009 Regional Course, Mombasa, Kenya, 5 July – 3 September 1999'. https://bit.ly/40BI41O [Accessed 8 December 2010].
73 Abungu. 'ICCROM and Africa', 65.
74 Ibid., 123.
75 Abungu. 'ICCROM and Africa'.
76 Ibid.
77 King. 'Final Report of the Africa 2009', 2.
78 Ibid., 2.
79 Ibid., 5.
80 Ibid., 5.
81 Ibid., 7.
82 B. Rakotomamonjy. 2010. 'Conservation in Immovable Cultural Heritage: Final Report, 2010'. https://bit.ly/42Yw247 [Accessed 3 August 2010].
83 Abungu. 'ICCROM and Africa', 63.
84 King. 'Final Report of the Africa 2009, 2010', 10.
85 Ibid.
86 Ibid, 8.
87 Abungu. 'ICCROM and Africa', 69.
88 Ibid.
89 Ibid., 69.
90 Ibid., 68.
91 King. 'Final Report of the Africa 2009, 2010', 20.
92 'UNESCO World Heritage Convention Global Strategy'. http://bit.ly/40SbCYF [Accessed 20 May 2010].
93 Ibid.
94 Ibid.
95 Ibid.
96 Abungu. 'ICCROM and Africa', 67.
97 Ibid., 68.
98 King. 'Final Report of the Africa 2009, 2010', 20.
99 Ibid., 26.
100 L. Steiner & B.S Frey. 2011. 'Imbalances in World Heritage List: Did the UNESCO Global Strategy Work?'. *Working Paper*, No. 14, University of Zurich, 3. https://bit.ly/3nFJlWR [Accessed 17 February 2010].
101 Ibid., 3.
102 Ibid., 7.
103 Ibid., 2.
104 Ibid., 7.
105 Ibid., 8.
106 Ibid., 7.
107 CHDA Brochure, 6.
108 King. 'Final Report of the Africa 2009, 2010', 26.

109 'Centre for Heritage Development in Africa'. https://bit.ly/40AdPs1 [Accessed 23 June 2010]. The training it has conducted, as stated on its website, includes: Training in Conservation of Movable Heritage, Training in Conservation of Immovable Heritage and Fund-raising; Training in Public Programming and Education; Training in the Development of Nomination Dossier for World Heritage List; Training in Heritage Impact Assessment; Training in Exhibition Design; Training in Collections Management and Storage; and Training in Stakeholder Participation.

110 The stated objectives of the course are "to give competence to African natural and cultural heritage professionals, thereby improving the quality of African nomination dossiers submitted to the World Heritage Committee; to increase the number and diversity of African heritage properties on the World Heritage List. To reinforce the network of heritage professionals working on African World Heritage sites and set up a support and follow up mechanism to facilitate delivery of expected outcomes". https://bit.ly/40AdPs1 [Accessed 23 June 2010].

111 Smith. Uses of Heritage, 37.

112 I. Karp, C.A. Kratz, L. Szwaja, T. Ybarra-Frausto with G. Buntinx, B. Kirshenblatt-Gimblett & C. Rassool (eds.). 2006. 'Introduction'. *Museum Frictions: Public Cultures/Global Transformation*. Durham: Duke University Press, 15.

113 J.R. Glaser & B.C. Craig (eds.). 'Birth of the International Council of African Museums'. *Information on Training, Newsletter of ICTOP: the ICOM International Committee for the Training of Personnel*, 16(2): November 1999-2001. https://bit.ly/3nFdGVO [Accessed 9 July 2010].

114 Ibid.

115 G. Saouma-Ferero. 2006. 'Africa 2009: A Story of African Empowerment'. *Museum International*, 58(1-2):87. https://doi.org/10.1111/j.1468-0033.2006.00554_1.x

116 Ibid, 87.

117 See CHDA definition of Heritage discussed earlier, CHDA Brochure 2011.

118 Abungu and Arinze stated specifically that PREMA was developed to prevent the deterioration of collections and Africa 2009 to address immovable heritage increasingly at risk. See Abungu. ICCROM and Africa, 63.

119 Proposal to Rockefeller Foundation for the Development of An African Programme in Museum and Heritage Studies: Submitted by the Cape Higher Education Consortium, February 2003. Cape Town: CHR archives, UWC).

120 Ibid.

121 L. Witz. 2001. 'Museum and Heritage Studies: An Interim Position. Workshop on Mapping Alternatives: Debating New Heritage Practices in South Africa, 25-26 September. Cape Town: Project on Public Past, History Department, UWC and RESUNACT, UCT, 12.

The Transformation of Museum and Heritage Studies in South Africa 5

To appreciate the extent to which the RITP-APMHS orientation to Museum and Heritage Studies is innovative, radical, and progressive compared to other pre-existing programmes in South Africa and the rest of the continent as discussed in the previous chapter, it is necessary to trace the history of Museum and Heritage Studies in South Africa specifically. This exploration is necessary as it will both identify how RITP-APMHS is different from other programmes of Museum and Heritage Studies in South Africa and the continent and show the limits and possibilities that it may open for a critical Afrocentric turn in AMHS. Discussing the history of Museum Studies and training in South Africa also allows us to explore the kind of training and studies required and appropriate for dismantling the colonial museum as a means to transform and decolonise Museum and Heritage Studies from its racist exclusionary ethos to a decolonised African-centred orientation that responds to the need for epistemic and social justice. Although more needs to be done in decolonising and transforming Museum and Heritage Studies, it is undeniable that there has been immense tangible transformation in the heritage sector in South Africa. The extent to which heritage is decolonised depends on how far it is on the Afrocentric turn of dismantling the colonial museum. To what extent is the RITP-APMHS transformative of Museum and Heritage Studies in South Africa and what is its distinctive edge compared to previous and current programmes of the study of museum and heritage in Africa?

A way of answering these questions is to explore the origin and history of the development of museum training and Heritage Studies[1] in South Africa through its intellectual history and sociology of knowledge at different stages of its development. This exploration will entail an investigation of how the education and training in South African museums evolved, which theories and ideas underpinned it, what its ethos was, and how its ethos was inculcated in the training and education of museum workers. Here, ethos refers to the underlying fundamental guiding values and beliefs that reflect the ideology underpinning and sustaining its activities and is projected by the peculiar specific disposition of museums. This ethos which drives the orientation and operations of the museum is systematically inculcated in its operators through informal apprenticeship training and formal study and training programmes, structure, and pedagogy. At any historical period, the prevailing cultural political ideology dictates the principles that determine the museum ethos which the Museum Studies and training inculcate and project through its curriculum and study programmes.

As the history of museum development in South Africa and its accompanying studies and training reveals, the ideology of white supremacy dictated the founding ethos of the museums, which was geared towards sustaining and projecting this ideology. The ethos of transformation towards decolonisation thus requires a different ideological aptitude. It must be matched by the requisite technical training and critical theories of race and heritage to undertake the task of transformation. This transformation needs to overturn the legacy of the colonial Museum and Heritage Studies through scholarship and training tailored for redress and social justice. We dig into the intergenerational cultural resistance archive of the African resistance tradition that blossomed in the struggle against apartheid.[2] We aim to locate the archive of/for the training of a different museum and heritage ethos and assess the extent of how this ethos of culture as an act of freedom pervaded the realities of the transformation of Museum and Heritage Studies in South African museums, which has hitherto held its collections exclusively "for the future welfare of the race".[3]

Development of Museum and Heritage Studies in South Africa

Given the intrinsic symbiosis of museums' strategic orientation to the kind of studies and training required to actualise its objectives, we can determine what types of training were required, desired, and undertaken at different stages of museum development in South Africa through its documented histories. While the records of the South African Museum Association (SAMA) chronicle the timeline of the development of museums in South Africa, from which one can narrativise the development of the types of museum training and studies in the country, Mxolisi Dlamuka's study of the origin of museums in South Africa, specifically KwaZulu-Natal, allows us to extrapolate it to the history of Museum and Heritage Studies in South Africa.[4] This periodisation of museum history in South Africa into different eras dictated by the prevailing political ideology is important because it allows us to identify the prevailing ethos of the training offered and to critically engage the distinctions between the different periods in the history of museums in South Africa. This is necessary as a means to evaluate and assess the differences between the colonial, apartheid, and democratic periods and to identify, assess, and reflect on what has changed in the democratic dispensation from 1994.

The questions at the heart of this chapter's discussion is: To what extent has the ethos of the museum changed, transformed, and decolonised, what are its prospects of sustainability, and what are the possible challenges to its future? We thus critique the defining ethos of the different periods in the development of museums in South Africa to understand its accompanying Museum Studies and training. This allows us to highlight the fundamental difference between the pre-1994 period and the contemporary post-1994 dispensation. By focusing on the post-1994 period, we can determine how the variant of the post-1994 Museum and Heritage Studies in South Africa laid the foundation for the current discourse to decolonise museums and heritage through critical Heritage Studies and the Afrocentric turn in AHS. Although the periods seamlessly overlap, for analytical purposes, we have divided the history of the development of Museum Studies and training in South Africa into two periods: pre- and post-1994. Although the first museum in South Africa was established in 1825, we begin our discussion of pre-1994 Museum and Heritage Studies from 1935 when SAMA was established, because it marked the beginning of formal Museum Studies and training in the country. The post-1994 period focuses on the changes that happened in the sector because of the political imperatives of the democratic transformation.

We start in 1935 when the idea of a formal association of museum professionals in South Africa was mooted, then jump to its eventual inauguration in 1936 in Kimberly to show the development of South African museums and Heritage Studies and training before and during the apartheid period. We want to make an argument that there is a link between the Carnegie Corporation Report of the Poor White Problem in South Africa,[5] the Carnegie Corporation Report on the Museums and Art Galleries of British Africa,[6] the British Museums Association, and the subsequent development of Museum Studies and training in South Africa. What if part of the strategies as identified by the Carnegie Reports for solving the poor white problem in South Africa was to use education through the museum to teach white supremacist consciousness, given the role of museums as institutions and spaces for teaching and the cultivation of citizenry? Given the critical importance of historical consciousness to human survival, is it preposterous to think that what the report on poor whites found as part of the causes of those conditions was that they lacked historical consciousness of white supremacy and the privileges that it possesses, and that the museum can be marshalled to correct it through the projection of white supremacist history? Based on the acknowledged fact that the report on poor whites laid the foundation for apartheid, can the other reports, specifically the Museum Report by the same institution in the same year, avoid equal criticism of a white supremacist agenda?

Elda Grobler and Fransjohan Pretorius' article which described the relationship of the Carnegie Corporation and the British Museum Association (BMA) in the development of SAMA urged "today's museum fraternity in South Africa [to] recognise the role played by the British Museums Association and Carnegie Corporation in the 1930s and pay tribute to their vital contribution to museum matters in those early days."[7] This appreciation is appropriate because it was through the connection of these two institutions that Museum Studies and training in South African museums were initiated. In the next section, we explore how the Carnegie reports' recommendation for the formation of SAMA can be construed as laying the foundation of Museum Studies and training in South Africa.

While the report on poor whites was the most popular and most commented on, prior to it and the museum report, there was a report on libraries which also recommended "the establishment of a library association, modelled on the Library Association of the United Kingdom, to foster library development and to promote professional education and training of librarians". As noted by M. Nassimbeni, this points to the longstanding connection between the Carnegie Corporation and South Africa by showing that "prior to the establishment of the Corporation in 1911, Andrew Carnegie had made generous gifts to several South African communities, among them Vryheid and the town of Harrismith, for the construction of libraries, an endeavour that became a hallmark of Carnegie's world-wide philanthropy."[8] Therefore, although the Carnegie Report covers the British Empire, there was a greater emphasis on South Africa in the Africa survey.[9] Apparently, this bias in favour of South Africa was justified by the racist belief that "the Union of South Africa was a predominantly white area."[10] Thus, despite mentioning the evidence of museum appreciation by Africans through a museum leaflet in isiXhosa to attract an African audience to the East London Museum for instance, the report was premised on the racist belief that museums "were only likely to thrive where there was a large white or other literate population."[11]

This position taken by the report, and considering the connection of the poor white report and the museum report, begins to reveal how the museum was co-opted and marshalled to serve the exclusionary racist white supremacist ideology of the empire. This allows us to see not only the ethos projected by the museum during this era but also the basis of projecting white supremacist ideology and the reasons for the dehumanising depiction and exclusion of Africans from the museum cemented during the formal apartheid period. As argued by Jeremy Seekings, the concern with the condition of poor whites was not out of any altruistic reasons by the rich whites nor was the concern "rooted in the militancy of 'poor whites', but rather in the combination of their voting strength and their importance to other white classes as allies in the defence of 'civilisation', that is, white supremacy."[12] Basically, what drove the concern of white elites for poor whites is that they erode and degrade white supremacist arrogance of inherent superiority.

The five volumes of the Carnegie Corporation report of 1932 were "informed by ideology and prejudice more than research"[13] and covered the economic, psychological, educational, health, and sociological aspects of the 'poor white' phenomenon. Significantly, the report was motivated by the concern that unless something was done to help poor whites develop white supremacist consciousness, racial deterioration and miscegenation were inevitable. That is why the term 'poor whites' referred not only to those whites who are poor in material possessions but also those who lack personal development, white supremacist consciousness, and its accompanying privileges. The term 'poor white' was based on the racist assumption that whites were naturally expected to have a higher standard of living than the native or 'coloured' populations, so poverty among whites has less to do with material possessions than the fact that they are not conscious of their whiteness as a badge of superiority and privileges. According to the report, poor whites are deemed to possess "a narrow and confused outlook", thus "lacking enterprise, initiative and self-reliance".[14]

Therefore, the central thesis of the poor white report was that the condition of being white and poor in the midst of Africans is abnormal and due to psychological defects such as "poor intelligence or suffering from some physical infirmity, or failings of character."[15] For instance, 'The Race Welfare Society' went as far as suggesting that 'poor whites' were mentally defective and should be sterilised or, if sufficiently responsible, taught to use contraceptives.[16] Thus, central to the reasons for the problems of the poor whites contained in the report was "a feeling of inferiority and lack of self-respect, ignorance and credulity, leading to a lack of industry and ambition, and unsettledness of mode of life" among them.[17] The solution as emphasised in the report's recommendations is strident with white supremacist doctrinaire education for the inculcation of a white supremacist consciousness. As revealed by Seekings, the report resolved that the poor needed to be 'rehabilitated' by assisting them to develop new personal and psychological qualities, and not simply by providing them with opportunities. It emphasised that rehabilitation requires "a change in the person" and not just a "change of circumstances". It thus insisted that "the poor ought to be trained in thrift, self-help, temperance, health, solidarity and racial self-respect."[18] It is important to note the unapologetic racist agenda of the report through its emphasis of teaching solidarity and racial pride for inculcating white supremacist ideology so that the poor can regain "their lost character and self-reliance."[19] This project of raising white supremacist consciousness as a solution to the poor white problem is the point where the museum enters and links the two reports, and if we agree that the museum is an ideological apparatus, we can see how the museum was mobilised during this period to inculcate a white supremacist ideology as part of the solution to the poor white problem.

Although Grobler and Pretorius seem to imply that the poor white report and the museum report were divergent and unconnected, Nassimbeni argued that the combination of the poor white report, the South African libraries report, and the museum report, all funded and commissioned by Carnegie, almost concurrently and overlapping had far-reaching socio-political consequences for contemporary South Africa. This as she argued, was specifically because they laid the foundation for the perennial problem of the white supremacist ideology in South Africa, especially in its ideological and structural orientation of libraries and museums.[20] Further evidence of the connectedness of the reports can be seen in a recommendation to merge the South African library with the museum. As revealed by Nassimbeni in retrospect, "although the museum sector did not adopt one of the options recommended by Carnegie Corporation New York (CCNY) of becoming a section of the new South African library association, choosing rather to model itself on the British Museum Association, it is tantalising to imagine how different the consequences might have been for both these professions had the museologists followed the path of partnership with the librarians as at present there is little interaction between these two sectors both concerned with memory institutions."[21]

From a firm ideological commitment to the British African Colonial Empire, and imbued with an imperialistic fervour, with an eye on how the museum can serve and be part of the solution to the poor white problem in South Africa, the Carnegie Museum Report made some recommendations concerning funding, staff, research, and publications, and on the necessity of employing taxidermists. Given our concern with Museum Studies and training, we highlight the recommendation for the establishment of SAMA modelled on the BMA and its direct effect on the development of museums studies and training in this study. Significantly, as revealed by Grobler and Pretorius, it was made explicit that "the first duty of the Association was to serve the Empire and the British Association, and that the BMA should be regarded as the recognised authority and centre for museum interests throughout the Empire."[22]

In response to the Carnegie Museum Report's recommendation, the government, through the Secretary of Interior, invited officials of museums in South Africa to meet and form an Association of Museums in South Africa on the side-line of the South African Association for the Advancement of Science meeting in Paarl in 1935. The directive contained the structure and procedures to be followed including a draft constitution of the association to be approved by members. As stated in the SAMA 50 years commemorative publication:

> It was recommended that an annual conference of this body should be held so that contact and cooperation between the museums could be promoted. [...] [W]ith this first circular went a Draft Constitution of the proposed South African Museum Association, which stated that: The objects of the Association should be:
> (1) To encourage helpful relations amongst museums of all kinds, including art galleries, and persons interested in such institutions,
> (2) To improve and extend the museum service in South Africa,
> (3) To increase and diffuse knowledge of all matters relating to museums and art galleries, and to apply such knowledge to South African conditions, and
> (4) To organise short demonstration courses of instructions for the benefit of museums and art gallery assistants.[23]

While the fourth objective of the association to "organise short demonstration courses" directly points to the origin of Museum Studies and training in South Africa through the formation of SAMA, the connection to the poor white report can be seen clearly in the third objective of the association: "increase and diffuse knowledge of all matters relating to museums and art galleries, and to apply such knowledge to South African conditions". If one reads between the lines and unpacks the deeper meaning, one understands that the South African condition that informed the recommendation to form a museum association was based on a racist agenda of using the museum as an ideological apparatus to inculcate a white supremacist consciousness.

This first attempt at forming the association in Paarl in 1935 was unsuccessful due to the low turn-out of participants, but through the committed effort of Dr C.J. Swierstra, then Director of the Transvaal Museum, who became the first President of SAMA, and funding from Carnegie, SAMA was eventually established in 1936 in Kimberly. The constitution of the association, drafted by the Secretary of Interior, was adopted along with the format of an annual conference suggested in the circular. Thus, unlike most professional associations which are usually formed by the initiative of its members to project and promote its interests, SAMA was a government-initiated, BMA-constituted, and Carnegie-funded initiative. It should be noted, however, that although SAMA was government initiated and approved, it broke ranks with the government's apartheid regime from 1975 to 1995 when it renamed itself the 'Southern' rather than the 'South' African Museum Association. This was meant to remove the exclusive focus on South Africa to accommodate the sub-region, but also to escape the confines of the dictates of the apartheid government. This defiance of the apartheid policy costed SAMA, with regard to government recognition and support during this period. The history of SAMA as an organisation is an interesting field of research beyond the scope of this book, and our focus is limited to the origin and historical development of Museum and Heritage Studies as it pertains to the history of SAMA. In furtherance of its founding objective, staff training was a key focus of the association and the formal process of museum training in South Africa began when an Educational Committee was formally inaugurated in 1955 through the efforts of Dr John Pringle, who became its first chairman from 1955 until 1971.[24] To better situate the RITP-APMHS, we will briefly discuss the chronology of the development of Museum Studies and training in South Africa, starting with the BMA Diploma and Technical Certificate.

British Museum Association (BMA) diploma

The BMA diploma, established in 1935, constituted the foundation of Museum Studies as a professional qualification for museologists throughout the British Empire and its conferment was "evidence of knowledge and experience in the principles of museum service, administration and museum technique."[25] A university degree was desirable and encouraged for enrolment in the diploma, but not compulsory. The curriculum of the diploma consisted of courses in museum history and philosophy, museum organisation and management, and a choice of selected academic subjects: history, palaeontology, administration, museum techniques, and a specialised demonstration course. It was described as "a syllabus featuring instruction in general museum work and more specialised branches of museum work, as well as many practical elements – including a dreaded final exam in which students were presented with a table of assorted objects to identify."[26]

The beginning of formal Museum Studies and training in South Africa, seemingly the first on the African continent, can be located as an outcome of the Carnegie report that recommended the establishment of SAMA. According to SAMA's archival records, the culmination of the effort of the SAMA education committee which was inaugurated in 1955, was the facilitation of the award of the BMA Diploma and technical certificate for its members. Necessitated by an increasing training requirement of its members because of an extension of the educational functions of the museum and the professional value of the BMA diploma, and obviously not unconnected to the Carnegie Corporation's existing relationship to BMA and SAMA, "SAMA sought the assistance of the British Museum Association for training support."[27] This set the process of official training programmes of museum professionals in South Africa through the BMA in motion. Beginning in 1955, six members of SAMA were accredited as fellows of BMA to moderate the awarding of the BMA diploma and 13 applications were received for the first batch of students, although only 10 were qualified. The facilitation programme of acquiring the BMA diploma through SAMA continued late into the 1980s. However, it was discontinued for logistical reasons amid the growing political reactions to the crisis of the apartheid situation in the 1980s, which drove the intensification of efforts to launch a South African national museum diploma as we show later in this section. The facilitation of the BMA award from its inception incorporated a parallel SAMA technical certificate. As revealed in the minutes of a meeting of the SAMA executives in April 1956, the origin of the "SAMA Technical Certificate" was to accommodate applicants who did not qualify for admission to the BMA diploma. As recorded in the minutes of the SAMA education committee, "several applicants for registration as student members of the Diploma award has not been accepted as they had not matriculated and consequently, were ineligible. But they might be considered for the technical certificate award. After consideration it was resolved to adopt the technical certificate scheme."[28]

The technical certificate

Right from the inception of the BMA diploma, SAMA was advised by BMA to organise its own technical certificate award, modelled on the BMA technical certificate, in response to an inquiry of how to accommodate applicants who lack matriculation certificates as this was the minimum qualification required for eligibility to the BMA diploma programme. The SAMA technical certificate programme started in 1963 to meet the demand for technical training of staff for the budding museum sector. It was modelled on apprenticeship training in the museum, with a tutor at the same institution as the student appointed to mentor the student and ensure that the student is exposed to training courses and recommended literature.[29] Ten subjects were offered for the examination with zoological preparation toppling the number of registrations followed by artwork and cultural history. Other subjects included: archaeology, biology, ethnology, geology, palaeontology, photography, and general techniques.[30] The technical certificate was the longest training programme in South Africa, operating uninterruptedly from 1963 till 1995.

The National Diploma in Museum Technology

In 1972, SAMA initiated discussions on collaboration with the Cape College for Advanced Technical Education to explore the pioneering of a post-matric National Diploma in Museum Technology, which after many frustrating administrative delays culminated in a National Diploma in Museum Technology at the Cape Technikon in 1978. The three-year National Diploma, which is equivalent to a bachelor's degree, graduated its first cohort of seven students in 1981. It was suspended in 1982 and resuscitated in 1983 but seemed to have finally discontinued as the Education Committee chairman's report of 1985/6 indicated.[31] A correspondence version of the National Diploma in Museum Technology was subsequently offered by Technikon RSA in Johannesburg in the early 1990s, but this was also discontinued in 2001 after 12 years due to low student intake from museum staff.

Postgraduate diploma in Museology

Concurrent with the national diploma for technicians' initiatives, and ongoing enrolment for the BMA diploma by museum professionals, the University of Pretoria (UP) started a postgraduate diploma programme in Museology in 1974 and Stellenbosch University (SU) followed in 1976. These postgraduate diploma courses offering academic training were oriented towards the Human Sciences for professionals in museums as compared to the technical diploma course for technical museum staff. The Museology course at SU for instance was based at the Department of Afrikaans Cultural History and UP's' course also tilted towards cultural history with an emphasis on archaeology and ethnology. These two programmes ran into the 1990s. UP still offers Museum Studies programme which incorporates Heritage Studies,[32] while SU's course has since fizzled out. As noted in a SAMA 1979 Education Committee report on the Museum Studies course offered by UP in 1978/1979 which was structured as an extra-mural class compared to the full-residential SU course:

> The impression gain[ed] was of a Diploma of a very high standard with students having an excellent background in Museology. All aspects of museum work were well covered and in addition basic principles of administration (so lacking in many museums) are also given. Ethics of collecting and other neglected fields are discussed.[33]

From 1984, the courses and programmes of Museum Studies and training in South Africa were primarily: the technical certificate that started in 1963, the National Diploma in Museum Technology offered by the Cape Technikon in 1978, Technikon RSA in Johannesburg, and the postgraduate diploma offered by both UP and SU, running from 1974 and 1976 respectively. In addition to these programmes, Rhodes University started offering a museological option in an honours course in history from 1992, which together with other existing programmes continues to form the complement to Museum Studies and training in South Africa.

Transformation of Museum and Heritage Studies: The Robben Island Training Programme (RITP)

As noted in an education committee report, Gerard Corsane was credited with the introduction of a Museum Studies course in 1993 at the History Department of Rhodes University. Corsane was rightly commended for this initiative of a history disciplinary orientation in Museum Studies because it is a departure from the existing Museum Studies and training which focused on technical skills and the (then dominant) archaeology and ethnology disciplines in Museum Studies. The contributions of Corsane in the transformation of Museum Studies in South Africa is significant because it was his initiative along with other actors that resulted in the establishment of the RITP, which, as we show below, transformed Museum Studies in South Africa. Although there are numerous avenues from which to trace the origin of the RITP as we explore below, we trace the origin of the RITP as chronicled by Khwezi ka Mpumlwana and Gerard Corsane. Corsane traced the origin of the RITP to the impression made on him by André Odendaal's presentation at the historic SAMA East London Conference of 1994. The talk, according to Corsane, who had been involved in the introduction of the Museum Studies at Rhodes University in conjunction with the Albany Museum, was "a call to action and the spark to his rainbow dream, which inevitably led him to Robben Island Museum."[34]

As a SAMA education committee member responsible for training, Corsane was mandated by the SAMA Council following its 1995 strategic meeting to conduct a survey of the state of Museum Studies and training in South Africa. This resulted in his drafting of a 'National Strategy for Heritage Training' which recommended the establishment of a National Heritage Training Institute. Due to the prevailing political climate and apparently the influence of the Mayibuye Centre with which Corsane was now associated, the plan for Museum Studies and training was incorporated into the planning of the Robben Island Museum project. As seen in Mpumlwana and Corsane's reflections on the origin of the RITP, it was through Corsane's connections to both RIM through André Odendaal and Gordon Metz at the Mayibuye Centre and UCT through his involvement in an existing Museum Studies course that allowed the RITP to take off in 1998.

While Corsane was pivotal to the SAMA connection in respect of the establishment of the RITP and seems to have been the liaison between SAMA, RIM, UCT, and UWC, the Department of History at UWC also had a complimentary version of the origin of the programme, especially as it relates to Public History, which we discuss in detail in the next chapter. Ciraj Rassool, the co-director of the RITP-APMHS, stated the motivation of UWC's Department of History in the convening of the RITP. According to Rassool:

> We are interested in those forms of disciplinary practice in history and archaeology which have sought expressly to transcend the bounds of the academy and to seek ways of negotiating historical and archaeological knowledge in a direct relationship with communities and other

publics as a means of empowerment, democratisation, access and critical engagement. […] we are concerned about opening up and strengthening the possibilities for critical engagement, scholarship and knowledge formation.[35]

This positioning is further seen in the reflections on the origin and history of the Diploma Programme by Leslie Witz, Carohn Cornell, Ciraj Rassool, and Erin Finnegan.[36] Engaging these critical reflections on the RITP is necessary to understand how the expanding research in the field of Public History at UWC has defined the pedagogical distinctiveness of the RITP-APMHS approach to Museum and Heritage Studies in South Africa compared to the other strands discussed above. Moreover, these reflections allow an understanding of how the RITP is related to the transformative impact of RIM and its implications for Heritage Studies as a terrain of public historical knowledge production. These factors, combined with the distinction claimed from other programmes on Heritage Studies in Africa, make a critical reflection of the sociology of knowledge and intellectual history of the programme necessary. This section of the chapter thus traces the history of the RITP, from its inception in 1998 to its branding as the African Programme in Museum and Heritage Studies in 2003.

Leslie Witz, the co-convenor of the programme, and Carohn Cornell, from the then Academic Development Centre at UWC, traced the context in which the RITP originated in the immediate post-apartheid political imperatives of transformation in the cultural heritage sector in South Africa.[37] They located the call for transformation in the heritage sector to Nelson Mandela's speech at the formal opening of RIM on Heritage Day in September 1997. In his speech, referenced in the introduction, Mandela deplored the prevailing situation in the immediate post-apartheid where museums glorified mainly white and colonial history.[38]

Part of the efforts to correct this uncomfortable climate in the heritage sector in South Africa condemned by Mandela was a series of initiatives, culminating in the establishment of the RITP, a postgraduate diploma in Museum and Heritage Studies in 1998. This diploma, jointly offered by UWC, UCT, and the Training Programme of RIM, was described as "an ambitious and exciting programme to provide training 'to effect change'in the museum and heritage sector"[39] by Leslie Witz who, as co-director of the programme, reflected on the postgraduate diploma in Museum and Heritage Studies[40] in its first four years.

Witz identified the three strands that constituted the establishment of the Diploma:
(1) the call by the Department of Arts and Culture Task Team (ACTAG) for a proper training strategy and recommendation by the South African Museum Association (SAMA) for the establishment of a National Heritage Training Institute.
(2) The Robben Island Museum's aim of becoming a leading player in providing heritage education.
(3) The growing interest and teaching in the sphere of Public History at the History Department of the University of the Western Cape.[41]

This perspective of the origin of the RITP was restated in more detail in a Swedish African Museum Programme (SAMP) conference paper co-delivered in August 1999 by Ciraj Rassool and Leslie Witz, the convenors of the programme since its inception. They presented a detailed intellectual configuration and sociology of knowledge that informed the convening of the Diploma in Museum and Heritage studies in 1998. According to them:

> The basis of the new postgraduate diploma in Museum and Heritage Studies – RITP – which emerged was a partnership between the academy and institutions in the public sphere. With the intention of the Robben Island Museum to create a platform for education, negotiations were entered into between the Robben Island Training Programme and representatives of the University of the Western Cape and the University of Cape Town. These representatives were academics in the disciplines of History, Art History, Fine Art, Archaeology, Literary Studies, Anthropology, Architecture and Urban Planning. In line with the goals of the transformation of Higher Education in South Africa, the partnership recognised the need to address historical inequalities between different universities. The creation of a partnership with the Robben Island Museum, and the involvement of representatives of other museums such as the District Six Museum and other heritage sectors, ranging from the built environment to national parks, ensured that the new area of learning would also constitute a space between the academy and the public domain. This has enabled us to think about training in Museum and Heritage Studies as linked to new possibilities of developing public scholarship. Such education would not involve the mere technical process of simply training people for job categories in museums but would emphasise an understanding of the conceptual challenges of transformation. If museums are going to take forward their objectives of transformation beyond limited frameworks, this will depend on the extent they are able to develop as sites of research, not only by academics, but by their own staff. This research needs to be rooted in their archives and collections.[42]

They further stated that the beginnings and origins of the Diploma lay in a convergence of different initiatives and developments. According to them, the origin of the RITP emerged from:

1. A meeting of interests in heritage education emerging out of a transforming South African Museums Association (SAMA) as well as new policy initiatives from within the Department of Arts, Culture, Science and Technology (DACST).

2. Its origins also lie in the opening of the space of 'Public History', particularly in the wake of Nelson Mandela's 'walk to freedom' through the 'prison gate' at Victor Verster Prison in February 1990. Previously, radical historians had been limited to attempts to popularise academic social history research, especially aimed at a working-class audience. Now 'Public History' embraced those arenas and institutional settings in which the public encounters productions of the past, particularly in visual form, each with its own codes. At the same time, the old ways in which historians have held on to notions of the inherent superiority of academic historical knowledge began to be called into question. These were some of the key issues which informed the way in which new courses in Public History and Visual History began to emerge at the University of the Western Cape. This was also connected to the development of research into museums, tourism, festivals, the TRC and photographic archives as sites of history.

3. At the same time, as well, the Mayibuye Centre came into existence at the University of the Western Cape. This was a project which sought to develop a museum of apartheid and an archive of resistance, and to provide a forum for discussion of heritage policy. The Mayibuye Centre, based on the archives of the old International Defence and Aid Fund (IDAF), which had been returned to South Africa, was a central institution, which lobbied for the transformation of museums, as well as other areas of heritage. The Robben Island Museum, 'cultural showcase of the new South Africa', can be seen as the culmination of the cultural work of the Mayibuye Centre and its antecedent institutions such as IDAF and even the Treason Trial Defence Fund of the 1950s.

4. More and more, institutions in the public domain were becoming sites of contestation over heritage and representation. New institutions such as the District Six Museum, which had developed as an independent museum space and an arena of knowledge production, began to see the need for educational programmes in heritage and the cultural work of museums.[43]

These statements of Rassool and Witz give an overview of the combination of factors that gave rise to the formation of the RITP and the different angles its history can be approached from. However, the point of departure for this study is tracing the origin of the RITP in the RIM project in connection to the Mayibuye Centre, now the Robben Island-UWC Mayibuye Archives, and its relationship with the Public History research project in the Department of History, and the Institute for Historical Research (IHR), now designated the Centre for Humanities Research (CHR), at UWC. Using RIM as a point of departure is important because it recognises that the involvement of a heritage institution with the academy in conceptualising a Museum and Heritage Studies programme in Africa is a significant marker of the transformation in Museum Studies, especially its combination with heritage in post-1994 South Africa.[44] Tracing the history of how this fusion of the academy and an institution of public culture (with its origins in anti-apartheid resistance history) in contest and collaboration with the dominant technical orientation of Museum Studies of SAMA and its ambiguous history of apartheid came to define the critical Public History approach to Museum and Heritage

Studies in the RITP-APMHS, is important to assess and measure the desirability, validity, and success or failure of the transformation project of Museum and Heritage Studies in South Africa.

The Robben Island Training Programme (RITP) and the postgraduate diploma in Museum and Heritage Studies

As seen in the activities at UWC, central to the RIM project was its aspiration for museum and heritage transformation in South Africa by positioning itself as a museum of public historical scholarship and research. This orientation informed numerous initiatives and projects as constituents of RIM. One of these initiatives was the development of a museum and heritage training programme to address skills transformation in the heritage sector. A precursor to this initiative was the survey of the demographic composition in the sector, and the review of the existing training programmes by Gerard Corsane in his capacity as the SAMA Education executive committee member. Significant findings of the survey were that there was virtually no black museum or heritage professionals in the sector, and that the few black people who were employed were in dead-end, low-level jobs without the prospect of upward mobility. The survey therefore suggested the need for developing a 'fast track' heritage management programme to train black heritage professionals.[45]

In December 1996, Corsane, who eventually became the first Robben Island Training Programme coordinator, and Gordon Metz prepared a business plan for the establishment of the Robben Island Training Programme (RITP) at the request of the Swedish International Development Agency (SIDA) who were considering seed funding for the project.[46] The background of the business plan noted that in all the policies on transformation issues relating to culture and heritage, "the provision of appropriate training opportunities has been identified as being vital for ongoing transformation in the heritage sector" and that "the opportunities which are available need to be constantly reviewed and updated to ensure that they meet the present needs, especially in terms of transformation and development of new approaches."[47] The proposal resulted in the establishment of the RITP with the objective "to train a core group of black heritage professionals and museologists who can take forward the process of transformation and champion the need for democratising the heritage sector, especially through the development of a co-ordinated training system based on accessibility, equality and redress."[48] Its main immediate objective was therefore to develop and present a 'fast track' affirmative action education and training programme, while its long-term vision was to provide a foundation for the establishment of the National Heritage Training Institute (NHTI).[49]

In line with the vision of a vanguard of heritage transformation through critical scholarship, the business plan stated that since "the Robben Island Museum will be different to any of the traditional museums in the country, it will consequently provide an ideal location for a new style of training programme", which will have "an important impact on capacity building and redress in the heritage sector" by offering a "fresh approach to established paradigms in Museum and Heritage Studies."[50] Nevertheless, this imperative for a new approach to Heritage Studies in the RITP adhered to museum and heritage training according to the 'Standards and Ethics for Museum Training Programmes' of ICOM's International Committee for Training of Museum Personnel (ICTOP).[51]

Crucially, the plan offered a rationale for the RITP partnership with UWC and UCT:

> With the development of the RITP in 1997, it soon became apparent that it would benefit potential candidates if the training was certified through a tertiary institution; it was felt that by acquiring certification through a recognised institution the training would be given status and credibility. This would be important, as the affirmative action candidates would receive a respected qualification, which would give them a solid foundation and the standing for their work in the transformation process.[52]

Based on the stated objectives, which were within the framework of the Odendaal proposal, the RITP approached the UWC Department of History with a proposal to co-convene a programme in Museum and Heritage Studies, which was accepted. This merger resulted in RITP-designed courses being restructured and incorporated as components of the postgraduate diploma programme in Museum and Heritage Studies, both its core course and electives.[53] The incorporated RITP curriculum, modelled on the ICTOP basis standard for Museum and Heritage Studies, consisted of an introductory orien-tation module and six other modules. The orientation module was designed to introduce students to the purpose and key concepts of museum and heritage. The second module incorporated into the core course was Heritage Institutions for a New South Africa. This included:

- Historical context: The development of heritage interest groups, heritage institutions, heritage organisations and museums.
- Philosophical context and contemporary issues: Changing philosophies and paradigms in Heritage Studies and Museology.
- Organisational structures: The history, role, structure, and status of governmental and non-governmental bodies and their interrelationships.
- Legal and professional context.[54]

The other modules of the RITP that became electives on the joint Diploma programme were:
- Heritage Management and Collections Management;
- Researching and Interpreting Heritage Material;
- Heritage and the Public I: Communications, Education, Exhibitions, Publications and Human Agencies;
- Heritage and the Public II: Tourism, Public Relations and Marketing; and
- Management in Heritage Agencies.[55]

The first two items of this RITP curriculum were incorporated into the core course of the Diploma programme in a fundamentally different way – the conceptual issues were included and the technical topics were dropped. The remaining four modules remained the same, except the topics on legal and professional context were added to the 'Management in Heritage Agencies' module to constitute the four UWC-accredited Robben Island Museum offered electives on the programme. According to Corsane, "this was a very important achievement as the Diploma will be one of the first qualifications in the country for which two universities will be equally involved in certification."[56] The programme had its first intake of about 41 students in March 1998, with personnel and resources drawn from the three convening institutions, and RIM and UCT's Michaelis School of Fine Arts as nodes for the diploma.[57]

RIM formally opened in September 1997 and the programme started in March 1998. On 8 July 1998, André Odendaal (then RIM Executive Director) circulated an updated version of his earlier 'Discussion Document',[58] titled: 'Discussion Document of the Joint UWC/RIM Working Group Re-Proposal for a Cooperation Agreement between the University of the Western Cape and the Robben Island Museum relating to the Mayibuye Centre and other Joint Arrangements'.[59] Although the new Discussion Document focused mainly on the incorporation of the Mayibuye Centre into RIM, significantly, one of its core recommendations was a section that is crucial to understanding the challenge of the structural location of the RITP and the disciplinary location of its approach to Museum and Heritage Studies. This section proposed that:
- The staff and administrative component of the Robben Island Heritage Training project are located at IHR at UWC, consolidating the UWC role in the new postgraduate diploma in Museum and Heritage Studies awarded jointly by UWC and UCT.
- The IHR and Department of History at UWC start a Robben Island Project together with RIM, initiating various postgraduate and undergraduate courses and research projects relating to Robben Island.[60]

Corsane subsequently prepared details for the operation of the proposal titled 'Positioning RITP in Relation to IHR at UWC and RIM'.[61] The document set out a structure for the RITP in the programme at UWC in respect of its physical locality within the IHR at UWC, except during contact time for the purposes of training on Robben Island for which office and accommodation space will be required for RITP personnel at RIM. It further stated that the head of the Robben Island Training Programme will be given the title 'Senior Lecturer' and the course coordinator, 'Lecturer'.[62] Specifically in relation to the centrality of Public History in the RITP, the document stated that "the Head of the Robben Island Training Programme will have a communication line with the director of IHR at UWC, through the Chair of Public History."[63]

One of the consistent points in all the discussions of the RIM-UWC working group in connection to the formation of RITP was the focus on Public History, especially expressed in the desire to endow a Chair in Public History at the UWC Department of History, in addition to acquiring the Mayibuye archival collections as a central component of its museum structure. This concern, however, was not without its own tensions between the Department of History and the IHR, and the RITP and the Department of History, over the disciplinary location of the proposed Chair of Public History and the location of the RITP in the Chair of Public History. In the 'Report of the Location of RITP', subsequently prepared by the Department of History's Gary Minkley for the UWC/RIM Working Group[64] in response to the RITP proposal, as requested in the minutes of the meeting, it is stated that the Department of History felt very positive about the relocation of the RITP to the University campus because it would:

- Strengthen the field of Public History in Historical Studies at UWC.
- Provide significant administrative support for the Diploma in Museum and Heritage Studies at the site of its administration.
- Provide an academic environment and a source of educational integrity for the RITP.
- Provide a more integrated Diploma and enhance the development of subsequent courses in related programmes.
- Add new staff members and expertise at a time when posts in the field of historical studies and at the University are under threat.[65]

Nevertheless, he pointed out the challenges and limitations of locating the RITP to the IHR and expressed the Department's opinion that locating what was essentially a teaching and training programme in an almost exclusively research-based institute was extremely problematic for two reasons:

- The absence of teaching environment, infrastructure, and engagement with the broad disciplinary aspect implied in the RITP; and
- The fact that the Department of History at UWC has led the way in the field of Public History and remains its area of concentration and development. This is apparent from the key role the Department plays in the Diploma, through its projected development within the programme structure planned for implementation from 1999 (and including CSD Public History team research projects and participation).[66]

Although the brief report warned of the staffing implications, in the context of the 'rightsizing' of academic positions then going on at UWC, it nonetheless proposed that "the RITP should be located within the History Department – as the teaching component of historical studies at the University rather than within the IHR – which primarily remains a research institute."[67] As the Annex C document prepared by Corsane reflected, the driving impetus for proposing that the RITP be located within the IHR at UWC was the desire to align the RITP approach to Heritage Studies, modelled on the ICTOP curriculum, to the Public History approach of Heritage Studies that was developing in the Department of History. The failure of the proposal that 'the Head of the Robben Island Training Programme will have a communication line with the director of IHR at UWC, through the Chair of Public History[68] is crucial. This is revealed in the tensions between the approaches to Heritage Studies not only of the RITP in relation to the Public History orientation of the Department of History to the technical conservation training of the Diploma, but also in the contestation of the location of the Chair of Public History between the Department of History and the IHR.

Nevertheless, the Public History approach to Heritage Studies and the ICTOP approach to RITP continued to co-exist as part of the Diploma until Corsane's departure in 1999. The challenges to fully integrate the RITP into the Public History approach of the Diploma came to a head with Corsane's departure.[69] Due to subsequent developments in the RITP structure, which affected its course delivery, caused the convening board to be "concerned over RITP teaching methods and support structure for students."[70] This necessitated hiring a consultant to assist the Robben Island team in reviewing the RITP in relation to its objective and founding intentions.[71]

One of the measures to remedy these concerns was the convening of an Academic Review Committee by the Education Department at RIM in 2005 to evaluate the RITP elective and provide academic quality assurance for the RITP. Members of the committee included the Head of the Education Department at RIM, Deidre Prins-Solani, and other RIM executives, academics in the field of Public History, professors Gary Minkley and Stanley Ridge, heritage conservation professionals, Dr Harriet Deacon, and also Sephai Mngqolo, an alumna of the Diploma, and in addition to a representative of the South African Heritage Resources Agency (SAHRA). More importantly, it included George Abungu from the PREMA/CHDA/Africa 2009 programmes, which is an indicator of the RITP African-focused approach to Heritage Studies. One of the key recommendations of the committee was the appointment of an academic coordinator to manage the RITP electives and provide synergy with the core course.[72] This was acknowledged as a sign that the "Robben Island Museum remains a committed and valuable partner on the programme in that they have taken significant steps to improve their coordination, quality assurance and evaluation."[73] According to Witz:

> The experience of the Diploma suggests that if Heritage Studies is to be conceptualised in a manner that consistently, critically and practically challenges the dominant ways in which pastness is presented (in the academy and public sphere) then there are several matters that need to be addressed. Firstly, there have been requests by role-players within the heritage sphere to widen the domain that the Diploma covers. In particular,

there have been calls to design courses or modules which will look at built environment, heritage management, the archives, and internet-based exhibitions (the virtual museum). Another matter that needs urgent attention is the relationship between different modules on the programme. At the moment there appear to be contradictions between some modules and the core course. Arguments and issues that are discussed in the core course are sometimes at odds with ideas presented (or taken as given) in some of the modules.[74]

Witz suggested a way out of these seeming contradictions in the programme curriculum and structures: "rather than seeing Heritage Studies as an interim position, a more fruitful engagement would be to develop a graduate programme that could provide different exit levels." This, he advised, should "build on the Diploma, evaluate its strengths and weaknesses, and see where improvements can be made, elements added or discarded, and where it might fit into a flexible degree."[75] However, he cautioned that this must be done without relinquishing the "emphasis on questioning and contesting heritage, which is at the core of the Diploma." He warned that without such an approach, there is a danger that Heritage Studies will become "a form of technical training and the new breed of heritage workers will continue to be the manual functionaries they were relegated to under apartheid."[76]

As explained here and as argued by Erin Finnegan, it was the nexus of Public History at the UWC Department of History, the Mayibuye Centre, and the IHR that pioneered research in the critical examination of the politics of historical production in the public domain as the appropriate approach to Heritage Studies.[77] Significantly, while it was through Public History as a driving paradigm that the programme came of its own, there continued to be latent tension between the technical ICTOP model approach of the RITP in the programme and the Public History approach. These inherent tensions between pedagogical approaches to Museum and Heritage Studies continued to be evident beyond the branding of the RITP as 'African' in 2003. According to Witz, one of the major recommendations of the Rockefeller-funded external evaluation "was that notwithstanding its palpable achievements, the programme needs to choose between an academic-intellectual and more practical-vocational direction. In addition, the evaluation recommended the need for a firm physical location of the programme."[78] According to Witz, the Convening Committee of the APMHS decided in response:

> That the appropriate location for the institutional home of the programme is the University of the Western Cape, because of its expertise, capacity and long-term commitment; to move towards extending the programme to embrace a Master's in Heritage Studies; and to secure greater, more formal buy-in from museums and heritage institutions, especially those of national status in South Africa.[79]

UCT opted out of the programme in 2009, leaving it to be convened by UWC and RIM only. The APMHS had apparently taken an academic-intellectual orientation by developing a master's degree programme and producing many doctoral dissertations in AMHS. The administration was moved to the Centre for Humanities Research (CHR), the RIM-appointed academic coordinator was based in the Department of History, and RIM continued to provide four electives in the technologies and modalities of heritage. RIM as an institution has changed significantly from its initial focus on public scholarship and research to one that is more slanted towards a tourist-management orientation. While this structural challenge has not affected RIM's overall support for the programme, the shift to a more 'tourist destination' orientation has hampered both the critical intellectual contribution of RIM to the APMHS, and the advantage accrued to it through its participation. The centrality of the Mayibuye Archives, the CHR, and Public History in the Department of History and APMHS nexus as a fundamental consistency of RIM as a museum of public scholarship and research, has been forgotten in its strategic management apart from being reflected on its financial balance sheet, which had usually been questioned as un-mandated expenditure.

This situation is defeating the vision and rationale for the programme which, according to Witz and Rassool, hopes to build on these initiatives of the nexus of Mayibuye Centre and Public History that "enabled us to think about training in Museum and Heritage Studiesas linked to new possibilities of developing public scholarship." Such education, they argued "would emphasise an understanding of the conceptual challenges of transformation." This is because "if museums are going to take forward their objectives of transformation beyond limited frameworks, this will depend on the extent they are able to develop as sites of research, not only by academics, but also by their own staff." Crucially, they argued, "this research needs to be rooted in their own collections."[80] The decline of the Mayibuye Centre as a public historical research hub at the nexus of CHR and Public History has had an impact on the programme in relation to its objectives as a terrain of critical public scholarship.

While it is agreed that a museum is a dynamic institution subject to constant change, the change from a museum of public historical scholarship and research to a tourist destination museum appears to be defeating the ideals of transformation on which the vision of the APMHS was built, which is both a challenge to and an indictment of the challenges of the complex relationship between RIM and UWC. This unique fusion of the academy and a national museum of public historical scholarship as an initiative transforming the terrain of Museum and Heritage Studies in Africa is central to the vision of RIM as a museum of the liberation struggle. The confluence of critical Public History in the Mayibuye nexus, and the intellectual resistance tradition symbolised by RIM, offer immense potential for socio-cultural-political transformation through the cultivation of a new space for public scholarship in the APMHS.

This chapter has attempted to better situate the criticism by the RITP-APMHS against emphasis on technical training as constitutive of Museum and Heritage Studies of programmes preceding it and critique the impact of the transformation of Museum and Heritage Studies in South Africa through the lens of the RITP-APMHS. We have briefly described and analysed the history and process of development of Heritage Studies and training in South Africa to bring to the fore how radical and disruptive the version of Public History was in pioneering critical Heritage Studies in South Africa through the RITP-APMHS. We argue that the RITP intervention not only engenders tangible transformation but, more importantly, planted the seed for a radical Afrocentric turn in Museum and Heritage Studies in Africa, and the global movement for rethinking the meaning, purpose, and relevance of heritage in Africa.

Endnotes

1. By this we mean all types of formal training and studies conducted and undertaken for the award of recognised certificates for staff of museums and heritage institutions.
2. See A.E. Coombes. 2003. *History After Apartheid: Visual Culture and Public Memory in a Democratic South Africa*. London: Duke University Press, 149-55. https://doi.org/10.1515/9780822384922
3. C.K. Brain & M.C. Erasmus. 1986. *The Making of the Museum Professions in South Africa, 1936-2016*. Cape Town: South African Museums Association, 34.
4. M. Dlamuka. 2003. 'Identities, Memories, Histories and Representation: The Role of Museums in Twentieth Century KwaZulu-Natal'. Unpublished (M.A.) Thesis. Durban: University of Durban-Westville.
5. F.W. Grosskopf. 1933. *The Poor White Problem in South Africa*. Report of the Carnegie Commission I. Stellenbosch: Pro Ecclesia Publishers.
6. H.A. Miers & S.F. Markham. 1932. *The Museums Association Survey of Empire Museums*. A Report on the Museums and Art Galleries of British Africa Together with a Report on the Museums of Malta, Cyprus and Gibraltar by Alderman Chas. Squire and D.W. Herdman to the Carnegie Corporation of New York, Edinburgh.;
The Museums Association (compl.). 1933. *Directory of Museums and Art Galleries in British Africa and in Malta, Cyprus and Gibraltar*. London: The Museums Association.
7. E. Grobler & F. Pretorius. 2008. 'The British Museums Association, The Carnegie Corporation and Museums in South Africa, 1932-1938: An Overview'. *S.A Tydskrif vir Kultuurgeskiedenis*, 22(2):65. https://doi.org/10.4314/sajch.v22i2.6370
8. M. Nassimbeni. 2014. *Building Resilient Public Libraries with Carnegie in South Africa (1927-2012): Regularities, Singularities and South African Exceptionalism*, Research Paper. Cape Town: University of Cape Town, 3.
9. Grobler & Pretorius. 'The British Museums Association', 47.
10. Ibid.
11. Ibid.
12. J. Seekings. 2006. 'The Carnegie Commission and the Backlash Against Welfare State-Building in South Africa, 1931-1937'. *CSSR Working Paper*, (159):32.
13. Ibid., 13.
14. Ibid., 49.
15. Ibid., 7.
16. See S. Klausen. 2004. *Race, Maternity and the Politics of Birth Control in South Africa, 1910-39*. Basingstoke: Palgrave Macmillan. https://doi.org/10.1057/9780230511255
17. Seekings. 'The Carnegie Commission and the Backlash', 7.
18. Ibid., 8.
19. Ibid., 12.
20. Nassimbeni. *Building Resilient Public Libraries with Carnegie in South Africa*, 7.
21. Ibid., 7.
22. Grobler & Pretorius. 'The British Museums Association', 61-62.
23. Brain & Erasmus. *The Making of the Museum Professions in South Africa, 1936-2016*, 3.
24. Ibid., 8.

25 The Museum Association's Diploma: Some explanatory notes in SAMA collection. Box 7, UNISA archives.

26 See History of the British Museum Association. http://bit.ly/437OsiT [Accessed 8 January 2022].

27 Brain & Erasmus. *The Making of the Museum Professions in South Africa, 1936-2016*, 31.

28 Minutes of SAMA Meeting held in the Transvaal Museum. Pretoria, 30 April 1956, Box 6, SAMA collection, UNISA archives.

29 S. van Zyl. 2016. 'The Growth of Professionalism in South African Museums'. In: C.K. Brain & M.C. Erasmus (eds.), *The Making of the Museum Professions in South Africa 1936-2016*, 31.

30 Brain & Erasmus. *The Making of the Museum Professions in South Africa, 1936-2016*, 28.

31 Education Committee Chairman Report, 1985-1986. SAMA collection, Box 5, UNISA archives.

32 B. Social Science Hons (Heritage, Museum and Preservation Studies). https://www.up.ac.za [Accessed 21 April 2022].

33 1978, SAMA collections, Box 14 UNISA archives.

34 K. Ka Mpumlwana & G. Corsane. 2021. 'Creating a New Generation of Heritage and Museum Leaders: The Inception of the Robben Island Training Programme (RITP)'. In: N. Lekgotla laga Ramoupi, N. Solani, A. Odendaal & K. ka Mpumlwana (eds.), *Robben Island Rainbow Dream: The Making of Democratic South Africa's First National Heritage institutions*. Cape Town: HSRC Press, 158.

35 C. Rassool. 2010. 'Power, Knowledge and the Politics of the Public Past'. *African Studies*, 69(1):79-101. https://doi.org/10.1080/00020181003647215

36 See L. Witz & C. Cornell. 1999. *From Robben Island to Makapan's Cave: Transforming Heritage and Museum Studies in South Africa*. Paper presented at the World Archaeological Conference, Cape Town, 10-14 January 1999, 1.;
C. Rassool. 2000. 'The Rise of Heritage and the Reconstitution of History in South Africa'. *Kronos: Journal of Cape History*, 26:1-21.;
E. Finnegan. 2006. *The African Postgraduate Diploma Programme in Museum and Heritage Studies: At the Confluence of Critical Theory, Public History and Socio-Political Transformation in South Africa*, September 2006. Robben Island Museum, Education Department, Academic Committee meeting brief, 30-31 October 2006.

37 Witz and Cornell. *From Robben Island to Makapan's Cave*, 1.

38 Nelson Mandela's speech at the formal opening of Robben Island Museum, Heritage Day, 24 September 1997. This statement echoes of 'little was said about ways in which the public could directly influence, alter and shape exhibits in the future'. In: L. Witz & C. Rassool. 1992. 'The Dog, the Rabbit and the Reluctant Historians', *South African Historical Journal*, 27(1):238-242. https://doi.org/10.1080/02582479208671748

39 Proposal submitted to Rockefeller Foundation.

40 L. Witz. 2001. 'Museum and Heritage Studies: An Interim Position'. Workshop on Mapping Alternatives: Debating New Heritage Practices in South Africa, 25-26 September. Cape Town: Project on Public Past, History department, UWC and RESUNACT, UCT.

41 Witz. 'Museum and Heritage Studies', 1.

42 C. Rassool & L. Witz. 'Transforming Heritage Education in South Africa: A Partnership between the Academy and the Museum'. *SAMP 2001: Strengthening the Network: A Meeting of African Museums of the Swedish African Museum Programme*, 22-27 August 1999.

43 Ibid., 1-2.

44 RITP report for 1998-2002. Robben Island: RIM Institutional records, Robben Island Museum.

45 Report of Survey conducted by Gerard Corsane in Robben Island Report 1998-2002. Robben Island: Robben Island Museum Institutional Archive.

46 G. Corsane & G. Metz. 'Business Plan for the establishment of the 'Robben Island Training Programme (RITP)'. Att the request of the Swedish International Development Agency (SIDA), December 1996, updated March 1998. Robben Island: Robben Island Institutional archives.

47 Ibid., 9.

48 Ibid.,1.

49 Ruth de Bruyn. 2001. Prepared Report on the SIDA-supported Robben Island Training Programme (RITP).

50 Corsane & Metz. 'Business Plan', 2.

51 Ibid., 10.

52 Ibid., 9.

53 G. Corsane & G. Metz. 'RITP Business Plan'. Robben Island: Robben Island Museum Institutional Archive, Education Department Records 1997-2003.

54 G. Corsane. Robben Island Training Programme proposed course outline submitted to the UWC History Department, 1997. Leslie Witz private collections.

55 Ibid., 2-3.

56 Corsane & Metz. 'Business Plan', 9.

57 Corsane & Metz. 'RITP Business Plan'.

58 A. Odendaal. 1998. 'Discussion Document of the Joint UWC/RIM Working Group Re-Proposal for a Cooperation Agreement Between the University of the Western Cape and the Robben Island Museum Relating to the Mayibuye Centre and Other Joint Arrangements, 8 July 1998. Cape Town: CHR archives, UWC.

59 Odendaal. 'Discussion Document of the Joint UWC/RIM Working Group'.

60 Ibid.

61 G. Corsane, 'Positioning RITP in Relation to IHR at UWC and RIM'. *Annex C – 1998*. Cape Town: CHR archives, UWC.

62 Ibid., 1.

63 Ibid.

64 G. Minkley. 1998. 'Report of the Location of RITP'. Prepared for the UWC/RIM Working Group. Cape Town: CHR archives, UWC.

65 Ibid., 1.

66 Ibid., 1.

67 Ibid., 1.

68 'Positioning RITP'. The proposal suggested that 'the Head of the Robben Island Training Programme will have a communication line with the director of IHR at UWC, through the Chair of Public History'. Cape Town: CHR archives, UWC.

69 In 2001, Ruth de Bruyn, the consultant that was hired, prepared a 'Report on the SIDA supported Robben Island Training Programme (RITP)'. The review noted that staff of the RITP (previously Gerard Corsane, now Ramzie Abrahams) has done excellent proactive work in gaining recognition for Heritage Management Studies. In presenting the Diploma with the UWC and UCT, the RITP has contributed to a 'significant achievement within the context of transforming higher education. With the departure of Corsane there appears to be a high staff turnover of RITP personnel. Between 2000 and 2002 the RITP had 3 coordinators in quick successions.; Lucy Alexander, who succeeded Corsane, who was then followed by Ramzie Abrahams in 2001, followed in 2002 by Bulelwa Mbangu and Zuleiga Rossouw as the successive coordinators. This obviously had a negative impact on the development and offering of the RITP courses offered as part of the electives on the Diploma and its relationship to constituent convening partners. The report noted that "RITP fulfilled the condition of the contract [to SIDA] very successfully'.; Nonetheless, it pointed out 'a number of factors' as the 'causes of current difficulties'. The main cause of the current difficulties facing the RITP, according to the De Bruyn report, was 'Gerard Corsane leaving the project – Mr Corsane appears to have been the mastermind behind the planning of the RITP projects from 1996 onwards. It is likely that several matters 'fell through the gap' in the period between his leaving for Leicester University in October 1999 and the appointment of new staff in 2000." See: Ruth de Bruyn. 2001. Prepared Report on the SIDA-supported Robben Island Training Programme (RITP).

70 Minutes of APMHS board meeting held at CHEC office, 15 March 2006. Cape Town: CHR archives, UWC.

71 De Bruyn Report
– To assist the Robben Island Team in reviewing the RITP in relation to its objectives and intentions,
– To assess the progress achieved so far on the 2009 and 1999 course, and its impact (short and long-term) on the present batch of students and their future possibility to get work within the museum sector, and
– For the consultant to try to identify measures to be taken by the RITP staff to improve selection/recruitment processes and procedures for future training in order to both get sufficient numbers of enrolled and students with the right background.

72 Minutes of APMHS board, 15 March 2006.

73 L. Witz. 2008. Graduate Programme in Museum and Heritage Studies (Postgraduate Diploma and Master's): A Proposal for a Joint Programme to be Offered by the University of the Western Cape and Robben Island Museum.

74 Witz. 'Museum and Heritage Studies', 11.

75 Ibid.

76 Ibid.

77 Finnegan. *The African Postgraduate Diploma Programme*, 3.

78 Witz. Graduate Programme in Museum and Heritage Studies, 6.

79 Ibid., 6.

80 Rassool & Witz. 'Transforming Heritage Education in South Africa', 2

Public History and Heritage Studies in South Africa

6

As shown in the preceding chapter, the question of how the field of Public History is related to a programme in Museum and Heritage Studies is evident, given the centrality of the Public History research project at the UWC Department of History to the establishment and development of the RITP Diploma in Museum and Heritage Studies. However, the questions of what Public History is and why it is related to a programme in Museum and Heritage Studies remain unanswered. To answer this question, this chapter will focus on the meaning and features of the distinct brand of Public History developed by the 'Troika' at the UWC Department of History and why it is definitive of the RITP-APMHS and the transformation of Museum and Heritage Studies in Africa, specifically in South Africa.

Heritage and Public History

Although the ACTAG report of 1995 called for a proper training strategy to transform the heritage sector from its image as the bastion of colonialism and apartheid, according to Witz and Cornell, the process of how this was going to be put in practice was left in rather vague terms.[1] Significantly, while a section of academic historians welcomed and were eager to engage with heritage as a field of study, there was uneasiness about academic engagement with and participation in Heritage Studies. A major reason for the lukewarm reception towards Heritage Studies by historians in South Africa was the ACTAG White Paper's definition of African heritage as naturally occurring marginalised, black living heritage.[2] The problem with this notion of heritage and its implications is that "heritage training revolves around acquiring professional and technical expertise in a particular field to discover, present, and influence [the] interpretation of these naturally occurring living heritage, [which] according to Witz and Cornell, led to 'intense debates' of what should be the appropriate approach towards Heritage Studies and training" by academic historians.[3] Witz, independently and as part of the 'Troika',[4] answered this question through the theoretical articulations and practices of a distinctive type of Public History, which we discuss in this chapter.

As explained by Witz, despite the tainted atmosphere created by the ACTAG's definition of heritage and prevailing uneasiness not only with the definition but the kind of Heritage Studies it implied, the stated need for "museum critical theory to develop heritage practitioners as independent thinkers, who would constantly challenge the underlying assumptions of heritage" was the point of convergence between the Public History perspective of Heritage Studies and the notion of heritage as the almost naturally occurring

African living heritage projected in the ACTAG report.[5] This Public History perspective dictates that the appropriate approach by academic historians towards Heritage Studies is to view "Heritage Studies as a field of studies in its own right", and to be concerned with understanding the conventions and means by which heritage is produced in the public sphere.[6] Hence, the appropriate approach by Public History towards Heritage Studies is to discover different areas and modes of heritage production and to analyse the meanings which are produced through them, and the cultural politics that informs them and are projected through them.[7]

In the paper, 'Museum and Heritage Studies: An Interim Position?'[8] presented at the 'Workshop of Mapping Alternatives: Debating New Heritage Practices in South Africa', Witz reflected on the minutes of a meeting in September 1997 of the first convening committee of the RITP which he was requested to collate in July 2001. He noted that he was concerned with an item in the minutes of that first meeting which stated: "Leslie Witz agreed to be the interim Chairperson of the Convening Committee until the Chair of Public History at the University of the Western Cape assumes this position next year."[9] This item, according to Witz, led him to question not only "whether I am [he was] legally still the 'interim Chairperson?',[10] but more importantly:

> What, for instance, was being meant by 'Public History' and what does it mean to be a public historian? Why and how is this field of Public History related to a programme on Museum and Heritage Studies? And is Public History and its association with Heritage Studies merely an interim phase until one return[s] to the word of 'real history', in the archive and lecture room?[11]

By answering these questions, which offers an appreciation of the specific strand of Public History that distinguished the RITP from other programmes of Museum and Heritage Studies, we critique how Witz himself along with the Troika has answered these questions: What is 'Public History'? What does it mean to be a public historian? Why and how is the field of Public History related to a programme on Museum and Heritage Studies? And is Public History and its association with Heritage Studies merely an interim phase until one returns to the word of 'real history' in the archive and lecture room?

What is Public History according to Witz? In a Michigan working paper, Witz engaged the dilemmas that have been presented around the category of history in the academy and the museum and placed them together as a way to think through the role of the public historian.[12] He indicated that what distinguished the Troika's perspective of Public History is a disavowal of the 'trickle down' process that relies on ideas of outreach, upliftment, and access while holding on to academic expertise enshrined in the notion of Public History which "refers to academically trained historians imparting their skills and knowledge to institutions such as museums."[13] This position was reinforced by the Troika in their description of their specific notion of Public History, and how it is different from the projects of popularising history and the distinctive brand of Public History in the United

States. They emphasised their understanding of Public History as the questioning of "prevailing and dominant understanding of the past, either in the academy or public domain, where [the] heritage/history dichotomy loomed large."[14] These discussions, debates, and research around the politics and poetics of representation in the public domain constitute Public History, "broadly defined as Heritage Studies", which according to Witz describes a field of:

> ... 'heritage scholarship' where important issues about the ways that histories come to be constituted in the public domain are critically examined, where the politics of the production, circulation, representation and reception of heritage in a variety of sites are analysed. Some important issues covered in this scholarship are the meanings and politics surrounding the construction of memorial projects and landscapes; how often these are aligned with contemporary political and commercial concerns; the ways several artists have consistently resisted the easy binaries and, through their work, have opened up history to debate and enquiry; frictions between claims to academic expertise and knowledge production in museums; how the museum and heritage field can be read as reflecting transformations in society; the productions of historical meanings in new museums and exhibitions; and, most recently, how heritage is re-shaping the post-apartheid city, both disturbing and re-affirming the desire lines of modernist planning.[15]

This articulation of Public History as Heritage Studies and as a recognised field of study by Witz makes the field of Public History as Heritage Studies a scholarship born of struggle. This is because of the initial reluctance among academic historians in South Africa to associate themselves with Heritage Studies which they see as uncritical, static, error-filled depictions of the past. Significantly, Witz rejected Jane Carruthers' critcisim of historians' involvement in Heritage Studies, as lapses into inaccuracies, exaggeration, myth-making, omission and error, a forced move necessitated by the decline in numbers of students studying history in South African universities.[16] Against Carruthers, Witz argued that in the conception of Heritage Studies, and other ways of producing pastness suggested by Carruthers, Heritage Studies is located at the periphery, while 'basic history' is at the core of knowledge production of the past.[17] Witz challenged this perspective where:

> Heritage was seen as somehow a lesser field to history, which is regarded as a critical search for truths that were constantly open to scrutiny, debate and discussion, compared to Heritage which was subject to distortions and manipulations in the interests of politics and/or commerce, often seeking to cast the past as immutable.[18]

According to Witz, despite the opportunities offered by the "University of the Witwatersrand in 1992 when the History Workshop hosted a conference entitled 'Myths, Monuments, Museums: New Premises?' for popular history to seek ways for their histories to enter the public domain on a much wider scale through engagement with Heritage Studies, 'the conference organisers' hopes that historians and other academics would engage in debates about Public History were largely unfulfilled."[19]

'Popular history' which is "based on a notion of discovery, recovery and revelation of a hidden history, a past that has been subordinated by oppression and exclusion during the days of colonialism and apartheid from historical record", which was until then the dominant trend in democratising history, missed the opportunity to engage or question the issues of academic power involved in the production of historical past, which reveals its limitations.[20] According to Witz, "[t]his was a question of the politics of historical production in the public domain and it was noticeable that social historians, who over the past decade have attempted to make their work popular, seem unwilling to enter the tainted atmosphere of policy formation and the world of lived history."[21]

This was reasserting the argument in the 'Dog, the Rabbit and the Reluctant Historians', a paper, co-authored with Ciraj Rassool, co-convenor of the programme, warning historians who "have chosen to regard 'Heritage' [Studies] as an inferior domain [as having] not understood the changed nature of their field."[22] They suggested that "it was high time the concern for popularising the past be shifted into the institution and medium of Public History."[23] Public History is thus the production of historical knowledge through the transaction of knowledge between the academic historian and the publics of museums and heritage practices. As he further elaborated in the conceptualisation of Public History as definitive of critical heritage scholarship, two ideas are crucial features of public historical scholarship: firstly, an emphasis on history as representation and secondly, how histories are represented and created in the public domain. Taking history as representation ensures engagement with the "museums, as one of these locations of history, and not merely as institutions of conservation, display and education but rather as sites that are underpinned by, and present, 'notions of what the world is or should be' and concerned with forms and contents of representation allows us to investigate the different forms, practices, genres, methodologies and social contexts that went into the production of histories."[24]

What does it mean to be a public historian? According to Witz, it is firstly fundamental "that history is taken beyond the academy into the world of museums, monuments, memorials, television, tourism, heritage sites, government commissions, comic books, festivals and so on. Secondly, it was no longer adequate to understand these presentations in the public domain as being prior to history, but as historical practices within different genres characterised by different sociologies and modalities."[25] Crucially, the public historian subverts "the neat hierarchies of historical knowledge formation in which the academic has entered the public domain as research experts, the bases of popular history and most importantly public historians understand and interrogate how these different sites are constituted. How they articulate with each other and the relations of power in the production of public historical practices."[26]

However, Witz also cautioned that "being a public historian involves more than investigating the poetics of representation and the politics of production." He suggests cognisance of the cultural political dynamics embedded in "the processes and regimes of exclusion and domination that lead to individuals and events not making the 'cut of history'" as essential to being a public historian.[27] A public historian is therefore an historian who "instead of acting as a consultant who conveys history (usually defined as an empiricist who can verify facts) to the public, is concerned both with understanding the politics of production and the relationships with, and immersion in, the cut and thrust of making history".[28] In essence, this means a public historian is defined by cognisance of the cultural politics of heritage. As noted by Witz, while Popular History broadly "refers to academically trained historians imparting their skills and knowledge to institutions such as museums", ideally based on a 'shared authority' over making 'meanings', in practice, it is the methodologies and expertise of the academy that are paramount.[29] However, as Witz argued the practise of Public History in the RITP, the academics "enters into discussions and debates with these institutions as a series of knowledge transactions, where one's expertise as an historian is constantly being challenged, shaped and re-shaped in the negotiations over the past as different historical knowledge are evoked and articulated and 'the mystique of scientific knowledge' is, consequently, shattered."[30]

Rassool emphatically rejected the position of "scholars who understand the relationship between the academy and public culture bodies as hierarchical, indeed as an order of knowledge". He argued that this relationship between Public History and Heritage Studies was due to "practices of memory work and scholarship in the public domain which have demonstrated [an] enormous capacity for original research and critical knowledge engagement."[31] Pointing towards the District Six Museum as an example of a museum as space for critical public scholarship, Rassool maintained that:

> The domain of heritage and Public History, required serious examination, for it is here that attempts were being made to fashion the categories, images and stories of the post-apartheid South African nation. It was in the public domain that dominant versions of historical narrations and practice have been questioned as museums have emerged as significant arenas to exercise the authorship of history and to pose questions about the politics of location of historical expertise.[32]

As argued by Rassool, "far from South Africa having seen a retreat from history", what was happening was that "the place of the past was being redefined in the spaces of Public History and heritage construction."[33] According to Rassool, the domain of Public History that was emerging in South Africa was an assemblage of arenas and activities of history-making that were as disputatious as the claims made about the character of academic history. What was needed, he argued, "was a sociology of historical production in the academy, as well as the public domain, and an enquiry into the categories, codes and conventions of history-making in each location with all its variability."[34]

Witz argued that the Public History orientation in the RITP Diploma challenges the dismissive approach to Heritage Studies in the academy by "suggesting that Heritage Studies like other methods [of producing history], can open up possibilities for critical engagement of how histories are constituted and provide the underpinning to historise history itself."[35] Therefore, the Public History approach defended Heritage Studies as a genre of historical production that enriches the discipline of history because it ensures that "the study of museums and the worlds of heritage are approached in a manner that consistently, critically and practically engages with and challenges the dominant ways in which heritage is presented" in the academy and public discourse.[36]

The dismissal of Heritage Studies because of arguments that "heritage emphasises nostalgia, which exposes heritage to appropriation in support of the status quo and as another web of illusion to enmesh an unthinking populace"[37] and as a "state sanctioned nationalist rhetoric"[38] was challenged by David Harvey. He argued instead that "heritage is a vehicle for both conservative and radical/progressive movements searching for an answer to the perceived evils of modern society"[39] and insisted that there remains a case for a critical and evaluative approach to the study of heritage.[40] This conclusion by Harvey, which the RITP-APMHS is taking seriously by developing a critical Heritage Studies programme in the academy, is especially poignant.[41] This is because the concept and practice of heritage, in whatever configuration, is worthy of critical engagement on its own, as the curriculum of the APMHS reflected. More importantly, we argue that worthy of more critical engagement is the debate concerning the conceptual specificity of the approach to African Heritage Studies: 'African' by virtue of its ideological, epistemic positioning in the study of Africa and 'critical' by its methodological, self-reflective criticism of and challenge to the hegemony of the AHD approach to Heritage Studies in Africa.

David Harvey's arguments for an historical appreciation of the concept of heritage are useful as a framework for locating the underlying ideological assumptions of the unfolding notions of heritage and the Public History approach to Heritage Studies in the RITP-APMHS curriculum. The historical imperative of the idea and praxis of Heritage Studies provided by Harvey offers a critical framework for situating the notion of heritage in the RITP-APMHS, and for conceiving an alternative approach to Heritage Studies beyond the totalising notions of Heritage Studies, and for tracing its African historical and conceptual specificity. This search for ideological, epistemic specificity of Heritage Studies in Africa relies on the imperative for an historical perspective of the idea and practice of Heritage Studies charted by Harvey. Harvey argued that the "use of the past to construct ideas of individual and group identities is part of the human condition, and throughout human history people have actively managed and treasured aspects of the past for this purpose."[42] However, according to him, what is distinctive about the particular strand of heritage discourse that emerged in 19th-century Europe that has achieved hegemony as a 'universalising' discourse in the 21st century is its origin in the specific European history of modernity and nationalism.[43] As Ashworth noted:

> Nineteenth-century conceptualisations of heritage emerged in the ethos of a singular and totalised modernity, in which it was assumed that to be modern was to be European, and to be European or espouse European values was to be at the pinnacle of cultural achievement and social evolution. The acquisition of the adjective, 'modern', for itself by Europe was an integral part of imperialism and the pinnacle of heritage was to become the European metropolitan core of the imperial empire.[44]

The critical perspective offered by Harvey in his outline of a history of heritage is in terms of "a history of power relations that have been formed and operate via the deployment of the heritage processes."[45] He argued that notwithstanding the differing perspectives of the definitions of heritage, notably among Lowenthal, Tunbridge, Ashworth and Graham, Hewison and Samuel, their general agreement on the dating of the origin of the practice of heritage as a 'modern' 19th-century invention is erroneous, because it obscures "a comparatively rich historical contextualisation of heritage beyond the 19th century."[46] This view by Harvey of the need for "a deeper understanding of the historically contingent and embedded nature of heritage" is vital, because it allows a consideration of the possibilities of an approach to Heritage Studies in Africa that goes beyond its 19th-century hegemonic imposition. More importantly, it exposes questions of power and authority in the production of heritage and identity in society,[47] which informs the consideration of an alternative approach to Heritage Studies in Africa, as a challenge to the Eurocentric hegemony in Heritage Studies.

This argument for a longer historical trajectory of the practice of heritage as a "process, a verb, related to human action and agency and as an instrument of cultural power in whatever period of time one chose to examine"[48] is crucial for this study. It offers a framework to explore the possibilities of conceptual and historical specificity of Heritage Studies in Africa beyond the approach to Heritage Studies unfolding in the RITP-APMHS. Furthermore, it allows us to ask the question of what is conceptually and historically distinctive about the approach of Heritage Studies in the RITP-APMHS that makes it African, beyond the critique of notions of heritage as automatic, traditional, pre-colonial inheritance. Especially instructive for the search for an approach to Heritage Studies that is specifically African is the implication of Harvey's emphasis on the need for a historical, conceptual understanding of Heritage Studies. According to him:

> What this implies for (*African*) Heritage Studies is that we should not draw any lines of temporal closure, or see the entire heritage concept as a product of later 19th and 20th century cultural change without origin. Rather, we should supply (*African*) heritage with a history of its own; not in terms of recounting the story of the development of a particular modernist strand of heritage from a 19th-century icon, but in terms of examining the evolution of the heritage process over a longer term.[49]

The notion of heritage as a 19th-century invention tied to European modernity is inescapably dominant and definitive of the notion and process of heritage. However, a history of heritage, as suggested by Harvey, allows us to appreciate heritage not as a monolithic, hegemonic, cast-in-stone concept, but as a concept always subjected to contestation, appropriation, and challenges to its meanings, histories, and uses. More importantly, in the context of an interrogation of the approach to Heritage Studies in the RITP-APMHS, Harvey's theory "allows a much greater temporal depth",[50] offering a framework for exploring a deeper history of Heritage Studies in Africa that can define its conceptual specificity and accommodate its critical distinction. Crucially, Harvey agrees with Dennis Hardy's contention that a "distinction can be drawn between heritage used in a conservative sense and heritage as a radical concept."[51] This dissonant notion of heritage is important because it allows the conceptualisation of an alternative discourse on Heritage Studies in Africa, which, according to Ferdinand de Jong, is "committed to disrupting the 'Eurocentrism' that continues to underpin cultural heritage theory/practice through a contemporary 'politics of recognition', which is bound up in new, alternative, or 'parallel' characterisations of heritage."[52]

This understanding is linked to another critical relevance of Harvey's theoretical position for foregrounding an analysis of the Public History approach to Heritage Studies projected in the RITP-APMHS. His arguments on the relationship between history and heritage are part of a debate that is pivotal to the approach to Heritage Studies projected in the RITP-APMHS as revealed in the analysis of its theoretical assumptions. According to Harvey, the attack which labelled Heritage Studies a "destruction of history"[53] (by Hewison,[54] Hardy,[55] and Tunbridge and Ashworth)[56] was based on erroneous assumptions. These negative assumptions are "firstly that there is something called 'correct' historical narrative that heritage is busily destroying, and secondly that until very recently, all history, historical narrative and other relationships with the past were somehow more genuine and authentic than they have now become."[57] Thus, he argued, the "distinction between true history and false heritage may be more illusory than actual",[58] because "traditional memory, rather than having been ended and defeated by false heritage, had in fact been transformed through visual technological and archival development."[59] This position is concurrent with the notion of heritage in relation to history that entered the APMHS core course via the reading by Raphael Samuel prescribed in one of the sessions analysed later in this chapter.

Notions of heritage in the APMHS

Leslie Witz and Ciraj Rassool, co-convenors of the APMHS programme, provide background and grounding to the debates on approaches to Heritage Studies encapsulated in the RITP-APMHS, which formed the basis of this analysis. In a reflection on the beginning of the programme in 1998, Witz admitted that the "teaching of Heritage Studies was like entering a minefield where one is confronted by highly explosive issues of personal and group identities, and it's not clear which direction to take."[60] This challenging pedagogical indeterminacy, he argued, existed because:

> To define Heritage Studies is notoriously difficult. Firstly, the notion of 'doing' heritage embraces a wide range of activities, from stamp collecting [...] to collecting oral traditions and museum curating. Secondly, the meanings of heritage are intensely debated. As defined by the Arts and Culture task group (ACTAG), it refers to an almost naturally occurring phenomenon, 'that which we inherit', and 'a powerful agent for cultural identity, reconciliation and nation building'. In contrast, within a great deal of academic historical writing, heritage refers to constructed, imagined or invented collective pasts and presents.[61]

This dilemma of what notions of heritage should inform the approach to Heritage Studies in the programme was, as already mentioned, reconciled in the ACTAG report's[62] call for 'museum critical theory' as an essential part of skills development in Heritage Studies.[63] This reference to critical museum theory in the ACTAG report, according to Witz, allowed the convergence of a healthy tension between the prevalent notions of heritage as inheritance, and the critical perspectives of the notions of heritage in the academy. Challenging the negative notions of heritage in the academy as "a primary source of raw data subject to evidential scrutiny, dependent upon present concerns, necessarily biased, usually condensed to the point of distortion and driven by the need for public approval." Witz argued that in the programme "heritage is recognised as a specific type of history with its own modes and conventions."[64] The approach to Heritage Studies that thus informed the programme at its beginning, as stated by Rassool, was to "critically and practically engage and challenge the dominant ways in which heritage is presented and represented", and to "discover different areas and modes of heritage production and to analyse the meanings which are produced." As he clearly stated:

> I am concerned about opening up and strengthening the possibilities for critical engagement, scholarship and knowledge formation in both domains. In the academy I have sought to understand the forms of power which were entrenched within South African social history at the same time as they made claims for the democratising capacities of 'history from below' and the efforts of popular history to address wider publics. My work, together with that of my historian colleagues at the historically black, apartheid-created University of the Western Cape, have sought to build a space for rethinking History and historical practice beyond conventional disciplinary distinctions and hierarchies between primary and secondary source, voice and writing, orality and history, and heritage and history. [...] This broader approach to the production of historical knowledge also seeks to understand the practices and genres of history making outside the academy, as well as how these relate to the peculiar routines and rituals of academic practice.[65]

To appreciate the significance of this articulation of a critical Public History perspective of heritage and its implied Heritage Studies, we analyse selected readings prescribed in the first three sessions of the 2007 academic year curriculum of the programme. This analysis is necessary for understanding how the Public History approach to critical Heritage Studies in the curriculum unfolded. These readings offer insight into the critical notions of Heritage Studies projected through Public History in the APMHS, and their limitations for the projection of Afrocentric notions of 'African' in African Heritage Studies.

An analysis of the 2007 core course outline for the first and second semesters[66] reflects the search for an appropriate approach to Heritage Studies (that is, both critical and African) as an overarching concern of the curriculum. This is especially evident if one considers the very first session of the core course, which required students to evaluate different meanings of heritage and suggest which of them would be most appropriate for an approach to Heritage Studies.[67] This underlying concern reflected in this question is seen throughout the first semester sessions, which focused on debates about the meanings and histories of different notions of heritage, and the different approaches to Heritage Studies they dictate and how appropriate they were for transforming and decolonising museums and heritage in Africa.

Heritage as inheritance

While the first session of the core course curriculum was titled 'What is Heritage?', the actual debate of this question started only in the second session of the course.[68] This second session, titled 'Heritage as a Product', has remained largely unchanged, except for the omission from the 2001 curriculum onwards of the suggested extra readings.[69] An important pedagogical intervention was the suggestion that students read the texts in the sequential order provided for them to understand the dialectic of the debate concerning notions of heritage as they unfold in the texts.

The introductory abstract for the session stated that the objective was "to question the meaning of heritage and discuss how heritage is produced."[70] This reveals a constructivist perspective of the notion of heritage as a product[71] inherent in the curriculum of the programme. This implicitly challenged the notions of heritage in the ACTAG Report, in which heritage was defined as "that which we inherit" and George Abungu's notion of heritage as "a nation's or people's resources."[72] The theoretical challenge to these notions of heritage relied on Graeme Davison, who, from an Australian perspective, traced the history of the concept and argued that 'heritage', both as a concept and as a practice, is essentially a constructed, cultural political idea.[73] This debate also draws on Ashworth and Tunbridge's notion of heritage as "a created phenomenon continuously created anew according to changing attitudes and demands, in order to understand the different meanings attached to heritage and discuss which might be most appropriate in terms of an approach to Heritage Studies."[74]

The first notion of heritage debated in the curriculum was an excerpt from the ACTAG Report, presented to the Minister of Arts, Culture, Science and Technology in June 1995. In the excerpt, which focused on 'definition and description', the report introduced the notion of heritage as "that which we inherit, which is a powerful agent for cultural identity, reconciliation and nation building."[75] This assumed heritage, which "we inherit as agents for identity and nation-building" and that the report specifically stated refers to "cultural heritage, including the landscape we live in,"[76] was defined as the "sum total of wildlife and scenic parks, sites of scientific or historical importance, national monuments, historic buildings, works of art, literature and music, oral traditions and museum collections."[77] The report further identified what it referred to as four major disciplines of heritage: "(1) living culture, which is the wealth of untapped information in our oral traditions; (2) archives which conserve and interpret documents; (3) museums which conserve objects; and (4) heritage resources which are the present concern of the National Monuments Council and its former homeland equivalent."[78]

While the focus on ACTAG reflected the South African debate on the meanings of heritage, the next part of the session was an attempt to locate this notion of heritage in the discourse of dominant notions of heritage on the African continent, through setting a conference paper by George Abungu (archaeologist, ex-Director of the National Museum of Kenya, and a leading expert on conservation management in Africa) as prescribed reading for the session. This is an excerpt from "Heritage, Community and the State in the 90s: Experiences from Africa", presented at 'The Future of the Past' Conference, held at UWC from 10 to 12 July 1996. This was at the height of the critical debate on the meaning of heritage in the context of calls for transformation in the heritage sector in South Africa. In his paper, which has remained prescribed reading for the session through the years under analysis, he defined African heritage as follows:

> A nation's or people's resources – both natural and cultural – can be classified as heritage. Cultural heritage can take the form of either tangible or intangible resources [...] cultural heritage in Africa includes sites, architecture, remains of cultural, historical, religious, archaeological or aesthetic value, as well as song, dance, music, language, dress, food and religion.[79]

One of the criticisms of this idea of heritage is that apart from its notion of African heritage as traditional, pre-colonial essence destroyed by colonialism, it revealed little cognisance of the constructiveness of heritage as a resource. This perspective took the notion of heritage as given, and did not fully explore the cultural, political process of this construction, beyond criticism of the generally negative colonial impact on a supposedly inherited pre-colonial traditional culture as heritage resources. The approach to Heritage Studies dictated by this notion of heritage implied a focus on the acquisition of conservation, preservation, and presentation skills on the uses of these resources, with the objective of achieving recognition for this neglected heritage through increased representation on UNESCO's world heritage list.

Notwithstanding criticism of the notions of heritage and the approach to Heritage Studies it implied, engagement with both ACTAG's and Abungu's projected notions of heritage revealed not only the notions of heritage of which the RITP-APMHS is critical, but also its points of criticism. They were also instructive in revealing the notions of Heritage Studies that the RITP-APMHS projects, and its limitations for Heritage Studies from the Afrocentric turn perspective. The critical point of the session is the challenge to the approach to Heritage Studies implied in the notion of heritage as neutral, automatic, inherited resources projected by the Abungu and ACTAG perspectives. This point unfolded in the next prescribed reading, which challenged and rejected the approach to Heritage Studies implied in the notion of heritage as a given and natural occurring phenomenon and resources. This is argued to have lacked a critical interrogation of either the origin or the meaning of the concept; or contestation over its practices, especially given the inherent cultural politics it entails.

Heritage as a product

The next prescribed reading for the session, 'The Meanings of Heritage'[80] by Davison, not only traces the intellectual history of the concept of heritage, but critically challenges the notion of heritage as an automatically occurring resource or phenomenon by revealing the history of its intellectual and socio-cultural political construction as both a concept and as a set of practices. The text debunks the notion of heritage as a naturally occurring phenomenon by tracing the origin of uses of the concept, from its initial common use to depict material property, to its banal use in denoting any commodity that purports to produce nostalgic 'past-ness', to the use of the term as an intellectual inheritance and its use to denote the natural environment. Davison highlighted its more serious use in the notion of national heritage as "collections of folkways and political ideas that define national identities."[81] In a direct challenge to the notion of heritage as automatic inherited resources, Davison suggested that heritage, rather than being something naturally occur-ring that we must preserve or save, is instead something that we create and build.[82]

While Abungu seemed to have no problem with UNESCO's notion of heritage in Africa, as seen in his (justified) argument that "the non-recognition of the continent's rich heritage is well documented,"[83] Davison was cynical of the role of UNESCO in projecting a notion of heritage that eventually determined the notion of heritage as applied not only in the Australian context, but also globally. According to Davison, UNESCO's adoption of the term 'heritage' as "shorthand for both built and natural remnants of the past"[84] was crucial for the acceptance of the concept. Davison therefore recognised the deeply contested terrain of the meaning of heritage in postcolonial societies, and the challenges to notions of heritage of UNESCO and affiliated bodies in professionalising heritage through its emphasis on the objectification and systematisation of heritages. He argued that "though most heritage listing invokes the language of democracy and aspires to some kind of representativeness, the elitist values of the heritage consultants show through"[85] in the definition of what is and what is not heritage.

Construction of heritage

This notion of heritage as a process of conscious, present-centred construction through the activities of agents operating in a socio-cultural political context was the focus of the debate in the next prescribed reading. The reading, the first chapter in the book, *Dissonant Heritage*, by Tunbridge and Ashworth, argued for the intrinsic dissonance of heritage as both an idea and praxis. It traced the changing meanings of heritage and argued that "there are intrinsic dangers in the rapidly extending and stretching use of the word which leads to loss of precision" and "conceal[s] and magnifies problems intrinsic to the creation and management of heritage."[86] Signposting the distinction between history and heritage (a topic that was the focus of the next session), the text challenges the notion of heritage as automatically inherited resources by introducing the notion of heritage as a "product of the present, purposefully developed in response to current needs or demands for it, and shaped by those requirements."[87] In applying a mechanistic, industrial analogy of commodification to the notion of heritage as a process of production, the text showed how the activities of agents in selection and targeting through interpretation produced heritage resources.[88] This notion of heritage is especially important in challenging the ACTAG Report and Abungu's notions of heritage as automatically occurring resources, because it shows that while the resources of the past (in its varied forms) might be automatically occurring and existing, they are not in themselves heritage; rather, at best, raw materials from which to produce heritages. According to Tunbridge and Ashworth:

> The resource base from which heritage is assembled is a wide and varied mixture of past events, personalities, folk memories, mythologies, literary associations, surviving physical relics; together with places, whether sites, towns, or landscapes with which they are symbolically associated. These are raw materials which form a quarry of possibilities from which the selection [of heritage] occurs.[89]

The process of heritage production through interpretative selection, as articulated in the text, reveals the notion of heritage as a culturally constructed concept exclusive to a specific legatee.[90] The notion of heritage revealed in this conceptual distinction between heritage construed as automatically inherited artefacts of the past and as raw material of the process of production, and the produced resources of specific, culturally constructed legatees, is crucial for the approach to Heritage Studies it implied. If heritage is construed as the automatic, almost naturally occurring resources of the past, the implication for Heritage Studies is merely that they should take an antiquarian approach. However, for heritage as a process of production of exclusive legatees using cultural inherited resources as its raw materials, the focus of Heritage Studies will not only be the questioning of the criteria for identifying and selecting interpretations of these raw materials, but also the interrogation of the politics of its production processes and of the actual end-product. The critique of this approach to Heritage Studies, as a critical study of the process of cultural, political construction of identity to demarcate socio-political and spatial temporalities, informed the subsequent sessions of the curriculum.

History and heritage, heritage as history

The importance of the location of the RITP-APMHS in the UWC Department of History rather than in the Departments of Archaeology, Anthropology, or Cultural Studies (or even Environmental Studies), as is the norm in similar programmes worldwide, was reflected in the next session, titled 'History and Heritage: Rivals or Partners'. The session started with a discussion of the distinction between history and heritage and heritage as history, and, importantly, revealed the notion of critical Heritage Studies encapsulated in the RITP-APMHS. The session not only identified the different connotations of the concepts and practice of Heritage Studies as it relates to the academic discipline of history; it also engaged and interrogated the underlying theoretical assumptions of the notion of heritage as a genre of knowledge production of the past, different from and challenging the basic assumptions of history.

The reading prescribed for the session started with an internet debate prompted by Phillip Curtin's writing on the historical significance of Goree Island to the transatlantic slave trade, given its acceptance as heritage. We will focus briefly on the debate to identify the notions of heritage it highlighted, since it is the notion of heritage that it revealed distinct to that of history that is crucial for this analysis. More importantly, we have chosen to focus on the reading by Raphael Samuel, because as can be seen in both the Jane Carruthers and David Lowenthal texts prescribed for the session and the responses to them, Samuel remains a key referent in the debates.

The Curtin debate revealed three notions of heritage, two of which are worth mentioning for their importance in relation to the notion of heritage and the construction of identity, before focusing on the third notion of heritage, in relation to history, which was the focus of the debate. A notion of heritage as 'tradition' was emphasised in the editor's introduction to the debate, which explained that Curtin "raise[d] important issues for historians and humanities concerned with Africa", because "not only is there the issue of the creation of tradition, but also the purpose of and motives for such creation."[91] The equating of heritage in Africa with 'tradition', similar to the ACTAG Report and Abungu's notions of heritage in Africa, revealed the prevalent, underlying assumption of the notion of heritage in Africa as traditional pre-modern. In addition, the notion of heritage as ancestral roots was also revealed in the beginning of Phillip Curtin's contribution,[92] which presumes a notion of heritage defined by genealogical roots in temporal spaces, which is the underlying assumption of the notion of African heritage as automatic inheritance by virtue of its autochthonous root in Africa. Curtin also revealed the notion of museum as heritage in his dismissal of Goree Island (as an 'emotional' museum, as compared to a 'serious' museum).[93]

Significantly, in relation to the focus of this chapter, the approach of Public History as critical Heritage Studies encapsulated in the APMHS started to unfold in the main debate on the value of empirical historical methodology in the construction of heritage as knowledge and practice. In providing a clear example of what distinguishes history from Heritage Studies, the debate introduced the notion of Heritage Studies as a critical field of study with its own paradigm and methodologies. This approach of Heritage Studies as epistemology, with its own paradigm of knowledge construction challenged the authority of history as relying on empirical, verifiable archival sources, while heritage is a product of ideological consciousness and cultural, political expediencies.

Rejection of this approach to Heritage Studies as a critical discipline, with its own paradigm and methodologies, was apparent in the responses to Jane Carruthers' scathing criticism of the collusion of academic historians in the budding heritage fad in South Africa in the next prescribed reading for the session.[94] In accordance with her remarks on Johan Marnitz's distorted Afrikaner heritage presentation (as "incorrect, biased, in fact totally ahistorical"), Carruthers argued that "heritage is problematic and it poses a distinct theoretical challenge to the discipline of history" which should be avoided rather than embraced by academic historians because of its lack of methodological historical rigour.[95] Though not included in the readings, Carruthers' comments generated many responses. Peter Limb, for instance, a librarian, argued (in support) that while heritage is not evil, it certainly is distinct from history.[96]

The defence of the notion of heritage as a terrain of knowledge production with its own epistemology and methodological paradigm was the basis of the response by Ciraj Rassool to Carruthers' attack on academic historians' dubious engagement with heritage. While the paper in which this response was articulated was not initially added to the prescribed readings, it is essential to this analysis, because it clearly underlined the notions of heritage and critical Heritage Studies operative in the APMHS curriculum. Rassool (in response to Carruthers) argued that rather than avoiding heritage, historians should in fact embrace it, because, according to him, "the domain of heritage and Public History requires serious examination" since it is in this domain that post-apartheid South African identities are being fashioned and contested.[97] Here, Rassool introduced the notion of heritage as public historical terrain of identity contestations and argued that historians "who have chosen to regard heritage as an inferior domain" are lagging behind fundamental changes in their field.[98] This, he argued, was because new ways of thinking about the past and history are emerging that are challenging the hegemony of academic historical methodologies and authority in the production of knowledge of the past.[99]

To challenge the hegemonic modernist hierarchical paradigm of historical knowledge production, Rassool argued for a radical rethink of history as a "higher activity of systematic research" as opposed to heritage as "a type or genre of history produced by non-academics as innately subordinate to academic history in a hierarchal schema."[100] This, he argued, was because critical Heritage Studies offered the potential for the "fundamental reconstitution of the discipline of History." According to him, "professional historians, long used to a world of words – written and spoken – are being confronted with visual histories, whose code and conventions they are ill-equipped to read."[101] Rassool's perspective here reflected how the notion of Heritage Studies as a critical discursive terrain of knowledge production, challenging the hegemony of academic history in the contest of knowledge production of the past, unfolded in the curriculum of the APMHS. This is traceable to the inclusion of Lowenthal, who Rassool dismissed, along with Carruthers, as a heritage sceptic.[102]

The inclusion of Lowenthal in the prescribed texts for the session reflected the dialectical pedagogy of the curriculum. Lowenthal's text came after the text by Carruthers and was followed immediately by the text of Raphael Samuel, an advocate of heritage as a critical praxis, showing that Lowenthal's arguments were built into the debate only to be pulled down. In the reading chosen for the session, which is a chapter from his book, *The Heritage Crusade and the Spoils of History*, Lowenthal used the example of the Bermuda slave-breeding myth to show how "heritage can endure even when exposed as historically false", and argued that "heritage the world over not only tolerates but thrives on and even requires historical errors."[103] Lowenthal, like Carruthers, therefore rejected the notion of heritage as a source of knowledge of the past and warned historians of its conterminous dangers – not only for academic historical methodology, but also for its socio-cultural political implications.[104]

In defence of heritage

The defence against the disparaging views of heritage presented in the debate, of the relationship of the history discipline to the proliferation of engaging meaning and a practice (being designated heritage), was argued in Raphael Samuel's *Theatres of Memory*. Iain J.M. Robertson provided a background to the British heritage debate contained in the reading by Samuel. According to Robertson, the heritage debate had polarised audiences into heritage believers and heritage sceptics. On the sceptic pole, he positioned Robert Hewison,[105] David Lowenthal,[106] and Patrick Wright[107] as representing a notion that "sees heritage as an essentially conservative and nostalgia project" caught in an illusory "romanticised and idealised view of the past which is deployed to reinforce old certainties at a time of significant change."[108] On the optimist side, Raphael Samuel was positioned as champion of those who "recognise a more democratic form of heritage, where heritage is seen to emphasise the 'little platoons' rather than 'great society'."[109] Given the crucial influence of the notions of critical Heritage Studies revealed in Samuel's text in unfolding the underlying theoretical assumption of the notion of heritage and the approach to Heritage Studies in the RITP-APMHS curriculum, a brief analysis of the prescribed chapters in *Theatres of Memory* is pertinent.

The influence of Samuel's reading on the notion of heritage in the curriculum is especially apparent in the concordance of the notions of heritage revealed in both Witz and Rassool's[110] response to Jane Carruthers and in the response of Samuel to what he called 'the heritage baiter' in the British debate. Samuel was very critical of those he saw as 'heritage baiters', accusing them of "reifying professional historical narration as an objective practice that recounted a 'real' past, and being hypocritical in their description of the heritage industry."[111] He traced the debates between history and heritage to the:

> ... 'legacy of Romanticism' of the demarcation between memory and history, where memory was regarded as 'primitive and instinctual' and history as conscious; where memory comes naturally to the mind, while history is a product of analysis and reflection, and memory was regarded as subjective and history objective with history beginning where memory ends through the historical power of abstract reason and empirical proof.[112]

He rejected the artificial dichotomy between history and memory/heritage and argued that 'memory', rather than being merely a passive receptacle or storage system, an image bank of the past, is rather an active, shaping force that is dynamic. What it contrives symptomatically to forget is as important as what it remembers and that "it is dialectically related to historical thought, rather than being some kind of negative 'other' to it."[113] He therefore argued that "memory like heritage is a way of constructing knowledge after its own fashion."[114]

Samuel was especially critical of the academic historical discipline, accusing it of nothing less than being an appendage of power through incestuous inbreeding sectarianism that encourages autarchic tendencies of "a very hierarchical view of the constitution of knowledge".[115] This hierarchical view, according to Samuel, "fetishises the act of archival-based research, while denigrating other methods of engagement with the past. For example, the 'Antiquarians' – pioneers of record-based research – are denigrated by the use of a pejorative term"[116], local historians are denigrated as having a myopic, parochial outlook. In addition, Samuel challenged those who dismissed oral history "as being nothing more than naïve empiricism in which facts are supposed to speak for themselves",[117] and the oral tradition is "history's netherworld, where memory and myth intermingle, and the imaginary rubs shoulder with the real".[118] He equated oral history with the practice of memory "as an intellectual labour or conscious act of recollection which is historically and culturally conditioned",[119] and 'popular memory' can be regarded as the antithesis of written history.

Samuel traced the complex semantics of heritage to its 'lexicabilty', or ability to accommodate complex (and often divergent), ever-changing meanings within and between spaces and temporalities. Its definition has evolved from the archaic "God, King and the Law, the altar and the throne"[120] to its connotation as "the principal element in conveying tradition from generation to generation",[121] "as an alternative to tradition", and as "a vernacular, indigenous force, the natural heir to centuries of struggle."[122] In addition, Samuel mentions its "radical-patriotic version"[123] and its use as a metaphor for denoting the "environments and unspoilt countryside and wildlife and nature reserves and landscapes."[124] Aesthetically, he argued that as with history, "heritage is a hybrid, reflecting, or taking part in, style wars, and registering changes in public taste",[125] especially in its "association with corporate image-making."[126] Other uses he mentions include its use as a propaganda tool to promote an illusory 'Britishness' during and after the 1939-1945 European war[127] – to "today by contrast, where the past is seen not as a prelude to the present but as an alternative to it."[128] Samuel argued, thus, that "a genealogy of heritage might try to connect nature conservancy with the idea of preservation in the built environment",[129] to the "birth of the oral history movement"[130] and the "back to nature movements"[131] which rather than being the preserve of a minority is a "cultural capital on which all were invited to draw."[132]

Engaging with the intrinsic paradox of heritage as both a constraining/conservative process and a radical/progressive, emancipatory process, which are "historically symbiotic, complementary at the same time, or even two sides of the same coin, each testifying to a felt absence in the present",[133] Samuel responded to Patrick Wright's attack on heritage movement as "reactionary chic representing the triumph of aristocratic and reactionary nostalgia and part of the self-fulfilling culture of national decline."[134] Samuel similarly responded to Robert Hewison's rejection of heritage as an "aristocratic plot signalling the end of history"[135] and charges of heritage being part of the grand capitalist conspiracy that opiates the society through "a complex and purposefully selective process of historical recollection" as "a bid for hegemony, a way of using knowledge in the service of power."[136]

In addition, Samuel argued that the connotation of heritage as the 'blessed' right of specific individuals, lineages, and stock locally was linked to the racialised discourse of global British imperialism.[137] He showed how, chronologically and sociologically, "the rise of the heritage industry, far from heralding an epoch of feudal reaction, coincides, rather, in Britain as in other European countries, with political de-alignment and a collapse of the two-camp class divide"[138] in politics. This, he argued, had the "significant consequence of broadening what had hitherto been understood as heritage to a more pluralist and radically different version from the previous hegemonic version of heritage." Samuel thus defended heritage from attack from both the left, who believe heritage is a capitalist commodification of the past for tourist consumption and the right, who argued heritage blurs the line between entertainment and education.[139] In addition to its outright dismissal as a "fraud"[140] by Neal Ascherson, Samuel exposed the irony that "though the denigration of heritage is voiced in the name of radical politics, it is pedagogically quite conservative, and echoes some of the right-wing jeremiads directed against new history in the schools"[141] which assumed that the masses, if left to their own devices, are "moronic; their pleasures are unthinking; their taste, cheapo and nasty."[142] Therefore, for Samuel, "far from heritage being the medium through which conservative version[s] of the national past becomes hegemonic, one could see its advent [not only] as part of a sea-change in attitude which has left any unified view of the national past liberal, radical, or conservative in tatters",[143] but as a continuation of its history in preservation which "owes its origin as much to the Left as to the Right."[144]

Instead of disparaging heritage, historians should consider those areas or practices where "heritage has the edge on archive-based scholarship and research" according to Samuel.[145] He specifically mentioned visual awareness and oral history as areas of heritage that cast into question the narrow preoccupation with the written word as a form of historical knowledge construction. Samuel therefore argued that "heritage, if we adopted some of its procedures, could begin to educate us in the language of looks, initiate us into the study of colour coding and force us to become our own picture researcher."[146] More importantly, he argued for the appreciation of heritage based on its immense contribution in the creation of the space of Public History,[147] and also the history of the environment, where Heritage Studies seems to be uniting natural history with archaeological inquiry.[148] He also captured the contemporary, 'next-to-nothing' significance of heritage when he suggested that "heritage, in short, far from being a stationary state, is continually shedding its old character and metamorphosing into something else",[149] and added that:

> Heritage is in fact one of the few areas of national life in which it is possible to invoke an idea of the common good without provoking suspicion of party interest, and it is one of the few areas where notions of ancestry and posterity can be invoked without embarrassment or bad faith.[150]

Samuel was also to be found lurking in the background of Witz and Rassool's respon-ses to Carruthers[151] as he rejected the artificial dichotomy of history and memory/heritage, and argued that memory, rather than being merely a passive receptacle or storage system, an image bank of the past, is in fact an active, shaping force that is dynamic.[152] This argument, of the notion of heritage as a way of "constructing knowledge after its own fashion",[153] can be seen echoed in Witz and Rassool's notions of Heritage Studies as Public History as a terrain of knowledge construction within its own distinct paradigm.[154] Samuel's challenge to the academic historical discipline was also echoed in Witz and Rassool's response to Carruthers' warning to historians to avoid the murky world of heritage, especially Rassool's argument on the methodological advantages of heritage over academic history in its introduction of visual text as historical narrative.[155] Rassool's emphasis on the recognition of visual images as historical text echoes Samuel's specific mention of visual awareness and oral history as areas of heritage that question the narrow preoccupation with the written word as a form of authority on historical knowledge construction.[156] Most important is the influence of Samuel's notion of heritage as Public History on the APMHS, reflected in Witz and Rassool's promotion of heritage and rejection of the notion of heritage as an automatic, naturally occurring phenomenon. This is especially apparent in the projection of heritage as a terrain for the contestation of hegemonic representation of the past with academic history, rather than as automatic inheritance or an illusion imposed by power on an unthinking public.

Critical Heritage Studies and Public History

Laurajane Smith offered a connection between the critiques of the concept of heritage as masculine and the notion of its intrinsic gendered intangibility to expose further limitations to the notion of heritage as reflected in the British debate. According to Smith, Heritage Studies are at "remedial stage of feminist and/or gender awareness"[157] because "heritage is 'masculine' and tells a predominantly male-centred story, promoting a masculine, and in particular, an elite-Anglo-masculine vision of the past and present."[158] This, she argued, was because the "way heritage is defined, understood and talked about reproduces and legitimises gender identities and the social value that underpinned them."[159] According to Smith, the 1972 World Heritage Convention, which embodied a "particular understanding and conceptualisation of the nature of cultural heritage",[160] is definitive of the notion of national and international heritage. She argued that the "Western Authorised Heritage Discourse (AHD) that defines heritage as material (tangible), monumental, grand, good, aesthetic and of universal value dominates, if not underwrites, much of UNESCO's heritage policy."[161] According to Smith, the idea of heritage as intangible, as codified in the Intangible Cultural Heritage Convention ICHC 2003, "challenges the AHD both at a practical and philosophical level",[162] because it recognised that "heritage only becomes 'heritage' when it is recognisable within a particular set of cultural or social values, which are themselves intangible."[163]

The significance of Smith's notion of heritage as an intangible cultural process of making meaning is that in "drawing attention to the issue of intangibility, and in challenging the emphasis placed on the Western idea of material and the preservationist desire to freeze the moment of heritage and to conserve,"[164] she exposes and calls attention to the often unstated and under-studied underlying Western ideological assumption inherent in the notion and process of heritage in all its dissonant ramifications. This notion of the inherent intangibility of all heritages as an approach to critical Heritage Studies is of fundamental importance to this chapter, because of how the implications of Smith's notion of heritage as intangible for critical Heritage Studies was challenged by Gary Minkley, Ciraj Rassool and Leslie Witz revealed the specific critical notion of heritage and approach to Heritage Studies employed by the APMHS.

Despite accepting the merits of Smith's 'intangibility' notions of heritage, as representing a subversive departure from the hegemonic notion of heritage, Minkley, Rassool, and Witz[165] took issue with Smith in a critique of the South African heritage complex. They concluded that the critical notion of heritage as intangible "reproduces the logic of what it seeks to criticise",[166] because Smith's over-reliance on the role of expertise in legitimising heritage limits her approach to critical Heritage Studies.[167] According to them, "there is a profound sense" that the notion of heritage in the "new Heritage Studies" articulated by Smith, "continues to work with a sense of disciplinary hierarchies"[168] where the disciplinary practices and methodologies of history, anthropology, cultural studies, and architecture can translate agency, experience, memory, locality, and performance in and of community into heritage.[169]

The Troika thus challenged Smith's reliance on the methodologies of social history to situate critical Heritage Studies.[170] It is in this rejection of the notion of critical Heritage Studies suggested by Smith as "social history of a particular critical type" that the distinctive notion of critical Heritage Studies employed by the APMHS unfolded. According to Minkley, Rassool, and Witz, the limitation of Smith and much of critical Heritage Studies is that they "operate from the site of the academy or the professionals, where there is no appreciation, or even engagement of the public sphere, or of contested and constituted and re-constituting publics."[171]

As shown in the arguments for the rejection of Smith's notion of critical Heritage Studies, the relationships between the academy and the public in historical knowledge production is what distinguishes the notion of Heritage Studies used by the RITP-APMHS from the social history notion of Heritage Studies projected by Smith. For Minkley, Rassool, and Witz, the notion of Heritage Studies as popularisation of 'history from below', which the social history approach suggested by Smith implies, maintained rather than challenged the 'hierarchies of knowledge' in historical knowledge production.[172] Correlating this notion of social history with the notion of popular history in South Africa and the American perspective of Public History,[173] in order to capture the notion of Public History in the APMHS, Minkley, Rassool, and Witz stated that their specific perspective on Public History:

> ... [i]s to question prevailing and dominant understanding of the past, in either the academy or the public domain [...] we are concerned to show how the visualisation of pastness (something academic historians attempt to do through the written narrative) generates, in different ways and on several fronts, precisely what a history is about.[174]

This approach to Heritage Studies, which takes the knowledge transactional relationship between the academy and the public in the production and presentation of the historical past as definitive of the practice of Heritage Studies as public "historical practice, within different genres characterised by different sociologies and modalities of historical production",[175] "draw[s] on the methodologies of David William Cohen"[176] for its notion of critical Public History. This reliance on David Cohen is crucial because of his argument that "while academic guild historians debated methods and experience of handling specific texts, and also oral tradition generally, people across Africa were producing, using and actively debating their pasts in ways virtually inaccessible to guild interest in evolving something like oral historiography."[177] According to Minkley, Rassool and Witz, the critical importance of Cohen's theory of the production of history on their approach to Heritage Studies as critical Public History is "first, an emphasis on practice, and second, that the production of history was multiple and 'equal' in significance and possibility."[178] Thus, according to them, critical Public History recognised:

> That those outside the professional history fraternity are engaged in producing history, in a domain of public scholarship, where the public historian enters into collaborative research and works with institutions in the public domain. In these knowledge transactions, the expertise as a historian is challenged, shaped and re-shaped as different historical knowledges are evoked, articulated, negotiated and contested. Here the mystique of the scientific knowledge is shattered, while multiple histories are encountered, sometimes reduced, other times ignored, and at still other times emerge in critical frame over narratives of inclusion and exclusion, taxonomies and biographies of material objects, cartographies of jurisdiction, and the performance of insiders and outsiders.[179]

While it is not explicitly stated, Cohen's theory of the 'production of history', which he referred to as "the processing of the past in societies and historical settings all over the world and the struggle for control of voices and texts in innumerable settings which animate this processing of the past", is African-derived. This is not only because of his collaborations with E.S. Atieno Odiambo, but (as mentioned by Minkley, Rassool, and Witz) much of Cohen's theory, which was framed around production of history in post-colonial Africa, especially Kenya and Uganda, aimed towards an attempt at the reconstruction of African history.[180] It is precisely the engagement with the heritage dynamics of the production of history in post-colonial Africa which informed the criticism of what the Troika, following a Foucauldian reading by Tony Bennett,[181] called the South Africa heritage complex, that exposes the limitations of the critical Public History approach to Heritage Studies as 'African'. The heritage complex of post-anti-apartheid South Africa was argued by them to be framed within the discourse of 'one indigenous voice of freedom' for South Africa's past, while rationalising current forms of political governance of citizenship as 'African and liberated'.[182]

One crucial aspect of Cohen's influence on the critical notion of Public History as Heritage Studies in the RITP-APMHS is his concern with decolonising knowledge production about Africa, and his conclusion that the project of analysing the Western power system that Edward Said pioneered is far from complete, given the continued and deplorably Eurocentric state of production of African history.[183] Invoking Said's thesis of Orientalism, they argued that "the production of history has continued in all kinds of settings beyond the formal and quite visible institutional structure. In many of these settings, such as situations of decolonisation, the practices of liberating knowledge productions have themselves contained the impulse and grammar of the established imperial frameworks."[184]

As argued so far, it is a challenge to the approach to Heritage Studies implied in the notion of heritage defined as African projected in the ACTAG report and Abungu's paper that constitute the critical point of departure for the challenge to the dominant notion of heritage in Africa in the APMHS curriculum. However, both the British heritage debate and the criticism of Laurajane Smith, which the RITP-APMHS relied on for its projection of critical Public History as the best approach to Heritage Studies, seems to be inadequate as an approach to Heritage Studies that is both critical and African. The approach to Heritage Studies as public historical production adequately accounts for the conceptual methodological distinction between the APMHS approach to Heritage Studies and any other similar programmes.

However, this approach is limiting as an approach to Heritage Studies that is African by its ideological epistemic positioning in the study of Africa. The importance of notion of heritage derived from Cohen's work on the production of history in Africa as an approach to Heritage Studies in the APMHS, is how it allows consideration of another perspective, projecting a notion of Heritage Studies that is claimed to be not only critical, but also – more significantly – 'African'.

This finally allows the argument for non-engagement with an Afrocentric turn as the limit of the critical Public History approach in the APMHS. The concern with the Africanisation of heritage through a narrative of "resistance of and liberation of the oppressed", and indigenous culture against "paradoxically and problematically long-standing exclusionary and racist histories",[185] further revealed the APMHS's underlying preoccupation with the question of an approach to Heritage Studies that is both critical and African. More importantly, it allows an engagement with how the consideration of arguments for an Afrocentric turn can further contribute to this concern.[186]

Endnotes

1. L. Witz & C. Cornell. 1999. 'From Robben Island to Makapan's Cave: Transforming Museum and Heritage Studies in South Africa', World Archaeological Congress. Cape Town, 10-14 January, 3.
2. L. Witz. 2001. 'Museum and Heritage Studies: An Interim Position'. Workshop on Mapping Alternatives: Debating New Heritage Practices in South Africa, 25-26 September. Cape Town: Project on Public Past, History department, UWC and RESUNACT, UCT, 3
3. Witz & Cornell. 'From Robben Island to Makapan's Cave', 3.
4. The 'Trioka' consisted of Ciraj Rassool, Leslie Witz and Gary Minkley and developed from an academic collaboration formed at UWC in the late 80s, that pioneered a new radical interpretation and practice of Public History.
5. Witz. 'Museum and Heritage Studies', 5.
6. Witz & Cornell. 'From Robben Island to Makapan's Cave', 3-4.
7. Ibid., 4.
8. Witz. 'Museum and Heritage Studies', 1.
9. Ibid., 2.
10. Ibid.
11. Ibid., 1.
12. L. Witz. 2010. 'Museums, Histories and the Dilemmas of Change in Post-Apartheid South Africa'. *University of Michigan Working Papers in Museum Studies*, 3:3.
13. Ibid., 2.
14. L. Witz, G. Minkley & C. Rassool. 2017. *Unsettled History: Making South African Public Pasts*. Ann Arbor, MI: University of Michigan Press, 14. https://doi.org/10.3998/mpub.9200634
15. Witz. 'Museums, Histories and the Dilemmas of Change in Post-Apartheid South Africa', 6.
16. See J. Carruthers. 1998. 'Heritage and History', 20 October. *H-Africa, Africa Forum*, 2.
17. Witz. 'Museum and Heritage Studies', 10.
18. Witz. 'Museums, Histories and the Dilemmas of Change in Post-Apartheid South Africa', 5.
19. Ibid.
20. Witz. 'Museum and Heritage Studies', 2. Popular history is "based on a notion of discovery, recovery and revelation of a hidden history, a past that has been subordinated by oppression and exclusion during the days of colonialism and apartheid from historical record."
21. Witz. 'Museum and Heritage Studies', 3.
22. C. Rassool. 2000. 'The Rise of Heritage and the Reconstitution of History in South Africa'. *Kronos: Journal of Cape History*, 26:23.
23. Witz. 'Museum and Heritage Studies', 4.
24. Witz. 'Museums, Histories and the Dilemmas of Change in Post-Apartheid South Africa', 6.
25. Witz. 'Museum and Heritage Studies', 4.
26. Ibid.

27 Witz. 'Museums, Histories and the Dilemmas of Change in Post-Apartheid South Africa', 6.
28 Ibid., 7.
29 Ibid., 2.
30 Ibid.
31 Witz. 'Museums, Histories and the Dilemmas of Change in Post-Apartheid South Africa, 2.;
    Also see C. Rassool. 2010. 'Power, Knowledge and the Politics of Public Pasts'. *African studies*, 69(1):79, 80 & 101. https://doi.org/10.1080/00020181003647215
32 Rassool. 'Power, Knowledge and the Politics', 84.
33 Rassool. The Rise of Heritage, 5.
34 Rassool. 'Power, Knowledge and the Politics', 85.
35 Witz. 'Museum and Heritage Studies', 11.
36 Witz & Cornell. 'From Robben Island to Makapan's Cave'.
37 D. Harvey. 2001. 'Heritage Pasts and Heritage Presents: Temporality, Meaning and the Scope of Heritage Studies'. *International Journal of Heritage Studies*, 7(4):327. https://doi.org/10.1080/13581650120105534
38 See D.W. Cohen. 1994. *The Combing of History*. Chicago, IL: University of Chicago Press.;
    See also G. Minkley, L. Witz & C. Rassool. 2009. 'South Africa and the Spectacle of Public Pasts: Heritage, Public Histories and Post Anti-Apartheid South Africa'. Paper presented at the Heritage Disciplines Symposium, UWC, 8-9 October.;
    L. Witz & C. Rassool. 2008. 'Making Histories'. *Kronos: South African Histories*, 34(1):6-15. https://www.jstor.org/stable/41056600
39 D. Harvey. 2008. 'The History of Heritage'. In: B.J. Graham & P. Howard (eds.), *The Ashgate Research Companion to Heritage and Identity*. London: Routledge, 27.
40 Harvey. 'Heritage Pasts and Heritage Presents', 320.
41 Minkley, Witz & Rassool. 'South Africa and the Spectacle of Public Pasts'.
42 L. Smith. 2006. *Uses of Heritage*. New York: Routledge, 17. https://doi.org/10.4324/9780203602263
43 Ibid., 18.
44 B. Graham, E. Ashworth & G. Tunbridge. 2000. *A Geography of Heritage*. London: Arnold, 17. A point also made by Laurajane Smith when she argued that "the origin of the dominant heritage discourse is linked to the development of 19th century nationalism and liberal modernity" in Uses of Heritage, 17.
45 Harvey. 'The History of Heritage', 19.
46 Harvey. 'Heritage Pasts and Heritage Presents', 326.
47 Ibid., 321.
48 Ibid., 327.
49 Ibid., 326.
50 Harvey. 'The History of Heritage', 23.
51 D. Hardy. 1988. 'Historical Geography and Heritage Studies'. *Area*, 20(4):333-338. http://www.jstor.org/stable/20002646
52 F. de Jong & M. Rowlands (eds.). 2006. *Reclaiming Heritage: Alternative Imaginaries of Memory in West Africa*. Walnut Creek, CA: Life Coast Press Inc., 9.

53   See D. Lowenthal. 1996. *The Heritage Crusade and the Spoils of History*. London: Viking, 3.
54   J.E. Tunbridge & G.J. Ashworth. 1995. *Dissonant Heritage: The Management of the Past as a Resource in Conflict*. New York, NY: John Wiley, 6.
55   Hardy. 'Historical Geography and Heritage Studies'.
56   Ashworth & Tunbridge. *A Geography of Heritage.*; Lowenthal. *The Heritage Crusade and the Spoils of History*.
57   Harvey. 'Heritage Pasts and Heritage Presents', 325.
58   Ibid.
59   Ibid., 327.
60   Witz & Cornell. 'From Robben Island to Makapan's Cave', 2.
61   Ibid., 3.
62   ACTAG Report of the Arts and Culture Task Group, presented to the Minister of Arts, Culture, Science and Technology, Pretoria, June 1995. ACTAG is a task force created by the South African Minister of Arts and Culture to advise on policies for heritage transformation from its apartheid legacy to one that reflects the new, democratic 'rainbow nation'.
63   Witz & Cornell. 'From Robben Island to Makapan's Cave', 3.
64   Ibid., 4.
65   Rassool. 'Power Knowledge and the Politics of the Public Past', 79.
66   **Core course outline, 2007:**

   First Semester
   1. **What is Heritage? An introduction to the course and the internship**
   2. **The Production of Heritage**

      Some issues to be considered: The production of heritage; heritage as a construction.
   3. **Heritage and History**

      Some issues to be considered: Is 'history' the same as 'the past'? Is 'heritage' different from 'history'?
   4. **National Heritage**

      Some issues to be considered: How is 'national heritage' defined? Who determines what is 'national heritage'? Understanding power, ideology, and discourse.
   5. **Natural Heritages and Cultural Landscapes**

      Some issues to be considered: What is a 'natural environment'? Are natural environments constructed landscapes?
   6. **What is Living Heritage?**

      Some issues to be considered: Living heritage and intangible heritage – considering public memories, oral histories, lifestyles and the making of traditions. Are orality and literacy directly in opposition to each other or do they influence each other?
   7. **The Museum as Heritage**

      Some issues to be considered: How meanings are attached to objects.
      Stuart Hall has argued that "a museum does not deal solely with objects, but more importantly, with [...] ideas – notions of what the world is or should

be. Museums do not simply issue objective descriptions [...] They generate representations and attribute value and meaning in line with certain perspectives or classificatory schemes which are historically specific. They do not so much reflect the world through objects as use them to mobilise representations of the world past and present." What does Hall mean by this?

8. **Visual Strategies of Museum Exhibitions**

    Some issues to be considered: Ways of representation and presentation of visual material through exhibitions, and imagining new exhibitions and heritage displays. Examples will be drawn from Iziko Museums of Cape Town and other museums.

Second semester, 2007:

1. **Exhibition Analysis: 'Familieverhalen/Family Stories' and 'Memory of Congo'**

    'A Group Portrait from 9 South African Families', National Cultural History Museum, Pretoria, 2004 (formerly exhibited as 'Familie Verhalen uit Zuid-Afrika': South African Exhibition at the KIT, Tropemuseum, Amsterdam) and 'Memory of Congo: The Colonial Era', Royal Museum of Central Africa, Tervuren, Belgium, 2005.

2. **The Bushman Diorama: A History**

    In preparation for this class, in addition to your readings, you need to visit the South African Museum.

3. **Skeletons in the Cupboard: From the Diorama to Human Remains**
4. **Shadowed Ground: Sites, Locations, and Memorials**
5. **Memorials to Conflict**
6. **World Heritage and Global Systems**

    At the turn of the 21st century, the desire to acquire world heritage status has escalated, without sufficient attention to all the implications. In this class, we will consider of the category 'world heritage', its meanings, purposes, social constructions, and cultural politics. We are interested in thinking about the categories of World Heritage Site status, as well as the 'Masterpieces of Oral and Intangible Heritage of Humanity'. Other global dimensions of heritage involve tourism and legacies of colonial history.

7. **Slavery and Heritage in Ghana and South Africa**
8. **Robben Island: History and National Heritage**

    In preparation for this class, in addition to your readings, you need to visit the Nelson Mandela Gateway.

9. **The District Six Museum: Education in a Community Museum**

67 Preparatory questions, Core course, Session 1, 2009, Course reader, APMHS collections, CHR archives.

68 The first sessions observed from 2007 through 2009 dealt with students' orientation, formal introductions, and general introduction to the programme, the modalities of the internship component, and administrative logistics.

69 The readings omitted from the 2001 curriculum onwards were extra recommended readings that dealt with defining heritage and history and the relationship between them. These were:

K. Walsh. 1992. *The Representation of the Past: Museums and Heritage in the Post-Modern World.* New York, Routledge, especially chapters 4 and 5. https://doi.org/10.4324/9780203320570

R. Samuel. 1994. *Theatres of Memory: Past and Present in Contemporary Culture*. London: Verso, especially 259-273 and 288-312.

'History/Heritage', Mailbase United Kingdom, Internet discussion list, June 1997-October 1997. http://www.mailbase.ac.uk/lists/history-heritage

70   Introduction, Core course, Session 1, 2009, Course Reader. APMHS collections: CHR archives.

71   B. Graham & P. Howard. 2008. 'Heritage and Identity'. In: B. Graham & P. Howard (eds.), *The Ashgate Research Companion to Heritage and Identity*. London: Routledge, 2.

72   Introduction, Core course, Session 1, 2009, Course Reader. APMHS collections: CHR archives.

73   G. Davison. 1991. 'The Meanings of 'Heritage'. In: G. Davison & C. McConville (eds.), *A Heritage Handbook*. St Leonards: Allen and Unwin, 121. Third prescribed reading for Heritage as a Product, 1999, Core Outline, Issues in Museum and Heritage Studies (Leslie Witz private collection).

74   Introduction, Core course, Session 1, 2009, Course Reader. APMHS collections: CHR archives.

75   ACTAG Report of the Arts and Culture Task Group. Presented to the Minister of Arts, Culture, Science and Technology, Pretoria, 1995, 55.

76   Ibid., 55.

77   Ibid., 55.

78   Ibid., 56.

79   G. Abungu. 1996. 'Heritage, Community and the State in the 90s: Experiences from Africa'. Paper presented at the Future of the Past' Conference. Bellville: UWC, 10-12 July, 1.

80   Davison, 'The Meanings of 'Heritage''.

81   Ibid, 116.

82   Ibid, 117.

83   See Abungu, 'Heritage, Community and the State', 18.

84   Davison. 'The Meanings of 'Heritage'', 113.

85   Ibid., 125-126.

86   Tunbridge & Ashworth. *Dissonant Heritage*, 3.

87   Ibid., 6.

88   Ibid., 6.

89   Ibid., 7.

90   Ibid., 8.

91   Editor's note: Goree and the Atlantic Slave Trade, H-Africa discussion, 31 July-30 August 1995. hnet2.msu.edu-africa.threads.goree.html (Leslie Witz private collection).

92   P. Curtin opening comment. Goree and the Atlantic Slave Trade, H-Africa discussion, 31 July-30 August 1995 in 2007 Core Course Outline First Semester. Issues in Museum and Heritage Studies. hnet2.msu.edu-africa.threads.goree.html (Leslie Witz private collection).

93   **The Museum as Heritage**

      Some issues to be considered: How meanings are attached to objects.

Stuart Hall has argued that "a museum does not deal solely with objects, but more importantly, with [...] ideas – notions of what the world is or should be. Museums do not simply issue objective descriptions [...] They generate representations and attribute value and meaning in line with certain perspectives or classificatory schemes which are historically specific. They do not so much reflect the world through objects as use them to mobilise representations of the world past and present." What does Hall mean by this? – 2007 Course Outline, First Semester. CHR archives: UWC (Leslie Witz private collection).

94 Carruthers. 'Heritage and History', 2.
95 Ibid.
96 P. Limb. 28 October 1988. H-Africa@H-net.msu.edu (Leslie Witz private collection).
97 Rassool. The Rise of Heritage, 1.
98 Ibid., 23.
99 Ibid., 23.
100 Ibid., 5.
101 Ibid., 6.
102 Ibid., 6.
103 Lowenthal. *The Heritage Crusade*, 132.
104 "Heritage has been described as state-sanctioned nationalist rhetoric, and Heritage Studies as its uncritical voice", according to Minkley et al (2010). A position which echoes Patrick Wright's attack on the notion of heritage in the British debate as nationalist nostalgia of the imperial empire. See P. Wright. 1985. *On Living In an Old Country Again*. Oxford: Oxford University Press.
105 See R. Hewison. 1987. *The Heritage Industry: Britain in a Climate of Decline*. London: Methuen.
106 Lowentha. *The Heritage Crusade*.
107 P. Wright. *On Living In an Old Country Again*.
108 J.M. Robertson. 2008. 'Heritage from Below: Class, Social Protest and Resistance'. In: B. Graham & P. Howard (eds.), The *Ashgate Research Companion to Heritage and Identity*. London: Routledge, 143.
109 Ibid., 143.
110 Rassool, 'The Rise of Heritage'.;
    See also Witz & Cornell. 'From Robben Island to Makapan's Cave'.
111 Harvey. 'Heritage Pasts and Heritage Presents', 327.
112 Samuel. *Theatres of Memory: Past and Present in Contemporary Culture*, x.
113 Ibid.
114 Ibid.
115 Ibid., 4.
116 Ibid.
117 Ibid.
118 Ibid, 6.
119 Ibid.
120 Ibid., 205.
121 Ibid., 205
122 Ibid., 207.

123 Ibid., 208.
124 Ibid., 209.
125 Ibid., 211.
126 Ibid., 214.
127 Ibid., 218.
128 Ibid., 221.
129 Ibid., 228.
130 Ibid., 235.
131 Ibid., 237.
132 Ibid., 238.
133 Ibid., 294.
134 Ibid., 242.
135 Ibid., 242.
136 Ibid., 243.
137 R. Samuel quoted in J. Littler & R. Naidoo (eds.). 2005. *The Politics of Heritage: The Legacies of 'Race'*. New York, NY: Routledge, 3.
138 Samuel. *Theatres of Memory*, 246.
139 Ibid., 260.
140 Ibid., 242.
141 Ibid., 245.
142 Ibid., 247.
143 Ibid., 281.
144 Ibid., 288.
145 Ibid., 274.
146 Ibid., 246.
147 Ibid., 278.
148 Ibid., 277.
149 Ibid., 303.
150 Ibid., 292.
151 Both of them described Carruthers views as 'heritage baiting'. See Rassool, 'The Rise of Heritage.;
See also Witz & Cornell. 'From Robben Island to Makapan's Cave'.
152 Samuel. *Theatres of Memory*, x.
153 Ibid.
154 Rassool. 'The Rise of Heritage'.;
Witz & Cornell. 'From Robben Island to Makapan's Cave'.
155 Samuel. *Theatres of Memory*, 274.
156 Ibid., 278.
157 L. Smith & N. Natsuko (eds.). 2009. *Intangible Heritage*. London: Routledge. Smith used the example of how the commemoration of African-American women's lives in Los Angeles, and the Waanyi Women History Project of Northern Queensland, Australia. This challenged not only assumptions of women's place in heritage, but also how both "the nature and the fact of the permanence and visibility of andocentric nature of heritage show how commemorative spaces can be made and used, despite the absence of surviving built heritage."

158 L. Smith. 2008. 'Heritage, Gender and Identity'. In: B. Graham & P. Howard (eds.), The *Ashgate Research Companion to Heritage and Identity*. London: Routledge, 159.
159 Ibid., 161.
160 L. Smith & N. Natsuko. *Intangible Heritage*, 1.
161 Ibid., 3.
162 Ibid., 3.
163 Ibid., 6.
164 Smith. 'Heritage, Gender and Identity', 162.
165 Minkley, Witz & Rassool. 'South Africa and the Spectacle of Public Pasts'. Witz & Rassool. 'Making Histories'.
166 Minkley, Witz &Rassool. 'South Africa and the Spectacle of Public Pasts'.
167 Ibid., 13.
168 Ibid.
169 Ibid.
170 Ibid., 14.
171 Ibid., 15.
172 Ibid., 15.
173 According to them, "[p]ublic history in the United States provides a parallel to the attempt to do popular history in South Africa in the 1980s, and is characterised by the same tensions and separations. It appears to have a larger institutional presence outside the academy than popular history did in South Africa, but the issues remain ones of popularisation: of hierarchies of knowledge, discipline recognition and transmission." Minkley, Witz & Rassool. 'South Africa and the Spectacle of Public Pasts', 17.
174 Minkley, Witz & Rassool. 'South Africa and the Spectacle of Public Pasts', 21.
175 According to Minkley, Witz & Rassool, "engaging in Public History means engaging in practice", where "expert knowledge gets taken up, reformed, reduced and narrowed and never taken for granted." It is an engagement where historians are "careful not to impose their academic rituals and methodologies." See Minkley, Witz & Rassool. 'South Africa and the Spectacle of Public Pasts', 26.
176 Minkley, Witz & Rassool. 'South Africa and the Spectacle of Public Pasts', 22.
177 Cohen. *The Combing of History*, xv.
178 Minkley, Witz & Rassool. 'South Africa and the Spectacle of Public Pasts', 23. As argued by Witz and Rassool in a Kronos article aptly titled 'Making Histories': "By treating sources as histories, rather than as data to be mined ... Their work has questioned boundaries between history and anthropology through opening up issues of practice, particularly around area of fieldwork. A major concern of theirs is to think through relationship between processes of historicising and the field, as it comes to be constituted in both history and anthropology. The field, for them, is sites where different histories in a range of genres are produced, circulated and contested ... The power of their work lies in its attempts to comprehend the politics of a society, such as Kenya, around the different versions of history that were generated, where do histories circulate and for whom they circulate and for whom they mattered."
179 Minkley, Witz & Rassool. 'South Africa and the Spectacle of Public Pasts', 27.
180 Ibid., 22.
Works by D. Cohen & E.S. Atieno Odhiambo include:
1989. *Siya: A Historical Anthropology of an African Landscape*. London: James Curry.;

1987. 'Ayany, Malo and Ogot: Historians in Search of a Luo Nation'. *Cahiers d'Etudes Africaines*, 27(107-108):269-286. https://doi.org/10.3406/cea.1987.3406;
1992. *Burying SM*. Westport: Heinemann.;
2004. *The Risk of Knowledge*. Athens: Ohio University Press.
Works independently by David Cohen focusing on Africa include:
1986. *Toward a Reconstructed Past: Historical Texts from Busoga*. Uganda, Oxford: Oxford University Press.;
1991. 'A Case for Basoga: Lloyd Fallars and Construction of an African Legal System'. In: K. Mann & R. Roberts (eds.), *Law in Colonial Africa*. Portsmouth: Heinemann, 239-254.

181 T. Bennett. 1995. *The Birth of Museum: History, Theory, Politics*. New York, NY: Routledge.
182 Minkley, Witz & Rassool. 'South Africa and the Spectacle of Public Pasts', 29.
183 Cohen. The Combing of History, 243.
184 Ibid.
185 Rassool. 'The Rise of Heritage', 10.
186 See L. Dondolo & O. Morakinyo. 2021. *Afrocentric Turn in African Heritage Studies: Epistemology of Alterity*. Cape Town: Ace Publishers.

Conclusion

Neville Alexander remarked that, "[t]he dilemma – at once ethical and practical – confronting the creation of the 'new South Africa' has revolved around how much of the past to preserve and remember and how much to erase and forget."[1] Dotted with a trove of new and old heritage markers, the post-apartheid heritage landscape serves as a visual reminder of the tension and contestation between the battle of remembering and forgetting. During the early 1990s, when democracy supplanted an authoritarian regime, the ensuing transformation process held much promise as it was marked by invigorating debates, national dialogues, and consultative processes as both a means to contribute to the shaping of new legislation and a policy framework and a reimagining of the South African heritage complex through the reinvention of existing institutions by reframing public programming, collections and exhibitions; developing new heritage institutions, monuments, and training initiatives; and renaming landmarks. These are just a few of the ways in which transformation were addressed. Moreover, heritage institutions have attempted to remedy transformation through staffing, governance structures, policies, public programmes, changes in collections and exhibitions through acquisition and representation, access, and the development of diverse audiences.

There is little doubt that the government has invested a vast amount of material resources on transforming the heritage landscape across South Africa, some with varying degrees of success or no success at all, as demonstrated in the most recent transformation initiatives spearheaded by the current Minister of the DACST, Nathi Mthethwa, which was to install a monumental flag of 100 meters tall at a cost of R22 million.[2] This initiative was subsequently met with a considered measure of public indignation at the seemingly wasteful expenditure of public funds, especially when framed within the socio-political and economic realities of the present which have been exacerbated by the global Covid-19 pandemic and the impact of the global and transnational political economy. Specifically, more than two decades later, archives and heritage education and training initiatives continue to be haunted by the spectre of white minority rule, which is palpable in all spheres of life, whether it is through the resilient patterns of racialised inequality and poverty or through the representation of racial and gender imbalances in cultural, heritage, and memory institutions. The long shadow of colonialism and apartheid and the challenge of social cohesion in the post-apartheid aftermath[3] has also contributed to the anxieties of an uncertain future brought about by inadequate or lack of human and financial resources, poor leadership, chronic underfunding, limited training and opportunities for professional development, the deterioration of infrastructure, and challenges in respect of access, research, and preservation. Commenting on the slow progress of transformation, Gerard Corsane noted that "although the call for change has been heard, there are still some in the sector who have been slow to recognise the urgency for transformation and who desperately hold on to a now outdated museological paradigm."[4]

Although not an exhaustive study of the heritage sector, but rather offering a lens on the transformation within post-apartheid archives and the transformation of museum education and training initiatives through a focus on two post-apartheid archives in particular, such as the National Heritage and Cultural Studies Centre (NAHECS) at the University of Fort Hare (UFH) and the Mayibuye Centre for History and Culture which was later absorbed into the Robben Island Museum (RIM) and a post-apartheid heritage training course, the African Programme in Museum and Heritage Studies (APMHS) which was jointly convened by UWC and UCT. The intention was to provide an exposition of the intricate connection between heritage training and post-apartheid archives. Most of these institutions and figures instrumental to these initiatives played a key role in the transformation discourse by leading discussions in heritage transformation on the national stage, yet despite the proliferation of post-apartheid heritage initiatives, transformation has been painfully slow. Where transformation has happened, there have been varying degrees of success, especially when framed by prevailing socio-political and economic considerations, the promotion of a gendered, exclusive, and patriarchal approach to transformation in addition to transformation being rooted to the ideals of Mandela's notions of reconciliation and national unity which has led to a hands-off approach when it comes to symbolic reminders of the colonial and apartheid past.

Following a comparative history of post-apartheid archives in South Africa and Museum and Heritage Studies and training on the African continent and in South Africa, we traced how the project of Public History developed through the activist activities and public historical knowledge production of the Mayibuye Centre in particular, that opened discussions around the frictions, contestations, and contradictions in and around archives, museums, heritage professionals, and academics. This was not only radical for its time but also had a global impact, arguably similar to the #RhodesMustFall movement and subsequent fallist movements that emanated from South Africa. We further argued that the Public History orientation foregrounded by the Museum and Heritage Studies through the RITP-AMPHS postgraduate diploma course pioneered by the UWC Department of History was transformative of Museum and Heritage Studies on the continent. Against the lukewarm reception of Heritage Studies in relation to the discipline of history in the South African academy, and the dominant orientation in Museum and Heritage Studies that overly-emphasised the acquisition of technical skills of heritage conservation and collection management without addressing the underlying cultural-political power dynamics operating in the practice of heritage, we argued for an approach to transformation that is based on theory and practice, and more importantly, an African centred approach to heritage practice and scholarship.

Specifically, for post-apartheid archives, we argued that one of the first things to consider in transforming the archival landscape is for archives to adopt an institutional policy that makes provision for archival scholarship whereby archival staff are encouraged to write, present, and publish based on research within their own institutions and also other archives and collections. In this tumultuous time of archives being under siege, archivists need to take up the call to arms whereby they transform themselves from hoarders of ruins and relics to becoming active participants in knowledge production and social justice. Having explored the challenges that NAHECS and the UWC Robben Island Museum Mayibuye Archives have faced and continue to face, we should not believe that the transformation to post-apartheid South Africa has been completed or has even happened. The effects of colonialism and apartheid continue to reverberate in post-apartheid South Africa and plays itself out through inequality, representation, education, skills, accessibility, and so forth. Cast within this light, it becomes even more pertinent that archives are urgently transformed and reconstituted as creative, political, and intellectual projects for the future.

In distinguishing itself from other heritage training initiatives in Africa, RITP-APMHS stated that "through linking together theory with practice, it is able to challenge the emphasis of several African postcolonial AMHS which have tended to argue for creating mostly technically oriented museum professionals."[5] The APMHS approach to Museum and Heritage Studies was therefore premised on the objective of avoiding the "danger that Heritage Studies will become a form of technical training and a 'new breed of heritage workers' will continue to be manual functionaries"[6] as Arinze lamented. Notwithstanding this apparent rejection of a focus on technical training as an approach to Museum and Heritage Studies, despite its incorporation of training in conservation technologies, the Public History approach pioneered by the UWC Department of History is a fundamental distinction between the approach to Museum and Heritage Studies on the continent and the approach in South Africa. We described and analysed the history and process of development of Heritage Studies and training in South Africa to bring to the fore how radical and disruptive the version of Public History was in pioneering critical Heritage Studies in South Africa. We argued that the RITP-APMHS intervention not only engendered tangible transformation but more importantly planted the seed for a radical Afrocentric turn in Museum and Heritage Studies in Africa, and the global movement for rethinking the meaning, purpose, and relevance of heritage in Africa.

Our critique of post-apartheid archives and Museum and Heritage Studies transformation in South Africa is against the backdrop of how the transformation of heritage in South Africa set in motion seismic changes in the museum and heritage sector globally, which is engulfing Western museums as a result of the multipronged generational struggles by Africans for heritage justice. Within this vein, we briefly touch on how the transformation of the museum and heritage sector in South Africa laid the foundation for the process of decolonising the heritage sector through the current concerted effort to redefine the meaning and purposes of the museums globally through the concurrent process of restitution of African artefacts from European museums, plus the subtle acknowledgement of the destruction of African knowledge through the violence of looting objects during and as part of the war of conquest of African resources and knowledge. We argue that this project heralds a new global discourse of heritage and culture as a terrain of struggle which was inaugurated by heritage transformation in South Africa.

In responding to Mandela's challenge in his Heritage Day speech of 1997 to transform the museum and heritage sector in alignment with the ideals of democracy, human rights, and the Constitution, the government addressed this through several key pieces of the national heritage policy and legislation, such as the *White Paper on Arts, Culture and Heritage* (1996), the *National Archives Act* (1996), the *National Heritage Resources Act* (1999), and the *National Heritage Council Act* (1999). Although, well-intentioned, South Africa's national heritage policy and legislation were informed by international policies and heritage discourse, drawing heavily from the UNESCO and ICOM framework and in this sense, this Western inspired heritage framework, prevents heritage institutions and initiatives in South Africa to be "of Africa [that] need to be imbued with African qualities and African values and to reflect African experience."[7] Despite the transformative gains made in South Africa since 1994, heritage institutions and training opportunities continue to be haunted by the legacies of their own colonial and apartheid history as they remain locked in their Eurocentric custodial cloisters evident in their thinking, collections, exhibitions, training opportunities, and "their often old palatial-like museum buildings."[8]

More than just the issues of training, funding, poor leadership, aging equipment, and infrastructure which hinders transformation, it is our contention that there seems to be a lack of political and public interest in heritage institutions and training as they are competing with poverty, unemployment, political upheavals, and other crises which are not often represented as institutions continue to cling to representations of the past that bear no relevance to the present.

These are some of the failures of post-apartheid transformation, some systemic and some as unintentional consequences of limited funding, political interference, and limited professional training. However, as we argued, for transformation to be fully realised, there needs to be a rupture from the colonial vestiges that informs the approach to heritage on the African continent and in South Africa in particular. In moving towards transformation, one that is informed by an African-based decolonised approach to heritage, we should be able to have honest, in-depth, and critical self-reflections of policies, practices, roles, missions, visions, and continuing relevance. Rather than remaining spectators and passive custodians of history, collections should be cultivated and activated to assist in knowledge production but also to enrich the lives of those around it and in this way ensures its longevity and relevance in a society in flux.

Endnotes

1. N. Alexander. 2002. *An Ordinary Country: Issues in the Transition from Apartheid to Democracy in South Africa*. Durban: UKZN Press, 81-110.
2. 'South Africa to Spend R22 million on 100-metre Tall Flag'. https://bit.ly/41599tU [Accessed 12 May 2022].
3. S. Marschall. 2019. 'The Long Shadow of Apartheid: A Critical Assessment of Heritage Transformation in South Africa 25 Years On'. *International Journal of Heritage Studies*, 25(10):1089. https://doi.org/10.1080/13527258.2019.1608459
4. G. Corsane. 2000. 'What Can South African Museums Learn from the Work of the French Sociologist Pierre Bourdieu'. *SAMAB*, 24:26.
5. Proposal to Rockefeller Foundation for the Development of an African Programme in Museum and Heritage Studies: Submitted by the Cape Higher Education Consortium, February 2003. Cape Town South Africa (Leslie Witz private archive).
6. L. Witz. 2001. 'Museum and Heritage Studies: An Interim Position, Workshop on Mapping Alternatives: Debating New Heritage Practices in South Africa', 25-26 September. Cape Town: Project on Public Past, History Department, UWC and RESUNACT and UCT, 12.
7. 'Towards Transformation'. SAMA Eastern Cape News Sheet. 3, August 1998, 2.
8. J. Gore. 2005. 'New Histories in a Post-Colonial Society: Transformation in South African Museums Since 1994'. *Historia*, 50:98.

REFERENCES

Abungu, G. 1996. 'Heritage, Community and the State in the 90s: Experiences from Africa'. Paper presented at the *Future of the Past' Conference*. Bellville: UWC, 10-12 July.

Abungu, G. 2009. 'ICCROM and Africa: Changing the Cultural Landscape in Museums and Immovable Heritage'. *Museum International*, 61(3):62-70. https://doi.org/10.1111/j.1468-0033.2009.01694.x

Abungu, L. 2005. 'Museum and Communities in Africa: Facing New Challenges'. *Public Archaeology*, 4(2-3):151-154. https://doi.org/10.1179/pua.2005.4.2-3.151

Abungu, L. & Abungu, G. (eds.). 2006a. 'Africa: A Continent of Achievements'. *Museum International*, LVIII(1-2):229-230.

Abungu, L. & Abungu, G. (eds.).2006b. *Museum International: A Continent of Achievement*. Oxford: Blackwell.

Abungu, P. 2011. *The Role of Heritage Training in Community Development: The Case of the Centre for Heritage Development in Africa (CHDA)*. London: Lambert Academic Publisher.

Academic Planning Committee Working Group. 1986-1987. Reestablishment of Historical and Cultural Centre including an apartheid museum at UWC in Background Documents, Volume 1 (André Odendaal private collection).

ACTAG Report of the Arts and Culture Task Group. Presented to the Minister of Arts, Culture, Science and Technology, Pretoria, 1995.

Adande, B.A. & Arinze, E. (eds.). 2002. *Museum and Urban Culture in West Africa*. Oxford: James Currey.

'Advertisement for World Centre for Heritage Development in Africa'. Heritage Nomination Dossier Training. https://bit.ly/40AdPs1 [Accessed 23 June 2010].

'Agreement of Deposit: Memorandum of Agreement entered into by and between the African National Congress and the University of Fort Hare', University of Fort Hare (NAHECS, University of Fort Hare, Alice).

Alexander, N. 2002. *An Ordinary Country: Issues in the Transition from Apartheid to Democracy in South Africa*. Durban: UKZN Press.

'ANC Archives Project: An Update'. In: CCS . Alice: University of Fort Hare, NAHECS.

'ANC Policy for Transformation and Development of Heritage Resources (Museums, Monuments, Archives and National Symbols) for a Democratic South Africa'. Discussion paper presented on behalf of the ANC Commission for Museums, Monuments and Heraldry to the ANC Culture and Development Conference, Civic Theatre, Johannesburg, May 1993. Alice: University of Fort Hare, NAHECS.

Anderson, B. 1991. *Imagined Communities*. London: Verso.

Appadurai, A. 2016. 'Archive and Aspiration'. https://bit.ly/42Olhjy [Accessed 18 November 2021].

Appiah, K.A. 2011. 'Identity, Politics and the Archive'. In: X. Mangcu (ed.), *Becoming Worthy Ancestors: Archive, Public Deliberation and Identity in South Africa*. Johannesburg: Wits University Press.

April, T. 2012. 'Theorising Women: The Intellectual Inputs of Charlotte Maxeke to the Discourse of the Liberation Struggle in South Africa'. Unpublished PhD Dissertation. Bellville: University of the Western Cape.

Archival Platform. 2015. 'State of the Archives: An Analysis of South Africa's National Archival System'. https://bit.ly/414GbdJ [Accessed 21 November 2021].

'Archives at the Crossroads 2007' 2007. Open Report to the Minister of Arts and Culture from the Archival Conference 'National System, Public Interest', April. https://bit.ly/3ZCcVKe [Accessed 22 March 2014].

Arinze, E.N. 1987. 'Training in African Museums: The Role of the Centre for Museum Studies Jos'. *Museum International*, XXXIX (4):278-280. https://doi.org/10.1111/j.1468-0033.1987.tb00711.x

Arinze, E.N. 1998. 'African Museums: The Challenge of Change'. *Museum International*, 50(1):31-37. https://doi.org/10.1111/1468-0033.00133

Arinze, E.N. 2002. 'Museum Training Issues in Africa'. Research Paper, ICOM\ICTOP Study series, (10). https://bit.ly/3KEcYBe 1 [Accessed 26 February 2010].

Bachelard, G. 1994. *The Poetics of Space*. Boston: Beacon Press.

Benjamin, W. 1968. 'Theses on the Philosophy of History'. In: H. Arendt (ed.), *Illuminations: Essays and Reflections*. New York, NY: Harcourt Brace Jovanovich.

Benjamin, W. 1969. *The Work of Art: in the Age of Mechanical Reproduction*. New York, NY: Schocken Books.

Benjamin, W. 1989. 'Theses on the Philosophy of History'. In: S.E. Bronner (ed.), *Critical Theory and Society: A Reader*. New York, NY: Routledge.

Bennett, T. 1995. *The Birth of Museum: History, Theory, Politics*. New York, NY: Routledge.

Bernal, M. 1991. *Black Athena: The Afroasiatic Roots of Classical Civilization*. New Brunswick, NJ: Rutgers University Press.

Blouin, F.X. & Rosenberg, W.G. (eds.). 2011. *Processing the Past: Contesting Authority in History and the Archives*. Oxford: Oxford University Press.

Bolotenko, G. 1983. 'Archivists and Historians: Keepers of the Well'. *Archivaria*, 16:5-25.

Boylan, P.J. 1987. 'Museum Training: A Central Concern of ICOM for Forty Years'. *Museum International*, 39(4):225-230. https://doi.org/10.1111/j.1468-0033.1987.tb00698.x

Bradley, H. 1999. 'The Seductions of the Archive: Voices Lost and Found'. *History of the Human Sciences*, 12(2):107-122. https://doi.org/10.1177/09526959922120270

Brain, C.K. & Erasmus, M.C. 1986. *The Making of the Museum Professions in South Africa 1936-2016*. Cape Town: South African Museums Association.

'Briefing for Jakes, London, 4 June 1988. In: Academic Planning Committee Working Group regarding establishment of Historical and Cultural Centre, including and apartheid museum at UWC. Background Documents, Vol. 2, 1988-1990 (André Odendaal private collection).

Brothman, B. 1993. 'The Limits of Limits: Derridean Deconstruction and the Archival Institution'. *Archivaria*, 36.

Brown, R.H. & Davis-Brown, B. 1998. 'The Making of Memory: The Politics of Archives, Libraries and Museums in the Construction of National Consciousness'. *History of the Human Sciences*, 11(4):17-32. https://doi.org/10.1177/095269519801100402

Buchanan, A. 2011. 'Strangely Unfamiliar: Ideas of the Archive from Outside the Discipline'. In: J. Hill (ed.), *The Future of Archives and Recordkeeping: A Reader*. London: Facet Publishing.

References

Burke, F.G. 1981. 'The Future Course of Archival Theory in the United States'. *American Archivist*, 44(1):40-46. https://doi.org/10.17723/aarc.44.1.4853801307551286

Cappon, L. 1982. 'What, Then, is There to Theorise About?'. *The American Archivist*, 45(1):19-25. https://doi.org/10.17723/aarc.45.1.q03v972668401056

Carruthers, J. 1998. 'Heritage and History'. *H-Africa, Africa Forum 2*, 20 October.

'Centre for Heritage Development in Africa (CHDA)'. https://bit.ly/40AdPs1 [Accessed 23 June 2010].

Clarke, J.H. 1975. 'The African Heritage Studies Association (AHSA): Some Notes on the Conflict with the African Studies Association (ASA) and the Fight to Reclaim African History'. *A Journal of Africanist Opinion*, 6(2-3):5-11. https://doi.org/10.2307/1166439

Cohen, D.W. 1986. *Toward a Reconstructed Past: Historical Texts from Busoga*. Uganda, Oxford: Oxford University Press.

Cohen, D.W. 1991. 'A Case for Basoga: Lloyd Fallars and Construction of an African Legal System'. In: K. Mann & R. Roberts (eds.), *Law in Colonial Africa*. Portsmouth: Heinemann, 239-254.

Cohen, D.W. 1994. *The Combing of history*. Chicago, IL: University of Chicago Press.

Cohen, D.W. & Atieno Odhiambo, E.S. 1987. 'Ayany, Malo and Ogot: Historians in Search of a Luo Nation'. *Cahiers d'Etudes Africaines*, 27(107-108):269-286. https://doi.org/10.3406/cea.1987.3406

Cohen, D.W. & Atieno Odhiambo, E.S. 1989. *Siya: A Historical Anthropology of an African Landscape*. London: James Curry.

Cohen, D.W. & Atieno Odhiambo, E.S. 1992. *Burying SM*. Westport: Heinemann.

Cohen, D.W. & Atieno Odhiambo, E.S. 2004. *The Risk of Knowledge*. Athens: Ohio University Press.

Confidential Memorandum from Lieb Loots to the Rector, University of the Western Cape. In: Academic Planning Committee Working Group Reestablishment of Historical and Cultural Centre including an apartheid museum at UWC. Background Documents, Volume 1, 1986-1987 (André Odendaal private collection).

Cook, T. 1994. 'Electronic Records, Paper Minds: The Revolution in Information Management and Archives in the Post-Custodial and Post-Modernist Era'. *Archives and Manuscripts*, 22(2).

Cook, T. 1997. 'What Is Past Is Prologue: A History of Archival Ideas Since 1898 and the Future Paradigm Shift'. *Archivaria*, 43.

Cook, T. 2001. 'Archival Science and Postmodernism: New Formulations for Old Concepts'. *Archival Science*, 1:3-24. https://doi.org/10.1007/BF02435636

Cook, T. 2009. 'The Archive(s) is a Foreign Country: Historians, Archivists and the Changing Archival Landscape'. *The Canadian Historical Review*, 90(3):497-534. https://doi.org/10.1353/can.0.0194

Cook, T. & Dodds, G. (eds.). 2003. *Imagining Archives: Essays and Reflections by Hugh Taylor*. Lanham, MD: Scarecrow Press.

Cook, T. & Schwartz, J.M. 2002. 'Archives, Records and Power: The Making of Modern Memory'. *Archival Science*, 2:1-19. https://doi.org/10.1007/BF02435628

Coombes, A.E. 2003. *History After Apartheid: Visual Culture and Public Memory in a Democratic South Africa*. Durham: Duke University Press. https://doi.org/10.1515/9780822384922

Corsane, G. 1997. 'Robben Island Training Programme proposed course outline'. Submitted to the UWC History Department (Leslie Witz private collection).

Corsane, G. 1998. 'Positioning RITP in Relation to IHR at UWC and RIM'. Bellville: University of the Western Cape, CHR archives.

Corsane, G. 2000. 'What Can South African Museums Learn from the Work of the French Sociologist Pierre Bourdieu'. *SAMAB*, 24:25-30.

Corsane, G. & Metz, G. 1996. 'Business Plan for the establishment of the Robben Island Training Programme (RITP)'. At the request of the Swedish International Development Agency (SIDA). Robben Island: Robben Island Institutional archives.

Craig, B.L. 1992. 'Outward Visions, Inward Glance: Archives, History and Professional Identity'. *Archival Issues*, 17(2)L113-124. https://www.jstor.org/stable/41101829

Davis, R.H. 1977. 'Reviewed Work: Andrew Smith's Journal of his Expedition into the Interior of South Africa, 1834-1836: An Authentic Narrative of Travels and Discoveries, the Manners and Customs of the Native Tribes, and the Physical Nature of the Country by William F. Lye'. *The International Journal of African Historical Studies*, 10(2):320-322. https://doi.org/10.2307/217364

Davison, G. 1991. 'The Meanings of 'Heritage'. In: G. Davison & C. McConville (eds.), *A Heritage Handbook*. St Leonards: Allen and Unwin.

De Jong, F. & Rowlands, M. (eds.). 2006. *Reclaiming Heritage: Alternative Imaginaries of Memory in West Africa*. Walnut Creek, CA: Life Coast Press Inc.

Derrida, J. 1995. *Archive Fever: A Freudian Impression*, translated by E. Prenowitz. Chicago, IL: University of Chicago Press. https://doi.org/10.2307/465144

Derrida, J. 2002. 'Archive Fever'. Transcript of seminar at University of the Witwatersrand, August 1998. In: C. Hamilton, V. Harris, M. Pickover, G. Reid, R. Saleh & J. Taylor (eds.), *Refiguring the Archive*. Cape Town: David Philip, 38.

'Director's Annual Report 1995' (Executive Summary). In: File 'Mayibuye Centre', Box 258. Bellville: UWC Robben Island Archives.

'Discussion Document of the Joint UWC/RIM Working Group'. Reproposals for a co-operation agreement between the University of the Western Cape and Robben Island Museum relating to the Mayibuye Centre and other joint arrangements, 8 July 1998. In: Box 32. Bellville: UWC Archives,.

'Discussion Document on Future Possibilities for Mayibuye Centre'. The Institute for Historical Research, University of the Western Cape, 9 June 1997.

Dlamuka, M. 2003. 'Identities, Memories, Histories and Representation: The Role of Museums in Twentieth Century KwaZulu-Natal'. Unpublished (M.A.) Thesis. Durban: University of Durban-Westville.

Dominy, G. 1993. 'Archives in a Democratic South Africa'. *S.A. Archives Journal*, 35.

Dondolo, L.M. & Morakinyo, O. 2021. *Afrocentric Turn in African Heritage Studies: Epistemology of Alterity*. Cape Town: Ace Publishers.

'Draft progress report by co-ordinator'. UWC Historical and Cultural Centre project for meeting of Academic Planning Committee Working Group, Wednesday 26 June 1991. Annexure A: Appendices (André Odendaal private collection).

Eastwood, T. & MacNeil, H. (eds.). 2010. *Currents of Archival Thinking*. Santa Barbara, CA: ABC-CLIO.

Echevarría, R.G. 1993. *Myth and Archive: A Theory of Latin American Narrative*. Durham: Duke University Press.

'Education Committee Chairman Report, 1985-1986'. SAMA collection, Box 5. Pretoria: UNISA archives.

Eliot, T.S. 1943. *Four Quartets*. New York, NY: Harper.

Esterhuyse, W. 2012. *Endgame: Secret Talks and the End of Apartheid*. Cape Town: Tafelberg Publishers.

Farge, A. 2013. *The Allure of the Archives*, translated by T. Scott-Railton. London: Yale University Press. https://doi.org/10.12987/yale/9780300176735.001.0001

Feinberg, B. 2009. *Time to Tell: An Activist's Story*. Newtown: STE Publishers.

Field, L. 2021. 'Museum Hegemony, Postcolonial Collections and the Scars of the Colonial Process'. *Academic Letters*, 867.

Finnegan, E. 2006. 'The African Postgraduate Diploma Programme in Museum and Heritage Studies: at the Confluence of Critical Theory, Public History and Socio-Political Transformation in South Africa'. Academic Committee Meeting Brief, Robben Island Museum Education Department, October.

Fontein, J. 2000. 'UNESCO, Heritage and Africa: An Anthropological Critique of World Heritage'. Occasional Papers, Centre of African Studies, University of Edinburgh.

Foster, H. 2004. 'An Archival Impulse'. *October*, 110:3-22. https://doi.org/10.1162/0162287042379847

Foucault, M. 1972. *The Archaeology of Knowledge*. New York, NY: Pantheon Books.

Foucault, M. 2002. *The Archaeology of Knowledge: And the Discourse on Language*. Sussex: Psychology Press.

Freshwater, H. 2003. 'The Allure of the Archive'. *Poetics Today*, 24(4):729-758. https://doi.org/10.1215/03335372-24-4-729

Friedman, S. & Atkinson, D. 1994. *The Small Miracle: South Africa's Negotiated Settlement*. Randburg: Ravan Press.

Galla, A. 1999. 'Transformation in South Africa: A Legacy Challenged'. *Museum International*, 51(2):38-43. https://doi.org/10.1111/1468-0033.00203

Garber, M. 2001. *Academic Instincts*. Princeton: Princeton University Press.

Glaser, J.R. & Craig, B.C. (eds.). 1999. 'Birth of the International Council of African Museums'. Information on Training, Newsletter of ICTOP: the ICOM International Committee for the Training of Personnel, 16(2). http://www.icom.org/ictop/ [Accessed 9 July 2010].

Gore, J. 2005. 'New Histories in a Post-Colonial Society: Transformation in South African Museums Since 1994'. *Historia*, 50:75-102.

Graham, B. & Howard, P. 2008. 'Heritage and Identity'. In: B. Graham & P. Howard (eds.), *The Ashgate Research Companion to Heritage and Identity*. London: Routledge.

Griffin, S.H. & Timcke, S. 2021. 'Re-framing Archival Thought in Jamaica and South Africa: Challenging Racist Structures, Generating New Narratives'. *Archives and Records*, 43(1):1-17. https://doi.org/10.1080/23257962.2021.2002137

Grobler, E. & Pretorius, F. 2008. 'British Museums Association, The Carnegie Corporation and Museums in South Africa, 1932-1938: An Overview'. *S.A. Tydskrif vir Kultuurgeskiedenis*, 22(2):54-65. https://doi.org/10.4314/sajch.v22i2.6370

Grosskopf, F.W. 1933. 'The Poor White Problem in South Africa'. *Report of the Carnegie Commission*. Stellenbosch: Pro Ecclesia Publishers.

Ham, F.G. 1975. 'Archival Edge'. *American Archivist*, 38(1):5-13. https://doi.org/10.17723/aarc.38.1.7400r86481128424

Hamilton, C. 2011. 'Why Archive Matters'. In: X. Mangcu (ed.), *Becoming Worthy Ancestors: Archive, Public Deliberation and Identity in South Africa*. Johannesburg: Wits University Press, 119-144. https://doi.org/10.18772/22011085324.11

Hamilton, C. 2013. 'Forged and Continually Refashioned in the Crucible of Ongoing Social and Political Life: Archives and Custodial Practices as Subjects of Enquiry'. *South African Historical Journal*, 65(1):1-22. https://doi.org/10.1080/02582473.2013.763400

Hamilton, C., Harris, V., Pickover, M., Reid, G., Saleh, R. & Taylor, J. (eds.). 2002. *Refiguring the Archive*. Cape Town: David Philip. https://doi.org/10.1007/978-94-010-0570-8

Hardy, D. 1988. 'Historical Geography and Heritage Studies'. *Area*, 20(4):333-338. http://www.jstor.org/stable/20002646

Harris, V. 1997. 'Claiming Less, Delivering More: A Critique of Positivist Formulations on Archives in South Africa'. *Archivaria*, 44:132-141.

Harris, V. 2000a. *Exploring Archives: An Introduction to the Archival Ideas and Practice in South Africa*. Pretoria: National Archives of South Africa.

Harris, V. 2000b. 'They Should Have Destroyed More: The Destruction of Public Records by the South African State in the Final Years of Apartheid, 1990-1994'. *Transformation*, 42:29-56.

Harris, V. 2001. 'Seeing (in) Blindness: South Africa, Archives and Passion for Justice'. *Archifacts*. https://bit.ly/3mfZTof

Harris, V. 2002. 'The Archival Sliver: Power, Memory, and Archives in South Africa'. *Archival Science*, 2:63-86. https://doi.org/10.1007/BF02435631

Harris, V. 2003. 'Freedom of Information in South Africa and Archives for Justice'. Transactions of Public Culture Workshop. Bellville: University of the Western Cape, January.

Harris, V. 2007. *Archives and Justice: A South African Perspective*. Chicago, IL: Society of American Archivists.

Harris, V. 2011. 'Archons, Aliens and Angels: Power and Politics in the Archive'. In: J. Hill (ed.), *The Future of Archives and Recordkeeping: A Reader*. London: Facet Publishing, 107-126.

Harris, V. 2012. 'Genres of the trace: Memory, Archives and Trouble'. *Archives and Manuscripts*, 40(3):147-157. https://doi.org/10.1080/01576895.2012.735825

Harvey, D. 2001. 'Heritage Pasts and Heritage Presents: Temporality, Meaning and the Scope of Heritage Studies'. *International Journal of Heritage Studies*, 7(4):319-338. https://doi.org/10.1080/13581650120105534

Harvey, D. 2008. 'The History of Heritage'. In: B. Graham & P. Howard (eds.), *The Ashgate Research Companion to Heritage and Identity*. London: Routledge, 19-36.

Hayes, P., Silvester, J. & Hartmann, W. 1998. 'Photography, History and Memory'. In: W. Hartmann, J. Silvester & P. Hayes (eds.), *The Colonising Camera: Photographs in the Making of Namibian History*. Athens: Ohio University Press.

Hewison, R. 1987. *The Heritage Industry: Britain in a Climate of Decline*. London: Methuen.

Hicks, D. 2020. *The Brutish Museums: The Benin Bronzes, Colonial Violence and Cultural Restitution*. London: Pluto Press.

'Highlights: 1981-1994'. Alice: University of Fort Hare, NAHECS (Centre for Cultural Studies).

Hill, J. (ed.). 2011. *The Future of Archives and Recordkeeping: A Reader*. London: Facet Publishing. https://doi.org/10.29085/9781856048675

'History of the British Museum Association'. https://bit.ly/437OsiT [Accessed 8 January 2022].

Hodge, J.C. 1987. 'Museum Studies in Australia'. *Museum*, 156(4).

Hodson, J.H. 1972. *The Administration of Archives*. Oxford: Pergamon Press Ltd.

Hofmeyr, I. 1994. *We Spend Our Years as a Tale That is Told': Oral Historical Narrative in a South African Chiefdom*. Johannesburg: Wits University Press.

Hooper-Greenhill, E. 1992. *Museums and the Shaping of Knowledge*. New York, NY: Routledge. https://doi.org/10.4324/9780203415825

'ICTOP – International Committee for the Training of Personnel'. https://bit.ly/3nuxx9U [Accessed 10 August 2010].

'IDAF Publications and Audio-Visual Department Report on trip to South Africa'. 26 November-3 December 1990 in Barry Feinberg collection. MCH 89, Box 19, Historical Papers. Bellvill: UWC Robben Island Mayibuye Archives.

Jenkinson, H. 1937. *A Manual of Archive Administration*. London: Percy Lund, Humphries and Co Ltd.

Jimerson, R.C. 2006. 'Embracing the Power of Archives'. *The American Archivist*, 69(1):19-32. https://doi.org/10.17723/aarc.69.1.r0p75n2084055418

Jisheng, L. 1987. 'Museum Training in China'. *Museum International*, 39.

Josias, A. 2013. 'Methodologies of Engagement: Locating Archives in Post-apartheid Memory Practices'. Unpublished PhD Dissertation. Michigan: University of Michigan.

Ka Mpumlwana, K. & Corsane, G. 2021. 'Creating a New Generation of Heritage and Museum Leaders: The Inception of the Robben Island Training Programme (RITP)'. In: N. Lekgotla laga Ramoupi, S. Solani, A. Odendaal & K. ka Mpumlwana (eds.), *Robben Island Rainbow Dream: The Making of Democratic South Africa's First National Heritage institutions*. Cape Town: HSRC Press.

Karp, I., Kratz, C.A., Szwaja, L., Ybarra-Frausto, T. with Buntinx, G., Kirshenblatt-Gimblett, B. & Rassool, C. (eds.). 2006. 'Introduction'. *Museum Frictions: Public Cultures/Global Transformation*. Durham: Duke University Press.

Ketelaar, E. 2001. 'Tacit Narratives: The Meaning of Archives'. *Archival Science*, 1.

Ketelaar, E. 2002a. 'Archival Temples, Archival Prisons: Modes of Power and Protection'. *Archival Science*, 2:221-238. https://doi.org/10.1007/BF02435623

Ketelaar, E. 2002b. 'Archive as a Time Machine'. http://bit.ly/3zDB5cU [Accessed 5 May 2014].

King, J. 1999. 'Final Report of the Africa 2009 Regional Course', Mombasa, Kenya, 5 July-3 September. https://bit.ly/40BI41O [Accessed 8 December 2010].

Kirby, P.R. 1940. *The Diary of Dr. Andrew Smith, the Director of the "Expedition for Exploring Central Africa", 1834-1836*. Cape Town: The Van Riebeeck Society.

Klausen, S.M. 2004. *Race, Maternity and the Politics of Birth Control in South Africa, 1910-1939*. Basingstoke: Palgrave Macmillan. https://doi.org/10.1057/9780230511255

Laesk, A. & Fyall, A. 2006. *Managing World Heritage Sites*. London: Butterworth-Heinemann.

Lalu, P. & Murray, N. (eds.). 2012. *Becoming UWC: Reflections, Pathways and Unmaking Apartheid's Legacy*. Cape Town: Centre for Humanities Research.

Laplanche, J. 1976. *Life and Death in Psychoanalysis*. Baltimore: John Hopkins University Press.

Lekgotla laga Ramoupi, N., Solani, N., Odendaal, A. & ka Mpumlwana, K. (eds.). 2021. *Robben Island Rainbow Dreams: The Making of Democratic South Africa's First National Heritage Institution*. Cape Town: HRSC Press.

'Liberation Archives Project: An Institutional Plan'. Alice: University of Fort Hare, NAHECS.

Little, T. 2000. 'The Future of Heritage in South Africa: Collaboration and Partnership'. https://bit.ly/3ZHIAKh [Accessed 14 June 2010].

Little, T. (ed.). 2001. *PREMA and the Preservation of Africa's Cultural Heritage: PREMA 1990-2000*. Rome: ICCROM.

Littler, J. & Naidoo, R. (eds.). 2005. *The Politics of Heritage: The Legacies of 'Race'*. New York, NY: Routledge

Lowenthal, D. 1996. *The Heritage Crusade and the Spoils of History*. London: Viking.

Lynch, M. 1999. 'Archives in Formation: Privileged Spaces, Popular Archives and Paper Trails'. *History of the Human Sciences*, 12(2):65-87. https://doi.org/10.1177/09526959922120252

Maaba, B. 2013. 'The History and Politics of Liberation Archives at Fort Hare'. Unpublished PhD Dissertation. Cape Town: University of Cape Town.

MacNeil, H. 2007. 'Archival Theory and Practice: Between Two Paradigms'. *Archives and Social Studies: A Journal of Interdisciplinary Research*, 1(1):517-545.

Mangcu, X. (ed.). 2011. *Becoming Worthy Ancestors: Archive, Public Deliberation and Identity in South Africa*. Johannesburg: Wits University Press.

Marnoff, M. 2004. 'Theories of the Archive from Across the Disciplines'. *Libraries and the Academy*, 4(1):9-25. https://doi.org/10.1353/pla.2004.0015

Marschall, S. 2019. 'The Long Shadow of Apartheid: A Critical Assessment of Heritage Transformation in South Africa 25 Years On'. *International Journal of Heritage Studies*, 25(10):1088-1102. https://doi.org/10.1080/13527258.2019.1608459

Masao, F.T. 1987. 'The Balance Between Domestic Needs and International Aid in Museum Training'. *Museum International*, 39(4):275-277. https://doi.org/10.1111/j.1468-0033.1987.tb00710.x

Massey, D. 2010. *Under Protest: The Rise of Student Resistance at the University of Fort Hare*. Pretoria: Unisa Press.

'Mayibuye Book Launch'. Campus Bulletin, 24 July 1991. In: Mayibuye Centre for History and Culture. First Annual Report 1992, Bellville.

Mayibuye Centre for History and Culture. Second Annual Report 1993, Bellville.

Mayibuye Centre for History and Culture. Third Annual Report 1994, Bellville.

Mayibuye Centre for History and Culture. Fourth Annual Report 1995, Bellville (A. Odendaal private collection).

Mayibuye Centre for History and Culture, Fifth Annual Report 1996, Bellville (A. Odendaal private collection).

Mayibuye Centre for History and Culture, Seventh Annual Report 1998, Bellville.

Mazrui, A. 1986. *The Africans: A Triple Heritage*. London: BBC Publications.

Media Statement by the Minister of Arts, Culture, Science and Technology. The Future Management and Development of Robben Island, on Wednesday 4 September 1996.

'Memorandum of Agreement between RIM and UWC in respect of The UWC Robben Island Museum Mayibuye Archives', 4. In: Box 32. Bellville: UWC Archives.

'Memorandum: Working Conditions', 19 January 1996 to the Director in Barry Feinberg collection. MCH 89, Box 6. Bellville: UWC Robben Island Mayibuye Archives.

Miers H.A & Markham, S.F. 1932. 'The Museums Association Survey of Empire museums'. A Report on the Museums and Art Galleries of British Africa Together with a Report on the Museums of Malta, Cyprus and Gibraltar by Alderman Chas. Squire and D.W. Herdman to the Carnegie Corporation of New York, Edinburgh.

Minkley, G. 1998. 'Report of the Location of RITP'. Prepared for the UWC/RIM Working Group. Belliville: UWC, CHR archives.

Minkley, G. & Rassool, C. 1998. 'Orality, Memory and Social History in South Africa'. In: S. Nuttall & C. Coetzee (eds.), *Negotiating the Past: The Making of Memory in South Africa.* Cape Town: Oxford University Press.

Minkley, G., Witz, L. & Rassool, C. 2009. 'South Africa and the Spectacle of Public Pasts'. Paper presented at the Heritage Disciplines Symposium, UWC, 8-9 October.

Minutes of APMHS board meeting held at CHEC office, 15 March 2006. Bellville: UWC, CHR archives.

Minutes of SAMA Meeting held in the Transvaal Museum, Pretoria, 30 April 1956. Box 6, SAMA collection. Pretoria: UNISA archives.

Morrow, S. & Wotshela, L. 2005. 'The State of the Archives and Access to Information'. In: J. Daniel, R. Southall & J. Lutchman (eds.), *State of the Nation: South Africa 2004-2005.* Pretoria: HSRC Press, 313-335.

Mycue, D. 1979. 'The Archivist as Scholar: A Case for Research by Archivists'. *Georgia Archive*, 7(2):10-16.

Nassimbeni, M. 2014. 'Building Resilient Public Libraries with Carnegie in South Africa (1927-2012): Regularities, Singularities and South African Exceptionalism'. *Research Paper.* Cape Town: University of Cape Town.

Nelson Mandela Speech at the formal opening of Robben Island Museum, Heritage Day, 24 September 1997. https://bit.ly/42NIQLY [Accessed 21 April 2022].

Nesmith, T. 2004. 'What's History Got to Do With It: Reconsidering the Place of Historical Knowledge in Archival Work. *Archivaria*, 57:1-27.

Nkrumah, K. 1970. *Consciencism: Philosophy and Ideology for Decolonisation.* New York, NY: Monthly Review Press.

O'Barr, J. & Mudimbe, V.Y. (eds.). 1993. *African and the Disciplines.* Chicago: University of Chicago Press.

Odendaal, A. 1991. 'Developments in Popular History in the Western Cape in the 1980s'. In: J. Brown (ed.), *History from South Africa: Alternative Visions and Practices.* Philadelphia, PA: Temple University Press, 361-367.

Odendaal, A. 1996. 'Suggested Robben Island Action Plan for the Department of Arts, Culture, Science and Technology', 4 March. In: Mayibuye Centre, Box 258. Bellville: UWC Archives.

Odendaal, A. 1997. 'Discussion Document on 16 June 1997'. Bellville: UWC, CHR archives.

Orwell, G. [1949] 2013. *Nineteen Eighty-Four.* London: Penguin.

Osborne, T. 1999. 'The Ordinariness of the Archive'. *History of the Human Sciences*, 12(2):51-64. https://doi.org/10.1177/09526959922120243

'Our Story'. https://bit.ly/437OsiT [Accessed 8 January 2022].

Panitch, J.M. 1996. 'Liberty, Equality, Posterity?: Some Archival Lessons from the Case of the French Revolution'. *The American Archivist*, 59(1):30-47. https://doi.org/10.17723/aarc.59.1.an67076131u104kj

'People are the real Wealth of a Nation': Centre for Heritage Development in Africa (CHDA) Brochure. https://bit.ly/3M9dPe5 [Accessed March 2011].

Pickover, M. 2005. 'Negotiations, Contestations and Fabrications: The Politics of Archives in South Africa Ten Years After Democracy'. *Innovation*, 30:1-11. https://doi.org/10.4314/innovation.v30i1.26493

Pickover, M. 2014. 'Patrimony, Power and Politics: Selecting, Constructing and Preserving Digital Heritage Content in South Africa and Africa'. Conference paper presented at IFLA, Lyon.

Pohlandt-McCormick, H. 2013. 'Taking Risks in the Post-Colonial Archive: Towards a Post-Colonial Thinking of the Archive'. Unpublished seminar paper. South African Contemporary History and Humanities Seminar, Centre for Humanities Research. Bellville: University of the Western Cape, 13 April 2013.

Pohlandt-McCormick, H. & Burton, A. 2005. *Archive Stories: Facts, Fictions and the Writing of History*. Durham: Duke University Press.

Portelli, A. 1998. 'What Makes Oral History Different'. In: R. Perks & A. Thomson (eds.), *The Oral History Reader*. London: Routledge.

'Preparatory Project: Archives and Museum of Resistance'. Alice: University of Fort Hare, NAHECS (Centre for Cultural Studies, UFH)

'Preventive Conservation in Museums of Africa'. Special programme of ICCROM (International centre for the study of the preservation and restoration of cultural property) for African museums south of the Sahara. http://bit.ly/3GiS5ZC also available at http://bit.ly/3ZMFnJD [Accessed 20 April 2012].

'Progress Report from Working Group'. Re UWC Historical and Cultural Centre to Academic Planning Committee, 4 March 1991 (André Odendaal private collection).

Proposal to Rockefeller Foundation for the Development of An African Programme in Museum and Heritage Studies. Submitted by the Cape Higher Education Consortium, February 2003. Bellville: UWC, CHR archives.

Rakotomamonjy, B. 2010. Conservation in Immovable Cultural Heritage: Final Report, 2010. https://bit.ly/42Yw247 [Accessed 3 August 2010].

Ramoupi, N.L., Solani, S., Odendaal A. & ka Mpumlwana K. (eds.). 2021. *Robben Island Rainbow Dreams: The Making of Democratic South Africa's First National Heritage Institution*. Cape Town: HRSC Press.

Rapaport, H. 1998. 'Archive Trauma', Review Article. *Diacritics*, 28(4):68-81. https://doi.org/10.1353/dia.1998.0030

Rassool, C. 2000. 'The Rise of Heritage and the Reconstitution of History in South Africa'. *Kronos: Journal of Cape History*, 26:1-21.

Rassool, C. 2004. 'The Individual, Auto/Biography and History in South Africa'. Unpublished PhD. Dissertation, Bellville: University of the Western Cape.

Rassool, C. 2010. 'Power, Knowledge and the Politics of the Public Past'. *African Studies*, 69(1):79-101 https://doi.org/10.1080/00020181003647215

Rassool, C. 2015. 'Human Remains, the Discipline of the Dead, and the South African Memorial Complex'. In: D.R. Peterson, K. Gavua & C. Rassool, *The Politics of Heritage in Africa Economies, Histories, and Infrastructures*. Cambridge: Cambridge University Press, 133-156. https://doi.org/10.1017/CBO9781316151181.008

Rassool, C. 2018. 'Building a Critical Museology in Africa'. In: T. Laely, M. Meyer & R Schwere (eds.), *Museum Cooperation Between Africa and Europe: A New Field for Museum Studies*. Bielefeld: transcript Verlag, xxii-xxiii. https://doi.org/10.1515/9783839443811-005

Rassool, C. & Witz, L. 1999. 'Transforming Heritage Education in South Africa: A Partnership Between the Academy and the Museum'. Paper, Swedish African Museum Programme, 22 August.

Report on the SIDA supported Robben Island Training Programme (RITP), prepared by Ruth De Bruyn, 2001.

'Report of Survey conducted by Gerard Corsane in Robben Island Report 1998-2002'. Robben Island: Robben Island Museum Institutional Archive.

Richards, T. 1993. *The Imperial Archive: Knowledge and the Fantasy of Empire.* London: Verso.

Rico, T. 2021. 'Heritage Studies After Said', Public Books. https://bit.ly/3nErWhx [Accessed 21 November 2021].

Ridener, J. 2009. *From Polders to Postmodernism: A Concise History of Archival Theory.* Duluth, MN: Litwin Books.

Riouful, V. 2000. 'Behind Telling: Post-apartheid Representations of Robben Island's Past'. *Kronos*, 26:22-41.

'RITP report for 1998-2002'. Robben Island: RIM Institutional records, Robben Island Museum.

'Robben Island Business Plan'. In: Box 35. Bellville: UWC Archives, Robben Island Gateway.

Roberts, J.M. 1987. 'Archival Theory: Much Ado About Shelving'. *The American Archivist*, 50(1):66-74. https://doi.org/10.17723/aarc.50.1.l357257455776g52

Robertson, J.M. 2008. 'Heritage from Below: Class, Social Protest and Resist'. In: B. Graham & P. Howard (eds.), *The Ashgate Research Companion to Heritage and Identity*. London: Routledge, 143-158.

Rookmaaker, K. (1797-1872). 'The Zoological Contributions of Andrew Smith with an Annotated Bibliography and a Numerical Analysis of Newly Described Animal Species'. *Transactions of the Royal Society of South Africa*, 72(2):105-173. https://doi.org/10.1080/0035919X.2016.1230078

Rundell, W. & Herbert Finch, C. 1977. 'The State of Historical Records: A Summary'. *The American Archivist*, 40(3):343-347. https://doi.org/10.17723/aarc.40.3.fm4qj3613841k014

Sachs, A. 2006. 'Archives, Truth and Reconciliation'. *Archivaria*, 62.

Samuel, R. 1994. *Theatres of Memory: Past and Present in Contemporary Culture.* London: Verso.

Saouma-Ferero, G. 2006. 'Africa 2009: A Story of African Empowerment'. *Museum International*, 58(1-2):83-94. https://doi.org/10.1111/j.1468-0033.2006.00554_1.x

Schellenberg, T.R. 1956. *Modern Archives, Principles and Techniques.* Melbourne: Cheshire.

Schwartz, J.M. 2007. 'Having New Eyes: Spaces of Archives, Landscapes of Power'. *Archives and Social Studies: A Journal of Interdisciplinary Research*, 1:321-362.

Seekings, J. 2006. 'The Carnegie Commission and the Backlash Against Welfare State-Building in South Africa, 1931-1937'. CSSR Working Paper No. 159.

Segger, M. 1996. 'Introductory Remarks, ICOM International Committee for the Training of Personnel'. Annual meeting, Lubbock, TX. https://bit.ly/3G9257U [Accessed 21 March 2021].

Segger, M. 1996. 'Message from the Chairperson'. *IT Newsletter*, 13(2).

Serequeberhan, T. 1994. *The Hermeneutics of African Philosophy: Horizon and Discourse.* London: Routledge

Shearing, C. & Kempa, M. 2004. 'A Museum of Hope: A Story of Robben Island'. *The Annals of the American Academy of Political and Social Science*, 592(1):62-78. https://doi.org/10.2139/ssrn.2720241

Singleton, H.R. 1987. 'Museum Training: Status and Development'. *Museum International*, XXXIX(4):221-224. https://unesdoc.unesco.org/ark:/48223/pf0000079452

Smith, A. 1849. *Illustrations of the Zoology of South Africa. Consisting Chiefly of Figures and Descriptions of the Objects of Natural History Collected During an Expedition into the Interior of South Africa, in the years 1834, 1835, and 1836*. London: Smith, Elder and Co. https://doi.org/10.5962/bhl.title.10416

Smith, L. 2006. *Uses of Heritage*. New York, NY: Routledge. https://doi.org/10.4324/9780203602263

Smith, L. 2008. 'Heritage, Gender and Identity'. In: B. Graham & P. Howard (eds.), *The Ashgate Research Companion to Heritage and Identity*. London: Routledge 159-180.

Smith, L. & Natsuko, N. (eds.). 2009. *Intangible Heritage*. New York, NY: Routledge.

South African Museums Association. 2016. *The Museum Profession in South Africa, 1936-2016*. Cape Town: South African Museums Association.

'South Africa to Spend R22 million on 100-metre Tall Flag'. https://bit.ly/41599tU [Accessed 12 May 2022].

Steedman, C. 2002. *Dust: The Archive and Cultural History*. New Brunswick, NJ: Rutgers University Press.

Steedman, C. 2008. 'Romance in the Archive', Presentation. https://bit.ly/40JmKXK [Accessed 14 November 2021]

Steiner, L. & Frey, B.S. 2011. 'Imbalances in World Heritage List: Did the UNESCO Global Strategy Work?'. Working Paper, 14, University of Zurich. https://bit.ly/3nFJlWR [Accessed 17 February 2010].

Stoler, A.L. 2002. 'Colonial Archives and the Arts of Governan'. *Archival Science*, 2:87-109. https://doi.org/10.1007/BF02435632

Stoler, A.L. 2009. *Along the Archival Grain: Epistemic Anxieties and Colonial Common Sense*. Princeton, NJ: Princeton University Press.

'Study Leave Report by Andre Odendaal'. 1990. Department of History, 1. In: Fakulteit Lettere en Wysbegeerte Verslae: Studieverlof, konferensie/kongresse bygewoon (Ciraj Rassool private collection).

Summers, R.F.H. 1975. *A History of the South African Museum, 1825-1975*. Cape Town: Balkema.

Taylor, H.A. 2003. 'The Discipline of History and the Education of the Archivist'. In: T. Cook & G. Dodds (eds.), *Imagining Archives: Essays and Reflections by Hugh A. Taylor*. Metuchen: Scarecrow.

The Museums Association (compl.). 1933. *Directory of Museums and Art Galleries in British Africa and in Malta*. Cyprus and Gibraltar, London: The Museums Association.

Timcke, S. 2015. 'Discourse, Memory, and Post-apartheid South African Archives'. *SSRN Electronic Journal*. https://doi.org/10.2139/ssrn.2630403

Tomose, N.G. 2008. 'The Viability of South African Museums in the Post-1994 Landscape'. *Research Report*. Johannesburg: University of the Witwatersrand.

Tuck, E. & Yang, K.W. 2012. 'Decolonization is Not a Metaphor'. *Decolonization: Indigeneity, Education & Society*, 1(1).

Tunbridge, J.E. & Ashworth, G.J. 1995. *Dissonant Heritage: The Management of the Past as a Resource in Conflict*. New York, NY: John Wiley.

Tunbridge, J.E., Ashworth, G.J. & Graham, B. 2000. *A Geography of Heritage*. London: Arnold.

'UNESCO World Heritage Convention Global Strategy'. https://bit.ly/40SbCYF [Accessed 20 May 2010].

Van Zyl, S. 2016. 'The Growth of Professionalism in South African Museums'. In: C.K. Brain & M.C. Erasmus (eds.), *The Making of the Museum Professions in South Africa*, 30-36.

Velody, I. 1998. 'The Archive and the Human Sciences: Notes Towards a Theory of the Archive'. *History of the Human Sciences*, 11(4):1-16. https://doi.org/10.1177/095269519801100401

Viljoen, J. 1992. 'Legacy of Apartheid'. *The Argus*, Monday, 12 October 1992, 4. In: Mayibuye Centre for History and Culture First Annual Report 1992, Bellville (André Odendaal private collection).

Walsh, K. 1992. *The Representation of the Past: Museums and Heritage in the Post-Modern World*. New York, NY: Routledge. https://doi.org/10.4324/9780203320570

Williams, D. 2001. *A History of the University College of Fort Hare, South Africa – the 1950s: The Waiting Years*. New York, NY: Mellen Press.

Williams, K. 1992. 'Closed Chapter for SA's Book Publishers'. Southside, 15. In: Mayibuye Centre for History and Culture, First Annual Report 1992, Bellville.

Witz, L. 2001. 'Museum and Heritage Studies: An Interim Position, Workshop on Mapping Alternatives: Debating New Heritage Practices in South Africa'. 25-26 September, 2001. Cape Town: Project on Public Past, History department, UWC and RESUNACT, UCT.

Witz, L. 2006. 'Transforming Museums on Post-apartheid Tourist Routes'. In: I. Karp, C. Kratz, L. Szwaja & T. Ybarro-Frausto with G. Buntix, B. Kirshenblatt-Gimblett & C. Rassool (eds.), *Museum Frictions: Public Cultures/Global Transformations*. Durham: Duke University Press, 107-134. https://doi.org/10.2307/j.ctv11cw1hd.10

Witz, L. 2008. 'Graduate Programme in Museum and Heritage Studies (Postgraduate Diploma and Master's): A Proposal for a Joint Programme to be Offered by the University of the Western Cape and Robben Island Museum'.

Witz, L. 2009. 'Towards a History of Post-apartheid Pasts in South African Museums'. Research Paper, Re-imagining Postcolonial futures: Knowledge Transactions and Contest of Culture in African Present. Bellville: University of the Western Cape, 8-11 July.

Witz, L. 2010. 'Museums, Histories and the Dilemmas of Change in Post-apartheid South Africa'. University of Michigan Working Papers in Museum Studies, 3.

Witz, L. & Rassool, C. 1992. 'The Dog, the Rabbit and the Reluctant Historians'. *South African Historical Journal*, 27(1): 238-242 https://doi.org/10.1080/02582479208671748

Witz L. & Cornell, C. 1999. 'From Robben Island to Makapan's Cave: Transforming Heritage and Museum Studies in South Africa'. Paper presented at the World Archaeological Conference, Cape Town, 10-14 January.

Witz, L. & Rassool, C. 2008. 'Making Histories'. *Kronos: South African Histories*, 34(1):6-15. https://www.jstor.org/stable/41056600

Witz, L., Minkley, G. & Rassool, C. 2017. *Unsettled History: Making South African Public Pasts, Ann Arbor*. MI: University of Michigan Press. https://doi.org/10.3998/mpub.9200634

Wright, P. 1985. *On Living In an Old Country Again*. Oxford: Oxford University Press.

INDEX

A

activist 9, 11, 14, 38, 48, 55-56, 61, 63, 66, 70, 77, 79, 87-89, 182

Africa 2009 110-114, 116, 140

African civilisation 3

African Museum and Heritage Studies 14, 99-100, 112, 114

African Museum and Heritage Studies (AMHS) 8, 100-101, 104, 106-107, 113-116, 123, 142, 183

Afrikaner 6, 12, 163

afrocentric 2, 14, 105-106, 115, 123, 125, 143, 157, 159, 171, 183

Albany Museum 3, 132

Anglo-Zulu wars 3

apartheid 2, 6-9, 11-12, 14-15, 19, 20, 45-47, 52, 61-66, 68-74, 76-79, 81-84, 90, 99-101, 124-126, 129-130, 135, 141, 149, 152, 157, 170, 181-184

archaeology 4, 28, 106, 108, 130-132, 134

Archival Platform 51-53

archival transformation 1, 61

archives iii-iv, 1-3, 5-7, 9-14, 19-38, 45-56, 61-64, 66-72, 74-79, 81-82, 87-89, 90, 124, 134, 141, 150, 159, 167, 181- 183

archivist 1, 5, 9, 13-14, 20-22, 25-26, 33-38, 42, 45-48, 50-51, 53-56, 65, 69, 108, 183

B

Benin 3, 105, 109-110, 116

British Museum 5, 32

C

Carnegie Corporation New York (CCNY) 127

Centre for Humanities Research (CHR) iii, 9, 135, 142

colonial and racial violence 2

colonial archive 1, 3-5, 32, 62-63, 67

consciencism 100
cultural institutions 1, 8
cultural patrimony 2
culture 2, 5-7, 9, 19, 38, 51, 61, 63, 66-67, 69, 79, 107, 109, 113, 115-116, 124, 135-136, 153, 159, 166, 171, 184
custodial cloisters 15, 53, 184

D

decolonisation 1, 11-12, 100, 105, 124, 170
democracy 6, 8, 11, 14, 19, 51, 61, 64-66, 83-85, 105, 160, 181, 184
democratisation 7, 9, 26, 70, 133
District Six Museum iii, 10, 65, 82, 134-135, 153
Durban Museum 3

E

ethnographic study 4-5
Eurocentric 1, 8, 15, 104, 115, 155, 170, 184

F

fallist movements 11, 182
Foucauldian epistemology 21
Free State Republic Museum 3
Frontier War 3

G

geographical mapping 4
global capitalism 3
Great Trek 3

H

heritage iii, 1-2, 9-12, 14-15, 20, 30, 38, 46, 51, 61, 65-66, 69-71, 82, 84-86, 89-101, 104-116, 123-124, 133-137, 140-143, 149-171, 181-184
heritage complex 1, 168, 170, 181

heritage institutions 1, 8-10, 15, 65-66, 69-70, 78, 113, 137, 141, 184

history 2, 7-8, 10, 12-13, 15, 19, 22-25, 27-29, 35, 37-38, 45, 47, 49-50, 53-56, 66-67, 70-71, 73, 75, 79, 83-84, 87, 89-90, 99-100, 102, 105, 115-116, 123-125, 129-133, 135, 137, 143, 150-158, 160-171, 182-184

human rights 2, 8, 11, 19, 64, 184

I

inequality 2, 6, 19-20, 90, 181, 183

institutionalised racism 2, 19

Iziko Museums iii, 5

K

King William's Town Museum 3

L

liberation movements 7, 63, 66-69, 71-72, 76-77, 84

libraries 6, 67, 126-127

Lwandle Migrant Labour Museum 10, 82

M

Mayibuye Centre 10-13, 65, 67-68, 72-82, 84-90, 132, 135, 138, 141-142, 182

memory institutions 2, 6, 61, 128, 181

mnemonic devices 19

monument 3, 6, 8, 10, 19, 28, 62, 65, 69, 71, 105, 152, 159, 181

Museology 99, 101, 103-104, 106, 131, 137

museum iv, 1-6, 8,-12, 14, 19, 65, 67- 69, 74-75, 78-79, 82-90, 99-109, 114-116, 123-131, 133-137, 139, 141-142, 149-154, 157-159, 162, 182-184

museum and heritage sector 1, 9-11, 79, 106, 108, 133, 183-184

museum as weapon 2

museum education and training 182

N

National Archives of South Africa Act 7, 51
nation building 84, 157-158
natural history 1, 4, 8, 167

P

People's History Project 12, 73
Post-apartheid 1, 5, 7, 9-11, 13-15, 19-20, 32-33, 46, 61-63, 65-67, 73, 79, 82-83, 89-90, 133, 151, 153, 163, 181-184
postgraduate diploma in Museology 131
postgraduate diploma in Museum and Heritage Studies 9, 133-134, 136, 138
Public Historical Scholarship 9, 86, 136, 142, 152
Public History 11, 13, 15, 73, 78, 85-86, 101, 132-135, 139, 140, 141-143, 149,-157, 162-163, 167-171, 182-183

R

reconciliation 6,-8, 10, 14, 19-20, 61, 65-66, 69, 82-84, 89, 157-158, 182
redress 6, 9-11, 51, 61, 66-67, 99, 124, 136-137
Robben Island Museum (RIM) iii, 8-10, 14, 62, 65, 80-83, 85-90, 99, 116, 132-140, 142, 182-183

S

scientific expedition 5
social cohesion 10, 19, 181
social justice 2, 14, 48-50, 55-56, 66, 99, 123-124, 183
South African Contemporary History and Humanities Seminar 9, 92
South African Museum of Natural History 4
State Archives Service (SAS) 6, 7, 63, 65, 67

T

technical certificate 129-131
The National Diploma in Museum Technology 131

transformation 1, 2, 7, 9-15, 19-20, 22, 29, 32-33, 46, 51-52, 55, 61-62, 65-67, 69-70, 78, 82, 90, 105-106, 116, 123-125, 132-137, 142-143, 149, 151, 159, 181-184

transformation discourse 6, 10, 13, 19-20, 66-67, 182

U

Union of South Africa 6, 126

W

white supremacy 2, 8, 10, 124-126

www.ingramcontent.com/pod-product-compliance
Lightning Source LLC
Chambersburg PA
CBHW080602170426
43196CB00017B/2882